THE LAST
BRITISH
BULLFIGHTER

Frank Evans was born in Salford Lancashire on 18 August 1942. He was educated at St James' Roman Catholic School for Boys, Salford.

The only recognized British matador in the world, he made his debut in the bullring in 1966 and went on to gain the widespread admiration of his fellow matadors, critics and audiences, who nicknamed him 'El Inglés'. His career spanned four decades and has included appearances at 93 *Festivales*, 38 *Novilladas* and 40 *Corrides de Toros*. He completed his 'Alternativa' to become a *matador de toros* in 1991, and has performed not only in Spain, but also in France, Venezuela and Mexico.

He speaks four languages and is married to Margaret, his wife of forty-two years. They have two sons, Matthew and James, and five grandchildren, Tom, Jack, Megan, James and Lola.

He played Rugby for Sale FC, and De La Salle where he was 1st team captain in 1980. He lives in Marbella on the south coast of Spain.

THE LAST
BRITISH
BULLFIGHTER

Frank 'El Inglés' Evans

MACMILLAN

First published in Great Britain 2009 by Macmillan
an imprint of Pan Macmillan Ltd
Pan Macmillan, 20 New Wharf Road, London N1 9RR
Basingstoke and Oxford
Associated companies throughout the world
www.panmacmillan.com

ISBN 978-0-230-74330-4

1 3 5 7 9 8 6 4 2

A CIP catalogue record for this book is available
from the British Library.

Printed and bound in the UK by
CPI Mackays, Chatham ME5 8TD

Every effort has been made to contact the copyright holders
of the photographs reproduced in this book. If any have been
inadvertently overlooked, the publishers will be pleased
to make restitution at the earliest opportunity.

For my sons –
Matthew for whom there was
never a negative moment
and James who was never
quite so sure.

CONTENTS

INTRODUCTION

The crowd roared as the bull raced into the ring. It looked magnificent and fierce. The best and wildest bulls run right into the middle of the arena – it's not a good sign when they run round the boards. It charged into the centre, and the crowd went up. They were on their feet cheering, clapping and roaring their approval, they knew they were going to be in for a good fight. This bull was a charger. It was going to put on a good display. My stomach was turning somersaults, and my mouth was dry. I could hardly move, but through the nerves, the raw emotion and the adrenalin that coursed through my body I managed to start towards this fiercest of beasts. A hand held me back: 'Not yet, Frank. Wait.'

I was watching it all the time. In fact, I couldn't stop staring at it. I could hear the words of my bullfighting trainer Garrigos ringing in my ear: 'Never take your eyes off a bull,' he would say to me, 'Even if it's dead you must always be on guard, because even a dead bull can still have you, and it can still take you out. Until the bull is a piece of meat don't trust it; never let it out of your sight.'

This was a talk he gave to every young bullfighter on his debut, and I was no exception. He sat me down on the field where I trained in Valencia, looked me in the eye and said, 'In the world's greatest arenas bulls have exacted revenge on their killers even after they have drawn their last breath and are lying dead in the sand. Bulls are dangerous; they are unpredictable and they will get you.'

I listened intently as he added, 'In Valencia a matador with a reputation for being unlucky stepped into the bullring to fight a bull, a 600-pound powerhouse of aggression and fury that would have fought its own shadow to a standstill. The fight was a triumph, and the matador dispatched this monster to huge acclaim. Then he took his eye off it. He took his eye off the dead bull, a big mistake. Never take your eyes off a bull. The horses came out to drag the animal from the ring on a sling attached to a piece of rope. As the horses pulled the rope the sling with the dead bull on it swung round, and the bull's horns smashed into the matador's leg, severing a main artery. He had taken his eye off the bull and paid the ultimate price.'

I kept my eyes on the bull and waited for what seemed like an eternity, but was actually only a couple of minutes.

'Right, Frank, go now. Go and fight the bull. It is ready for you.'

The voice spoke, but I couldn't feel my legs as I strode across the ring. The crowd fell into a hush. This was the highlight of their day; a young bullfighter making his debut in the bullring. But it was madness! Madness because I'd never fought any live beast before. Normally bullfighters making their debut get to fight dozens of cows before entering the ring. I'd fought none, and people close to me, including my manager, were expecting a massacre. It was suicidal for me to step into a bullring with so little experience.

As I strode towards the bull I caught its scent. It was the musky, sweet smell of sweat that all bulls give off, but it was a completely new sensation to my nostrils. We were close to each other now. I held out the cape in my ever-so-slightly trembling hands. The bull turned its head. Its eyes, as black as the night, looked at me, then they focused on the cape. It began to move, almost in slow motion; it moved towards the cape. Then, head down, displaying its horns as sharp as knitting needles, it charged.

This was it: the moment had arrived. I was a bullfighter.

Chapter One

SALFORD LAD

'**Mam, I've made my mind up;** I'm going to be a matador!'

'No you're not,' she said. 'Stop being so stupid.'

'I am, Mam. I'm going to fight bulls,' I replied, totally serious.

'This is Salford, not Spain.'

'But that is what I want to do. I want to be a bullfighter.'

She didn't take much notice, and why should she have? It's not as though Salford in the early 1960s had any bullrings. Neither did Britain come to that. But I was determined to live a dream that had grabbed hold of me and had now become an obsession. The long road to becoming a *matador de toros* had begun, and I was about to take the first tentative steps on a journey that would take me around the world.

Little events had come together to get me to this momentous decision: Dad being stationed in Gibraltar during the Second World War and seeing bullfights was one; a Spanish family coming to live on our street was another; there was a wedding in Spain; a holiday to Ibiza; and in every one the fighting of bulls was a prominent feature.

Of equal importance was being born in and living in Salford, which seems a bit odd, because the city isn't really a hotbed for matadors. I came into the world in 1942, and the one thing you did when you lived in Salford during the 1940s, 50s and 60s was dream of escaping it. The city was a major factory town and inland port during the eighteenth and nineteenth centuries. Cotton and silk spinning provided it with a strong economy. But by the time I arrived Salford was in decline and rapidly degenerating into one of the most socially deprived and violent areas in England.

My dad, Ralph Evans, was born in 1916, and two years later his dad was killed in France during the First World War. Dad was left with his mam and two sisters. His mam died of TB when he was seven, and he was moved to a family where there were already eight kids who lived in slum housing at Lower Broughton, near Manchester. He knew he had to do something to get out of the mess he was in because they had nothing. So he got a job aged six delivering papers. He also started smoking! When he was eleven he managed to pass his eleven-plus and get a place at De La Salle Grammar School, but he wasn't allowed to go, because his new family couldn't afford to buy him the books he needed to take with him. It was tragic, really. Getting married early to Mam was his way of escaping. She wanted to escape too. Her family had no money because her dad was a drunk who spent all the dosh on booze, so she was desperate to get out.

My mam, Agnes, was two years older than Dad. She lived in Rosa Street, which was in the middle of Hankinson Park in Salford, a real tough working-class district. This was where they filmed *A Taste of Honey* and other kitchen-sink movies of that era. It was slum housing built for people who worked in the factories that surrounded it. It was packed with green-grocers, bakers, butchers, ironmongers, off-licences and other shops of every description, because it was in the era before supermarkets, and on every street corner there was a pub.

The pub was the social hub of the area. Everybody congregated in there because beer was only a penny a pint. It was the one place people could escape to. There was no such thing as holidays in those days because nobody had anywhere to go to, or if they did, they didn't have the means to get there. It was a completely different world my mam grew up in to the one of today. The people were poor, but they were always decent in appearance and always made sure, however little money they had, that they wore clean clothes. But they were trapped in their social situation. The set-up at government level meant it was virtually impossible to borrow money. Those who had things left to them had a chance of upward social mobility, but if nobody left you anything you were basically stuck. And this situation went on right into the 1960s. So for my dad to get out of that and set up his own business really was quite remarkable.

Mam met Dad at a dance. When they got married she did all sorts of menial jobs, such as working in a laundrette, before becoming a bus conductress. She worked to put food on the table and clothes on our backs and was the steadying influence in our family. Dad was a bit on the wild side. He was more tempestuous and prepared to take risks.

After the war Dad was desperate to get out of the trap of

not necessarily being in poverty but never really having lots of money. He wanted more disposable income, and in those times, as maybe is the case now, richness was defined in not what you owned but what disposable income you had – basically how much you had to spend on a Friday night. That is why he wanted his own shop and set up Ralph Evans Butchers.

We lived in a row of terraced houses that was very Coronation Street. The toilet was at the bottom of the yard, and we had paper on a string to wipe our bums. That was until the mid-1950s, when it got posher, and very shiny toilet roll was introduced. But this was useless. You couldn't wipe your backside on that – it just skidded off! It was hardship, but in our area we were all in the same boat. But it was tough, especially in winter, when you'd be sat on the outside loo freezing your knackers off! Even the cats stayed in. Then there'd be family arguments over whose turn it was to get the coal in for the fire. One of us would have to go down to the yard and get it from the air-raid shelter, which everyone used to store their coal once the war had finished. Back then the threat was from nuclear bombs, and the flimsy air-raid shelters weren't going to provide protection from one of those monsters. But there was very much a community feel to living in that part of the world at that time, and this was epitomized by the Queen's Coronation in 1953.

During the Coronation the council organized a competition for the best-dressed street. Everyone was out in the days leading up to the big day, putting up bunting and banners and flags, and on the day the Mayor of Salford toured the streets and picked out which one was the best looking. Ours didn't win. That accolade went to one of the posh streets. But I suppose my family were a little bit posh compared to others because we were the first household on our street to own a television. We bought it specifically for the Coronation. It had a 12-inch screen with a big magnifying glass in front of it, and all the lights were turned off in our front room while we and the neighbours watched the proceedings in glorious black and white. There must have been about thirty people all crammed into our front room, and once that became full the rest stood outside and peered through the window.

After the Queen was crowned all the paraphernalia was put away, and life went back to normal again, which meant the football came out and about a dozen of us played soccer in the street. There was no thought of bullfighting then. I was ten and mad for football. But playing in the street meant quite a few windows were smashed. I remember playing a game when my Uncle Frank, who was in his forties, joined in. He kicked the ball and smashed someone's window. As soon as you heard the sound of breaking glass you ran inside your house so the victim had no idea who'd done it. My Uncle Frank was no different to the rest of us. As soon as the ball hit the window he scarpered.

I was beginning to discover myself at this age physically and emotionally. In my early years I was quite timid and shy, so much so that school was a real problem for me at first. At infant school they had to lock the school gates because of me. As soon as it was break-time I used to run home; I legged it all the way. I was dragged back again, but it became such a regular thing that eventually they had to lock me in. What saved me from the misery of school was the sudden discovery, when I was nine years old, that I could run quicker than anybody else my age. That gave me some kudos, especially when I set three city records as a hurdler. By the time I reached the age of eleven I was good at sport, and my confidence was sky-high. Other kids respected me because of my sporting prowess. I made the town team for football, rugby and athletics. The only thing I didn't make the town team for was swimming.

Twice a week I'd go for town team training. I'd meet the other lads at the bus stop – we'd been given tokens off our respective schools to get us there – and off we'd go. But on the way back we always walked, because the road the bus took us down passed so many different shops: butchers, confectioners, sweet shops and many more. This road was thriving, and as we made our way home we used to steal from these shops. I was the frontman when we walked in and I'd take my tu'ppence to the person behind the counter and say to him or her, 'How much is that over there, mister?' It was never 'mate' in those days, it was always 'mister'. While he had his back turned my lot rifled the shop.

They were a rum lot, my mates. John McGloughlin, who we nicknamed Glocky, was one of my gang. He was the cock of Salford and hard as nails. At the age of thirteen he had hairs on his chest, was having sex with girls and was smoking cigarettes. He was a tearaway but a brilliant kid to know, and really good at every sport, be it rugby, cricket, football – you name it, he could play it. But his family were slum poor. He'd turn up for school sports without a bag for his kit. His boots would be rolled up in newspaper. Sometimes, when his boots became too small for him, he'd play in his normal shoes, because his family couldn't afford a pair of new ones. He got picked to play for Lancashire at rugby but he didn't turn up. Most of those who played for the counties came from the grammar-school and private-school system, and I think he was too embarrassed to appear in case they looked down on him. This was a great shame, because he could've made it as a sportsman and probably earned quite a lot of money.

Nick was another great character. That was his nickname, not his real name. We called him Nick because he stole a lot. His dad was a rag-and-bone man, and one day Nick turned up in a great big overcoat his dad had got off someone while doing his rounds. He said to us, 'Look at this, lads, it's brilliant!' It had great big deep pockets and he added, 'I'll get some gear in this no problem.'

So after training we went and did some shops. Nick came out of one shop, an off-licence, and as well as the usual bubble gum and other things he had got two massive bottles of pop in both these deep pockets. But we were only nicking for mischief. When we got outside we gave most of the stuff away. Sometimes we didn't know what we were stealing. In one shop we came out with a box of what looked like white pads on strings. We didn't have a clue what they where or what to do with them, until a group of girls told us they were sanitary towels. Even when they told us this and told us what they were for we didn't believe them. We just thought they were winding us up.

We would swipe anything just for the thrill of thieving. None of us ever got in any big trouble. We just thought it was funny acting the goat. If we had got caught nothing would've really come of it. Most of the local Bobbies would've probably smacked us and told us to get lost. Now everything gets processed, and kids get dragged before the magistrates. Petty thieving is a period of life most kids will get over. There's no need to give them a criminal record. Back then any sort of mischief was dealt with on the spot, and our mams and dads had no idea. All the kids in Salford were looking for a buzz because Salford was such a grim, bleak, dark, depressing, cold and rainy place. But it benefited people in a bizarre way, because they learned how to survive in life and became tougher because of it.

They also developed a wicked sense of humour in adversity. Everybody had the Les Dawson kind of perspective on life – they'd say black when they really meant white, that sort of thing. People in Salford accepted from an early age that what they had was their lot in life, and they better just make the most of it. When Manchester bid for the Olympics in the early 1990s Salford was one of the places that held an open-air party. When the announcement that the games had gone elsewhere was made everybody sang 'Always Look on the Bright Side of Life'. That song typifies people who have been brought up in Salford. They're a rum lot with a great sense of humour which was a by-product of being brought up in difficult circumstances. None of us felt underprivileged, though, because we'd all been brought up in the same way and didn't really know anything about life outside the city boundary. And unlike today there were plenty of places for kids to play, mainly thanks to the Germans! We played on what were called crofts, which were big craters where the Nazis had dropped bombs during the war. They were filled with cinders and were brilliant for games of football, cricket and other ball sports.

Life was gradually getting better for me in those days; the old timidity was being replaced with a competitive and ambitious streak. But it was all focused on sport. Thankfully because of the sport I was beginning to enjoy school. I'd come to appreciate life and its challenges and adventures. Dad was a great help in this respect. He never actually gave me any money but he pointed me in the right direction and showed me how to get on in life. He taught me the importance of being reliable, to always turn up and always turn up on time. Dad was a firm believer in being well dressed at all times. He said it showed respect to others and gave you confidence and he insisted that having credibility was more important than having money. Dad reckoned the banks had all the money, and if you always paid your commitments on time and were credible you could borrow as much as you wanted. He always loved telling me not to deal in emotions, to beware of greed and had a saying: 'You can never afford a bargain.'

Dad was full of good advice, but what he couldn't show me was how to keep warm. And the one thing that really got me about life back then was the gnawing coldness of the place. I really do have abiding memories of being perished all the time. Going to school through slush and snow seemed to be a regular thing during my childhood. Mornings were the worst time because when I woke up for school the first thing I saw was my breath condense in the freezing-cold air of my bedroom. If I woke up in the night with my arm hanging out of the bed it'd feel like a block of ice. There was a shop on the corner of the street where I lived where a nice little old lady, Mrs Bradley, baked bread. The wall by the side of the shop was always hot, and I used to go and stand against it for hours to keep warm, pinning myself against the bricks. It was much better than being at home: that could be the equivalent of Ice Station Zebra at times. The coal fire at our house barely heated the room up. I'd warm myself in front of it only to find that my back was freezing. I'd have to wrap a blanket round my back if I wanted to keep totally warm.

The only escape from this freezing hell was through my imagination, and Dad's Second World War stories. I think this was where my love of bullfighting first came from. Through dad's stories, bullfighting suddenly appeared on my radar. Dad was in Gibraltar during the Second World War serving as an army chef. The Rock served a vital role in the conflicts in and around the Mediterranean in that it controlled all the naval traffic in that area. In addition to this it provided a strongly defended harbour from which ships could also oper-ate in the Atlantic. During the war the Rock did come under aerial attack from aircraft of Vichy France and Italy, but for those stationed there it was a nice posting, because the soldiers never really saw any action. So much so that my mother said it had changed him when he came back home. 'It ruined him, that bloody war,' she'd often say to me.

But he had some great stories. During the time he was sta-tioned there, on his days off he would walk across the bridge into Spain, where he watched bullfights. His descriptions of the matadors, dressed as they were in their gold suit of lights, taking on these giant beasts and armed with only a cape and a sword, seemed light years away from the harsh reality of living in northern England. He'd do impressions of the passes they made as I watched him in rapt attention. But at that early stage in my life it never really occurred to me that I could be a bullfighter; I was just amazed at all these wonderful tales.

He was in the Royal Scottish Regiment, which was a mixture of Scots kids and Salford lads; basically they were all lunatics. A lot of the Scots lot came from Glasgow, and there were the usual tensions between those who supported Celtic and the ones who followed Rangers, so much so that when the marchers held the 12th of July Orange Parade in Northern Ireland there were clashes in Gibraltar between Scottish Catholics and their Protestant counterparts. Dad said because of the constant tension and fighting within the army garrisoned at Gibraltar he actually held the record of time served as corporal without ever getting promoted to sergeant. Every day, he told me, somebody was on a charge, and he had to take them to be sanctioned. He could never get a good report because his boys were always fighting all the time, and it looked like he was unable to control them.

The worst incident involved the shooting-down of Wladyslaw Sikorski's plane. General Sikorski was Prime Minister of Poland's London-based government in exile and Commander-in-chief of its armed forces. His plane went down shortly after taking off from Gibraltar; he had been visiting Polish troops in the Middle East. The sixty-two-year-old died in the crash, prompting rumours that it was part of a Soviet, British or even Polish conspiracy. Even so his body was taken back to the peninsula, where the dockyard was lined with British troops, and his coffin carried and escorted by Polish servicemen. Dad was among those lining the route, and he watched in horror as some of his men started to attack the coffin. A story had been doing the rounds, which was totally untrue, that back in Britain the Poles who had fled there had been raping the British women. It was a madhouse. The men under his charge had only one thing on their mind: to antagonize whoever came in their path, friend or foe.

This came to a head when they took some Italian prisoners-of-war back to the Rock after capturing them in the Middle East. As the prisoners lined up for their food Dad would watch as they got served meat, potatoes and gravy; then a bright spark at the end slopped a big dollop of custard all over it, sparking a near riot. He often said it wasn't the Italians that needed locking up, it was the British. But the calm amidst this storm was the bullfighting. I found myself more interested in these stories than any of the others he told me.

Dad told me fantastic tales about watching Manolete fight. Manolete was the greatest bullfighter of his time, who died in the ring at Linares in 1947 after fighting a Miura bull, known for having killed more bullfighters than any other breed. In that period the top matadors would fight Miuras. They were big, well armed and dangerous. These bulls had what is known as *sentido*, the ability to quickly distinguish between the matador and the cloth. Once they had made that distinction they only went for the matador. This lethal strain, known as the Cabrera strain, has since been bred out of them.

As Manolete entered for the kill he was gored in the right

thigh as his sword went in and he died in the early hours of the next morning from massive blood loss. Dad had seen him, and I was in awe, because when Manolete died it made the papers across the world, and Spain went into mourning. Manolete was also friends with Churchill and once offered him the head of a bull he had killed. Churchill, rather diplomatically, turned it down. Dad also knew a bit of Spanish, so started teaching me the lingo: how to count to ten, how to say good morning, how to order drinks and all sorts of different phrases. The fascination with bullfighting and Spain had begun, and it would keep recurring with regularity until I made the decision to become a bullfighter.

Meanwhile there was the problem of how to keep warm and survive in Salford. My brother Bob, who is three years older than me, I took as a great example of how to survive in adversity. He has cerebral palsy caused by having the bad luck to have been born with difficulties at home and at a time when medical science wasn't as advanced as it is now. They got him out with forceps but ended up cutting his head to pieces and leaving him paralysed down his left side. Then, when he got to the age of twelve, he started having fits, which are now controlled by medicine. He is a tremendous example to me of how you should face life and get on with it, especially, like he did, if you got kicked where it hurts right at the very beginning. He has not once complained about his lot and he's held down a job all his life. When he left school at fifteen he got a job at Remploy; later he worked in a mail-order factory; then he worked as a gardener for Salford Parks Department, before retiring at sixty. He has a pension from the council and a state pension and financially he has never needed anyone's support despite his bad disabilities. Bob has motivated me. Whenever I have felt down I've looked at Bob and thought to myself: what have I got to feel sorry about? He inspired and instilled a work ethic in me even from an early age and proved that, whatever obstacles are put in front of you, be they physical or mental, you can always overcome them. You want to be a bullfighter but you live in Salford? No problem: go and chase your dream however overwhelming the odds are against you doing it.

Life was grim, but because Bob never complained, neither did I, and at eight years old I got my first job. My dad got me delivering meat on my bike. A couple of years later he bought the room above the shop, and we all lived there. It was much better than the terraced house: it had an inside toilet for a start – what a luxury that was. We were a cut above everybody then, and we also had a van, which dad used to pick the meat up. Suddenly we were mobile, and a whole new world opened up as every Sunday he'd take us on day trips to places like Blackpool, Morecambe and Southport.

He also taught me butchering skills from a very young age, and I loved it. Every now and then there would be a competition with all the other local butchers with prizes for things like who could cut and bone a shoulder of meat the quickest. I quickly got to know all the different cuts of meat. The only thing I didn't like about the job was having to get up at the crack of dawn every day to go with Dad to the meat market, though it did have some plus points because it was like walking into a new and wonderful world. I'd go outside, and the streets would be empty, totally deserted, apart from the odd milk float doing its rounds. Then I'd walk into Water Street abattoir, which was rather like Smithfield in London, and from the loneliness of a city in slumber everything would change in a flash to a scene of organized noise and commotion. There'd be thousands of butchers from across the North-west all buying meat and steam rising off the freshly cut carcasses. The meat was hauled across the hallway in carts, and I'd hear the carters crying at the tops of their voices, 'Mind your backs, mind your backs!' as they ran past.

We'd buy half a dozen lambs, a couple of sides of beef and maybe three pigs, and the sellers would always get you something on the side for ten bob, which is fifty pence in today's money. That was their little bit on the side, their tip almost. There were fiddles going on everywhere. The market was where I first saw animals being slaughtered. Harry Thorpe was the name of the slaughterman. We'd all go into a room at the back of the market, and they'd bring the cow in and tie it up, and Harry would shoot it in the back of the neck with a stun gun. Down it would go, and he'd open its jugular, and all the blood would spurt out. It was a shock seeing this at first, but I soon got used to it. What I could never get used to was the religious killings for things like Halal meat, where they were forbidden to stun it. They basically put the cow in a cylinder that trapped it so it couldn't move, and a religious man slit its throat from ear to ear, and it bled to death. It was like the biggest hosepipe you have ever seen. That really did take some getting used to. Some people criticize bullfighting for being cruel and inhumane in the way the animals are treated in the ring. Well, go into a British slaughterhouse and watch a religious killing if you want to see cruelty. I'm not having a go at the Jews or Muslims – they have to do it that way because their religious laws demand it – but try telling me the animal doesn't suffer by having its throat cut.

Outside the market, underneath a bridge, was a café which did a roaring trade at this time of morning. I loved going in there because it was packed with butchers all smoking unfiltered fags or roll-ups, eating dripping on toast and drinking huge mugs of tea. The windows were always steamed up so you could never see inside. But it was our world in there; the world of the butcher. Nobody else ever seemed to go in the place apart from butchers, and it was very male-driven and testosterone-fuelled with lots of joking and laughing and Mickey-taking. I've been in businesses where the people working have seemed a bit down, a bit lifeless and a bit low, and it makes me depressed. Inside this café every single bloke was happy because, when everybody is doing well, there's a buzz, and it's blinding. Life for these butchers was like that.

In 1950s Britain everybody had a job, consequently everybody had a bit of cash to spend, and they liked to spend money on fresh meat, because it was something that was in short supply during the war. These were safe, comfortable times for these lads. They were part of a working-class culture that got its money on a Friday night and spent it over the weekend so that by the time Monday came around they had very little left. When I got to an age where I could work behind the counter I found that the better-off would come in and order just half a pound of mince, say, and a couple of chops.

Whereas working-class Mrs Swift would come in and order brisket, legs of lamb, chickens and all sorts of things and basically spent the dough she had. People like her made the economy work. Whatever they earned they spent. Unlike the ones on higher incomes who saved up – for what I don't know. Everybody aspired to live in the places these rich sods lived, but whenever I saw them on their way to wherever they were going, they always seemed to live a miserable existence and had this sour look about them.

When we got the meat from the market we took it back to the shop, and I dressed the window. My main objection to this job, which I fitted in between my schooling and did on Saturdays, was that I'd see people going to work and I'd already been working two hours. Then, later in the day when they were all coming back from work, I was still at work taking the meat out of the window. But what that job did was instil in me a work ethic that I still adhere to today. And it kept me fit and gave me a voracious appetite. I could easily polish off a couple of steaks at dinner time and remember ploughing through fourteen chops and a big pile of spuds, so big that Mam could hardly fit everything on the plate. In this respect my parents were wonderful. They always made sure I ate well and ate the right sort of food. My dad wanted to make up for what he never had and worked his pants off to make sure we never went without.

He also did everything he could to help us get on. When I was fifteen I joined Sale Rugby Union Club. To get from Salford to Sale was very difficult because it was effectively a journey across two cities – Salford and Manchester. But you had to turn up for training on Mondays and Wednesdays to have any chance of being picked to play on Saturday, so Dad took me in his van, waited until I had finished and then brought me home again. He went out of his way to make sure I had the best chance to make it as a rugby player. He never gave me anything money-wise but he showed me how the system worked and how to be a good parent by taking an interest in my sporting prowess.

Rugby has always played a big role in my life. I was brought up 500 yards from The Willows, which is where Salford Rugby League Club plays. From being a small lad my father had followed Salford and seen all the great players, and it was every kid's ambition to play in the rugby league team or, if not for them, for Manchester United at football. I was OK at football. I got picked to play for Salford Boys against Manchester Boys when I was fourteen. We were due to play at The Cliff, where United used to train, and Nobby Stiles was captain of Manchester Boys – he also played for the England schools team. But at the same time I was chosen to play for Salford against Warrington at The Willows and had to make up my mind which I wanted to play. There was no competition, it had to be rugby. A kid called Kenny Harmon got my spot on the football team and never stopped thanking me, so I was a winner both ways really. Dad was convinced I was going to end up having a glittering rugby league career with Salford. He could see I had promise. But he also noticed that the kids who played rugby union as amateurs and were good got snapped up on bigger contracts by the rugby league clubs than those who simply joined rugby league as amateurs and then turned pro.

So he encouraged me to join Sale. Unfortunately I wasn't good enough to attract a rugby league club who wanted to give me a big contract, so I never switched codes and turned pro.

I went to Sale as a stand-off, but the coaches and powers-that-be had this idea that, because I was fast, I should play on the wing. Stand-off was where I really wanted to play, but no, they stuck me out on the wing, where I stayed for the rest of my playing days. But I also played at Salford, breaking all the rules about players not being allowed to play for two codes at the same time. At Salford I played for the A-team under an assumed name for a season. I decided to use the name Jim Roberts after the Sale and England winger who had run 9.8 seconds for the 100-yard sprint. Martin Offiah is the only player I've seen come close to his speed. So I became Jim Roberts, playing on the wing for Salford. I was at an ex-players' reunion at Sale in 2007, and Jim just happened to be there, and I said to him, 'Do you realize you played a season at Salford?'

He said, 'What are you talking about?' But the great man found it quite amusing when I told him, though I would've been in a hell of a lot of trouble if the authorities had found out at the time.

Playing rugby and working at the butcher's kept me out of trouble and kept me extremely fit. In 1962 I played for Salford second team for three months, because the rugby grounds in union were frozen solid – they used braziers to defrost the pitches in league, but they weren't so forward-thinking over at the rugby union clubs. Rugby league was always a lot more bruising, because there were some real hard cases out there.

You basically picked the ball up and ran and either you were hit by the opposition or you hit them. Almost everyone I came up against had most of their teeth missing. I was enjoying my rugby playing for both codes, and it really started to become a way of life before bullfighting took over.

All my friends were associated with rugby, and that was who I mixed with. Sale was a great club to play for, and I played against all the great sides: Northampton, Coventry, Wasps, Gloucester – it was country-wide experience. Sale always had a top-class fixture list and in the 1962/63 season I was second-leading try scorer for the club behind the great Bill Patterson, who played centre for England and the British Lions in South Africa. But I tended through the rugby to socialize with players a lot older than me, Freddie Griffiths and Eric Evans being prime examples. They used to take me to clubs, point a girl out to me and see if I could pull her. More often than not I did. I just had a lot of brass neck, as they say about over-confident people up north.

Playing for Sale was barmy. Most of the lads who were in the first team were university-educated, had decent jobs and were model citizens. But as soon as they got onto the rugby pitch they turned into complete nutters. I have memories of mass battles and punch-ups that will live with me until I die. We were playing Northampton at home in a big fixture and we were leading 3-0 – you got three for a try then – and there wasn't long to go when Fred missed a tackle on our twenty-five. Fred couldn't tackle for toffee; he was a bottler when it came to defence and would always blame his hands and go on about how he needed them for his job – he was a physio by profession. When he missed this particular tackle they went in to score, and we all got behind the line feeling pretty gutted. Fred was pointing to his hands and saying there was nothing he could do. So Eric walked up to him and smacked him as hard as he could around his ear hole. Fred almost went down and wasn't pleased, but he went in a bit harder in subsequent games and stopped blaming his hands for all his missed tackles after that. But that was Eric, up front and tough. He got knocked out in Paris playing for England against France in the days when you didn't have substitutes and had to come off for ten minutes to recover. After the game had finished I said to him, 'Did you get the fucker who did it?'

'Oh aye,' he said to me.

'Which one was it?'

'I don't know, I just went through the whole pack and battered the lot of them.'

That was his style. We played away at New Brighton when he was captain. New Brighton were hard Liverpool lads who had seen the rough end of life and would basically beat their opponents into submission. This day was no different. They were knocking seven shades out of us, and Roger Curtis, our second-row forward, had black eyes for ten days after the game. At half-time I went over to Eric and said, 'When are we going to do some of these tossers in?'

He turned on me and blasted, 'You go and do your job, I'll do mine.'

He'd blown me out. Five minutes into the second half there was a scrum, and as the ball came out I heard a loud crack. Looking across to the back of the scrum I saw our prop, Mike

Earley, out cold on the floor; his body was in spasm. He'd been given one hell of a smack. I was fuming and went to Eric and this time I didn't mince my words. I said, 'Fucking hell, Eric, if you don't do something—'

'Fuck off,' he said, cutting me short. 'I did it!'

He added later in the bar, 'I threw a punch to knock their prop out, and this sod put his head in the way.'

We had a great side during the early to mid-1960s. There was a giant of a player who joined the team called Peter Stagg. At 6ft 7in he was the tallest bloke I'd ever seen and he would go on to play for Scotland. He came to the club and said, 'Let me see the wingers.'

'Let me see how you throw the ball in,' he said to me.

He had been in America for a time playing American football. Before he came we threw the ball into the lineout using two hands. He taught me to use one hand and to treat the rugby ball like an American football. Pretty soon I became invaluable to the side because Peter and I controlled the lineout; we dominated it against every opponent. I was the accurate thrower; he was the player who always caught the ball. His coming effectively secured my place because we developed a good understanding of each other's game. But the first time he played at Sale didn't go quite as planned. We were playing at home, at the old Heywood Road ground. I threw the ball in from our first lineout, and he caught it no problem. The second time was again no problem. But the third time he didn't come up. The opposition second row had whipped his legs from underneath him, which is a dangerous thing to do because you can land on your head and break your neck. He was fuming about that. The next time we had a lineout he didn't go up again. Instead I heard a massive crack: he'd knocked this guy out cold who'd fouled him. I knew from that moment on he was going to make it as a rugby player.

Every good player who came into the region ended up playing at Sale, so the standard was sky-high, and as a result you had to fight to retain your place in the first team, because competition was fierce. Players who joined the club included Vic Harding, who was uncapped but eventually played for England at second row, Peter Stagg, who played for Scotland, Jim Roberts, who went on to play for England with Johnny Williams – the list went on and on as the years rolled by. But the one thing I noticed about all the players who went on to become internationals was they were all vicious bastards. If there was a ball on the floor and it was a fifty-fifty between them and another player they would rather beat their opponent to a pulp than lose out. It was a little thing I noticed, especially among the forwards. They had this streak in them where they were prepared to do anything, even risk major injury, to get the ball. I was never hard, but I played with some hard players, some proper head cases. But it taught me to be tough and gave me courage. In many respects it gave me the mental strength to stand in front of a fighting bull.

Chapter Two

MY FIRST TASTE
OF SPAIN

By the time I was twenty my family was moving up in the world. We'd moved out of the shop and into a house in Derby Road, Salford. It was a three-bedroomed quasi-semi, in the sense that it was a gable-end house but it was quite big and seen as posh for the area. Most houses in Salford at that time conformed to the two-up two-down image as portrayed on *Coronation Street*. But despite the fact that we had three bedrooms there was still an air of frugality. I still shared a bedroom and a double bed with Bob, because my parents would have thought it a waste to buy a bed just for me. I was still butchering, but I was getting itchy feet.

Because my dad set up as Ralph Evans Butchers a lot of people got to know him, including the local Conservative Party, who came knocking on his door and asked him to run as a councillor. They knew he had potentially great pulling power as a candidate because he was a popular member of the community and was heavily involved in things like Salford Rugby League Club, in what was predominantly a rugby area.

So he was put forward as a councillor in a largely Labour-voting district and won with a record majority of about 1,500 votes. A few years later my mam ran for council and got a bigger majority than he did! He eventually became Mayor.

It was through politics we were put in touch with a Spanish family, the Rocarruigs, who lived just round the corner from us and needed help with visa applications and work permits. I was sixteen and got to know them well, so well that I'd go round to their house for dinner. The food they ate was so different to what I was used to. It was very Mediterranean, with lots of olive oil. In Salford most people used olive oil to clean their ears out. You could only buy it in a chemist. They also made wonderful paellas, and various tapas-style dishes such as *albondigas*, which are meat balls in a rich tomato sauce.

It was unusual at that time to go to night school, but living in close proximity to the Spanish family and hearing them talk in their lingo made me want to understand it. So I enrolled on a night course at De La Salle. I believed that if I wanted to speak the language I'd have to learn the grammar, and the only way to do it was to enrol on an O-level course.

A friend of the family who had moved over with them, Paco Montes, a flamenco dancer, would tell me wonderful stories about a matador known as El Cordobés. Paco regarded him as the greatest bullfighter that ever lived. Fate ensured he was around at the right moment when bullfighting really took off big time in Spain in the early 1960s. And in Spain he became as big as the Beatles and Muhammad Ali. There's a photo in a Valencia bar of him being man-handled out of the ring by the police. He had jumped in from the crowd to have a go at the bull and make some passes, long before he ever became a matador, but nobody knew at the time he was going to become Spain's most famous bullfighter and the first one to earn one million pesetas a fight. In his younger days he got arrested many times because he was so poor he had to thieve to eat. I was enthralled by these stories of El Cordobés, because he was a maverick. Every time I went round to their house I'd say to Paco, 'Tell me another story. What was El Cordobés really like? How wild was he?' and Paco would be off recounting tale after tale – I think he appreciated having such a rapt audience.

This Spanish family were obsessed by him, and because I'd hear all these wonderful stories told to me by Paco I too became obsessed. El Cordobés lived the life. I wanted to be part of it but had absolutely no idea how to get there or what to do. By the age of twenty I hadn't even travelled abroad. I needed a lucky break. It came thanks to the Spanish family. Paco's sister Maria was going to get married to an English lad, a local businessman called Noel Booth, and the wedding had been planned to take place during the Feria de Corpus in Granada. I was invited along and jumped at the chance. I couldn't wait to see Spain and packed my bags.

In 1963 I was off to Granada to join Paco's lot for this wedding on my first trip abroad. But I never envisaged how much of a slog it would be to get there. I got the train to London and from there flew to Valencia, where I boarded another train to Granada. This was the hard bit. Thirteen hours on a train that travelled at a snail's pace, sat on seats that were made from big blocks of wood. There was no padding on the seats, and to make things worse there were people on the train who brought chickens with them that they allowed to roam about the carriage. It was more like a barn than a train. I'd never seen anything like it. This was real peasant country and totally detached from anything I'd ever experienced back home. I practised my Spanish, which I had been learning at home in college, by talking to a group of young lads. When I told them I was learning the lingo and was off to a wedding in Granada they did the usual trick of teaching me all dreadful things to say to my host when I met him at the station, rude phrases and swear words. But I could see through it because they were whispering these words. They didn't want anybody else on the train to hear them, so I knew they must have been bad.

For the next week and a half I had the time of my life, it was brilliant. On the day of the wedding the bride walked down a street lined with flower petals. She walked half a mile to the church, and every step of the way she trod on petals, it was magical. I was the only Englishman with the bride's lot. The groom's family were all English, and there was a group of them who, if truth be told, were struggling to come to terms with the change in culture between Britain and Spain. As I was on the Spanish side I got a real taste for their ways. And my Spanish came on massively over there. Every day when I woke up the bride's father, Miguel, would drag me off to the local bar to get drunk with his mates and all the other OAPs. The conversation was always about two things: bullfighting and the Spanish Civil War. When they talked to me about bull-fighting it was to tell me things that helped me to understand the art of it better, things that my dad wouldn't have known about. I soaked it all up, as well as the numerous glasses of white wine that they helped to throw down my neck. They would tell me there were only two really great matadors, El Cordobés, who I have mentioned, and Manolete, a favourite of my father.

Paco had already told me about El Cordobés. He broke away from how a traditional matador should look like and how he should behave. He had long hair, as opposed to the short style adopted by the matadors of that time; he disliked authority and was constantly in trouble with the police. But he represented the true feelings of the people who, at that time, were still being suppressed by Franco. So his unorthodox methods were seen by the people as a small act of rebellion and non-conformity, and they loved him for it. There's a certain way of behaving in a bullring, the matador should always show the bull respect. El Cordobés didn't. He was extremely disrespectful to the bull and would do things like put the sword in and then jump on the animal's back. This was his general way of behaving. He revelled in breaking all the rules. When you fight bulls you should walk to the bull with grace, you should confront the bull with your chest and present the *muleta* forward of your body and bring it gracefully through to execute a pass, the *muleta* ending up behind you. Then you link a few more passes together, and it becomes even more graceful and entertaining. El Cordobés didn't do anything like that. He held the *muleta* almost behind his body and really made it look a lot more dangerous because his body, rather than the cape, was now exposed to the bull. Then, when he had executed a pass, he didn't finish it in the correct way by standing in the correct position. He'd stand in a position where the bull could get hold of him, and often it did. He got tossed around more than anybody had ever seen in bullfighting before.

Some people do make a name for themselves by stepping outside the zone. El Cordobés became very famous for doing this. Even as a *novillero*, before he'd even become a fully fledged matador, he was hot property. His big break came in the most controversial fashion imaginable. The phone rang as he was making love to a girl in a hotel bedroom. He answered it, and it was a representative of the Barcelona bullring offering him a date in the capital city. Everything was agreed until it came to his fee. They offered him 100,000 pesetas, which, at £500, was a fortune in 1961. He said it had to be 200,000 pesetas. The representative said he'd have to check with his boss whether they could go up to this. El Cordobés told him if he put the phone down and had to ring him back with confirmation the price would go up to 300,000 pesetas. The representative rang back five minutes later to say 200,000 pesetas would be fine.

'No,' said El Cordobés, 'the price is now 300,000, like I said, and if you have to put the phone down again and ring me back with confirmation it will go up to 400,000 pesetas.'

He ended up getting half a million pesetas for the fight. That was the character of the man. Nobody messed him about. He messed them about and he didn't suffer fools. He'd been arrested as a young man for climbing into the bullring, and in his mind it was payback time. Driving back from one fight he got into an argument with his manager over money. El Cordobés simply slammed the brakes on the car, threw his manager out into the pitch dark, miles from anywhere, and drove off.

It got to the point where the impresarios, who are the organizers of the bullfights, had had enough of him and they tried to cut him off. They got together and agreed he should be paid only 100,000 pesetas a fight or they wouldn't put him on. El Cordobés told them to get lost. He then bought his own portable bullring and, whenever these organizers staged a fight, he put his ring next to theirs and fought next to them. His ring was full, theirs were empty. They ended up begging him on their bended knees to come back to them and fight. He did, but on his terms.

Manolete, on the other hand, was a class act. He was the first matador to cross the bull. Nobody had crossed the bull's line of charge before his time. It was a new way of fighting that was quickly picked up on and adopted. Then there were the stories about the Spanish Civil War, which was still a major talking point because many of these people I drank with were still getting over the repercussions of it. Paco's father, Miguel, told me how his brother was taken out of his house in the early hours of the morning and shot because Franco's henchmen suspected he supported the other side. He told me he lived on a farm where they grew tobacco and other cash crops and every night following his brother's execution he went into the fields to sleep, just in case Franco's lot came for him – they only ever came knocking in the dead of night, so he knew he was safe during the day. He told me that every evening the family would huddle round a radio and listen to a bloke called 'Chuchi'. It was only after a few minutes that I realized he was talking about Winston Churchill. He was a big supporter of Churchill, because Churchill was opposed to Franco.

The Spanish Civil War seemed to touch every conversation in Spain back then. Hostilities came about following a Franco-led coup in 1936 against the elected Popular Front government that split the country and led to war. After Franco's victory against Republican forces three years later he established a right-wing authoritarian regime that lasted until 1978, three years after his death, when a new constitution was drafted. An estimated half million people died during the Civil War, with another 100,000 Republicans estimated to have been killed or died in prison in the post-war period. In the immediate aftermath of the war those opponents of Franco who escaped summary execution were rounded up and put to work on forced labour projects: building railways, draining swamps or digging canals. The Spanish intelligentsia, atheists and military and government figures that had remained loyal to the Madrid government during the war were the main targets for oppression. And the immediate aftermath of the Civil War was socially bleak. Many Republican supporters fled into exile, and Spain lost thousands of doctors, nurses, teachers, lawyers, judges, professors, businessmen and artists. The brilliant minds fled and they only came back with a gradual easing of the oppression which slackened following Spain's admittance into the United Nations in 1955. By the time I arrived in Spain the local population could be quite critical of Franco. The fear of arrest, torture and execution for speaking out had eased, though they were still careful not to be too critical, and anything negative to be said about Franco was still spoken in hushed tones.

But I did feel the place was secure, more secure than when he died and a democracy was established. Dictators behave dreadfully I know, but one thing they always manage to keep under control is street crime. It's the same in Cuba under Castro. If you're a young girl you could walk down any street in Havana at four in the morning, dripping in gold jewellery, and nobody would touch you because there are plain-clothed coppers on nearly every corner. In 1963, Franco's Spain was very much the model for Cuba today, even in the way it was opening up for the forthcoming tourism boom.

Another major cultural difference was their outlook on women and sex. In England it was the start of the swinging sixties, and everyone was at it like rabbits. But in Spain it was the complete opposite. The Spanish are great touchers, but not with the women. I was sat round a table during this Spanish holiday with a group of about twenty made up of husbands with their wives. As I talked to one woman I touched her on the arm only for her husband to stand up and say to me, 'Take your hands off my wife.'

He ended up getting a real roasting off his friends for not understanding my culture, but I learned very quickly not to touch women as a sign of friendship. Even so, it didn't stop the men going to brothels at every available opportunity. The police turned a blind eye to all this, even though it was illegal. The brothels were well run, and the girls were checked medically for diseases at least once a month. I found it slightly hypocritical on the men's part that you couldn't touch the wife or the daughter, who more often than not dressed in the old-style Spanish way, which was to cover up as much as possible, but these men could go out and do it with a prostitute whenever the fancy took them. I had a real problem with this and I still have it when it comes to selling sex. I just don't feel comfortable with the idea of paying for that kind of pleasure.

The closest I got was during this ten-day holiday when I saw a gorgeous girl in a bar. As soon as I started chatting to her she said that she wanted paying. Unfortunately my heart ruled my head, so I told her OK, and off we went to a hotel. But there's no romance in having sex for money, and this was preying on my mind as we walked through the streets. What was also on my mind was who was in the background, i.e. the pimps and hangers-on taking money off this poor girl. We went to a very cheap hotel, and this lovely girl went off to the bathroom and came out with no clothes on. She couldn't have been more than twenty. I was besotted with her, but it just didn't feel right, especially when she put this big daft yellow thing on my penis. I was standing there, wearing this horrible ugly condom, while she tried to turn me on. In the end I told her, 'I'm sorry, I just can't go through with this.'

'No, you have paid for it, you must enjoy it,' she said.

'No,' I said, 'I can't. Maybe one day we'll do it as mates. This isn't right.'

I gave her some extra money and told her to go, but I asked her to keep that extra money for herself and not give it to her pimp, and that is my only experience with prostitutes. She went into the night, and I never saw her again. I knew I shouldn't have done it from the moment I agreed. She was so pretty, though, and I was young, free and single.

In Granada at that time all the blokes were knocking off the hookers. It was a very Victorian way of behaving. They treated their women with great respect but they also didn't let them do anything. Spanish women were almost viewed like the men viewed their cars. They kept them very clean but never, ever let anyone drive in them or have a go, or put their hands on them. On the other hand, they were round the back of the garage paying for sex with some banger. A few years later I discovered prostitution was even more prevalent in Barcelona. The girls would line up along these dark, narrow bars, with their skirts hitched up so you could see their knickers and their boobs spilling out of these low-cut dresses, and you basically picked one and went into an upstairs room for sex. That was the first time I saw champagne served in flat glasses. The prostitutes would pour it and then swill it round with their fingers. I don't know if it was meant to turn the punters on, but I found it a little bit vulgar. It was even more vulgar when you found yourself presented with the bill for the champagne afterwards. It was wrong on every level.

But in Granada it was party time, and I was having a ball. I loved all the stories and their way of life and I stayed in that dark little bar with dark wood and sawdust on the floor all day listening to the tales of the old men. More often than not they'd end up carrying me back in the evening and putting me to bed. I have never been able to take my drink, and I think Miguel's wife realized this because during one of these sessions, as I was being carried back, she screamed at him in the street: 'Why have you done that to that young boy again?'

I was in heaven. This was a great way of living. All the English who had come on the groom's side didn't mix, didn't like the food and tended to stay in their digs. I was getting the full-on cultural insight into Spanish life and traditions including tapas, which back then represented tapas in the traditional manner. It was a small piece of bread put on top of your glass of wine. The flies would be attracted to the bread rather than the wine and you wouldn't end up with them floating in your glass. *Tapa* means cover. It was only years later it got reinterpreted to mean a small plate of food for human consumption. Even today, when people ask me if I want to go out for tapas, it conjures up images of people sat round eating food meant for flies. The white wine that these tapas covered was also very good. The image of Spanish white wine being rubbish is false. They may have sent all their bad stuff to Britain in the past, but what they kept was very nice indeed. I was drinking wine from Jerez, where they produce the sherry. The grape is the Pedro Ximénez variety, the first pressing of which is made into wine, and I remember tasting a hint of sherry in it. It was beautiful. Every morning when I woke up I couldn't wait to get into that bar and enjoy the company of these men, the youngest of whom was in his fifties.

Some of the English lot on the groom's side got Spanish tummy after a couple of days. That was the big thing then. Every holidaymaker who went to Spain got it. They blamed it on poor hygiene standards, but I blamed it on the daft sods getting dehydrated and drinking water from the tap, which was full of all sorts of rubbish that could easily give you an upset stomach. It's OK to drink now, but back then it was very dodgy. I had Spanish tummy from eating an ice-cream I bought off a street vendor, so I stuck to drinking wine after that and ate whatever they ate and I was fine. What made me laugh was the English lot constantly complaining that the food was swimming in grease. It wasn't grease, it was olive oil, and the Spanish swilled it over everything because it was so good for them.

I did more drinking than eating during those ten days. The trouble was that in Santa Fé, the town where I was staying, all the buildings were painted a brilliant white, which wasn't conducive to getting over a hangover when the sun was reflecting off them in the mornings. Every day I woke up to mad white buildings and the first thing I did was put on a pair of sunglasses. It became slightly tiresome in the end. But it was infinitely better than the ever-present grey stormclouds of Salford. The city had just come out of the worst winter on record, so to be in the warmth and sunshine of Spain was bliss. I always felt slightly euphoric over there and on a high, brought on by exposure to sunshine. It was certainly a change from living in grim, satanic Salford. And my diet improved in Spain as well. It was all fresh fish and seasonal vegetables or salad. I was learning a new way to live, one that was infinitely better than the life I had back home. And with all the fascinating stories about bullfighting it started to cross my mind that becoming a bullfighter would be a great way to earn a living. But I was English and I didn't believe any Englishman could ever break into a world dominated by Spaniards. I was enthralled by it but I couldn't yet comprehend how I could ever do it.

It was during my visit to Granada for Maria's wedding that I saw my first bullfight. Granada's annual holidays are based around the religious celebration of Corpus Christi. I was loving my first experience of Spanish life and I didn't want to leave Spain without seeing a bullfight. When I learned that the Feria de Corpus was taking place in the capital and that there was a bullfight every day I started to pester my new friends to get me to a bullfight. Paco's sister, the beautiful Rosario, offered to take me. She got the tickets and together with her friend we got the tram into town. Granada is a beautiful city. It is a visitor's dream with a great Moorish influence. The bullring is one of impressive splendour, and I wandered the streets and bars in the district before the fight with my two lovely companions enjoying the sunshine and the bustling atmosphere that surrounds a major bullring in the hours leading up to a bullfight.

When we entered the bullring I noticed the faint smell of cattle, and we walked from the ice-cool underpass into the glaring sunlight on the terraces. I found the view stunning. Maroon-coloured boards running round the amber-coloured arena marked with two pristine white circles and the bowl-shaped terraces resplendent with bunting and Spanish flags adorning the balconies. The President's alcove had a beautiful moquette tapestry draped over the front. The public had to come in their Sunday best: men in suits smoking robust-sized cigars and the women dressed fit for Ascot. There were vendors offering whisky and beer from ice-buckets. When the bullring clock touched 5 p.m. the President showed his white handkerchief, the band struck up a *paso doble*, and to warm applause the bullfighters entered the ring and lined up for the parade. I was totally absorbed and fascinated. I can't recall too many details but I do remember the matador Zurito. I sensed the emotion and control in his work, which was performed in what appeared to me to be great danger. I was sitting in a bull-ring for the first time in my life between two beautiful women and watching a matador transmit emotion to his audience through his style and personality. I had discovered a new passion and I was hooked for the rest of my life.

My conversion was to come in stages. I was very friendly at that time with fellow Sale player Freddie Griffiths, who has died recently. He was larger than life, very loud, very big and a real personality to boot. Freddie was thirteen years older than me; he had had trials for England and played for Lancashire. I was just breaking into the Sale side. I went on holiday to Italy with Freddie Griffiths, just after I'd returned from Spain, and we had a great time chatting up the beautiful Latin women and basically getting drunk, as young men do. We enjoyed it so much we booked another holiday soon afterwards. It was a time when package tours were just being introduced. We went to Ibiza with the legendary player Eric Evans, who had just retired as captain of England, and his new wife, Marion, together with Ken Nelson, who was captain of Sale, and his lovely wife, Greta. There were six of us, and it was party time. My Spanish was great, so all the locals loved us, and we could communicate with them. At night we hit the discos. At one disco it was always virtually pitch black, so you could never really see who you were dancing with. Freddie and I could just about make out two girls dancing together on the floor, and

Freddie was on to them like a shot. 'Come on,' he said to me, 'Let's go and pull these.'

Fred always wanted the best so he went for who he thought was the nicest looking. When the lights came up after the song had finished his face was a picture. I'd ended up with the equivalent of Miss Sweden and he'd chosen what I would politely say was a girl somewhat on the large side. I ended up with this girl for quite a few days – it was a real holiday romance – and Fred tried his best to stick with this other one and do the honourable thing, but in the end he couldn't take any more and let her down. Mine wouldn't let me have sex with her, though. I found the same thing with other girls I went with on that holiday. They did everything but have sex. It was very frustrating for a young lad like me. It got to the last night, and Fred, who also had the same problem, said to me, 'We can't go back home and tell the lads we never got a shag on holiday.'

So we went to our usual nightclub, but it was empty because it was changeover day when holidaymakers were either leaving or arriving. There was no chance of us pulling in there, so we walked forlornly back to the marina and to our hotel. Just as we were about to go into the hotel we noticed a small dingy café across the road still had a light on. 'Sod it, let's get a coffee before we hit the sack,' Fred said.

As we walked in two old women were sitting in a corner. Fred looked at them, then turned to me and said, 'It's got to be them. We can't go back without having sex with them.'

It turned out the woman I got was a forty-five-year-old canteen manageress from Glasgow who, when I was having sex with her, said to me, 'By the way, I have never done it before.'

She was a virgin at forty-five! When we got back to England it would've been better if we hadn't done anything, because Fred was telling everyone in the Sale dressing room how I'd had sex with a forty-five-year-old virgin.

But I had a great time in Ibiza, and it just so happened there were bullfights galore over there. There were two lads on the first bill we saw. One had grace and did things correctly, but the appreciation of the crowd was tepid. The second fighter was obviously influenced by El Cordobés's antics and was far more flamboyant. I had my heart in my mouth with some of the things he was doing, and he was the one who got the bigger applause because, despite being technically deficient in comparison with his colleague, he had provided an entertaining show. But what he wouldn't have realized and what I didn't know then was that the first lad with all the grace and technique was the one who had more chance of making it as a matador. The second lad would have got found out as soon as he went to fight in the major cities.

We went to five fights, but things didn't run smoothly because in the fifth Eric got arrested for throwing a cushion into the ring. The authorities had ordered a clampdown after a bullfighter called El Nacional had appeared in Spain and been particularly bad. Before the ban people showed their hostility by throwing things into the ring like oranges and bread, that sort of thing. Some idiot threw a bottle, and it hit El Nacional on the back of the head and paralysed him. Because of this a law was brought in which banned anything from being thrown into the ring. If you are going to throw a cushion into the ring that you have been sitting on it's fairly innocuous, but nevertheless it is still banned. Eric didn't know this and with a great big flourish said, 'All stand back,' as he threw this cushion. Seconds later a policeman tapped him on the shoulder, and he was hauled off in a lorry with about twenty other English tourists who'd also thrown something into the ring and fined 500 pesetas. His wife was so furious she asked a policeman if she could go into the cell with him because she wanted to give him a good hiding. When I saw him being carted off I wondered to myself: if only they knew they were arresting the captain of the England Grand Slam-winning rugby union side.

Freddie could see I loved bullfighting, despite the mishaps, and he said to me, 'When we get back to England I'll give you a book I've read that tells you everything you need to know about bullfighting.'

This was my wake-up call. This was where it would all come together. Freddie's book turned out to be Vincent Hitchcock's autobiography, *Suit of Lights*. It wasn't really much of an explanation of bullfighting. But to me it was the Eureka moment, because Vincent was English, and it suddenly occurred to me that it was possible for an Englishman to become a matador. It began to dawn on me that, if he could do it, then so could I. But it had been a long journey of discovery from my father, to the Spanish family, to the wedding, then Ibiza, and now this book. Initially everybody thought I was going to be a top rugby union player, and Sale wanted to play me in their first team when I was sixteen. But by the time I was twenty I wasn't making it at county level and I knew I would never go beyond club rugby. That was it for me then. I thought, sod the rugby, I'm going to do something different. I read Vincent's autobiography from cover to cover and wrote a letter to him that I sent via the publishers. A couple of weeks later he sent me a letter back, the gist of it being, 'Come down and see me.'

It was just after Christmas 1963. I'd been picked for Sale to play at Gosforth up near Newcastle, and he invited me to go and see him the day before. It was going to be a bit of a slog to get back for the game, but I couldn't miss this opportunity. I was reading Hemingway's *Death in the Afternoon* at this point. My mates noticed I was reading a lot of stuff on bullfighting but reacted in utter disbelief when I told them my ambition was to make it as a bullfighter. Mam convinced herself my trip to see Vincent was just another one of my whims.

But I flew down to London, hired a car and drove to Faversham in Kent, where he had his farm and where we'd arranged to meet in a pub. Outside this little old country pub he had a bright green Jag glistening in the driveway and he was stood at the bar with a few mates when I turned up. The first thing that struck me was how dashing he looked. He was very tall, very slim, extremely good looking and had a huge personality to match. I was struck by the pair of Spanish Campo boots he was wearing. I'd never seen anything like them before. They looked pretty cool on him. He took me back to his house and I met his wife, Jacquie, and then we talked bulls. Vincent had fought throughout the 1940s and 1950s and told me he was now planning a comeback after a number of years out of the game. He was lucky in that he came from a wealthy background, and, as I was to later find, without money and back-up you haven't got much hope of making it as a bullfighter. When Vincent left school he joined the merchant navy and worked as a bursar. He discovered bullfighting when his ship was docked in Gibraltar and he went to a fight. He got a taste for it, got his father, who was a jeweller, to fund his training and basically blazed a trail. Vincent never became a full matador, but he did fight in the great arenas of Madrid and Valencia. Unfortunately for him he failed at the top level. To make it in bullfighting you have to succeed in Madrid. And this is what tends to happen all the time: would-be matadors fail to get it right when they're first exposed in the imposing arena of Madrid and they fade into obscurity afterwards. You only get one chance in the big *ferias*. Vincent failed to take his chance. But he was willing to take a chance on me and invited me to his villa in Majorca, where he said he would teach me the basics. That was all I needed to hear. The next day I flew up to Tyneside and played for Sale against Gosforth. I remember standing on the pitch in the freezing cold and lashing rain and looking at the grass while my team-mates were bashing up the opposition and I thought: what the hell am I doing here?

My head had gone. The rugby had died. I just didn't want to be standing on that pitch. All I could think about was bullfighting. I wasn't focused on the game any more. I wanted to be in Majorca, being trained by Vincent. I wanted to be a matador. It sounds daft and did sound daft then, some bloke from Salford dreaming of fighting bulls, and even today when I'm on a plane going out to Spain and someone says, 'What are you going to Spain for?' I'd rather say, 'I'm on business,' than 'I'm going to fight a bull.'

But in the early 1960s that was my dream, and it was a dream I was determined to fulfil. Mam reacted in utter disbelief when I told her of my intentions, and even when I started packing my suitcase I still don't think it really sank in with her. She was of the opinion I'd be back home within a week. I was determined to prove her wrong. But as I went to leave she was there at the front door.

'You're not going,' she said. 'I'm not going to allow this!'

Chapter Three

A ROOKIE
IN VALENCIA

It was April 1964. I had a date to meet Vincent Hitchcock in Majorca. I'd sent him a letter to say I was coming, and he'd sent me one back saying he could always be found in a place called Vera's Bar Rodeo in El Terreno, which is just outside Palma. The only thing stopping me was my mam. As I was about to leave she collared me. She sat me down, looked me in the eyes and said, 'Listen to me, you can't do this, I can't let you go through with this, it's dangerous. You could end up being hurt. You could even end up getting yourself killed.'

For most of my life whenever Mam cornered me like that and gave me advice it was always for my own benefit. I've no doubt she was right to tell me that, but I was selfish, and it was my selfishness that gave me the drive to spur me on to become a matador. Nobody has benefited from it apart from me. And it was my own selfishness then that led me to totally disregard her advice. All she was bothered about was the danger. She was very nervous about things that were potentially foolhardy and she was never a reckless person. So what I was doing terrified her. But I couldn't let that stop me, because the desire to do this was too great. I flew into Majorca from Manchester, walked into the bar where I was due to meet Vincent, and disaster struck! The owner of the bar said Vincent had taken a boat to the mainland to promote a bullfight. She said she didn't know where he was based or when he'd be back. Effectively I'd wasted my journey. But I wasn't going back home – no way. I'd come to learn how to be a bullfighter, and a bullfighter I was going to be. So I decided to stay in Majorca and wait for Vincent to come back; whether that was in a week, a month or even a year.

I sought out a *sereno* to get me a room for the night. In those days the *sereno* was the night-watchman – he was often either old or disabled or both. He carried a stick and on this stick were keys for all the Spanish flats and houses he looked after. If you forgot your key this man would let you in. And if you needed a room he was the one who could tell you if anybody was renting one out. All you needed to do was walk into the middle of the street, clap your hands loudly and he'd appear. I did and out popped this little old *sereno*: 'I'm looking for a room,' I said in my best Spanish.

'Ah, come with me,' he replied, and it was that simple.

I was put up with a Spanish family who rented their room for something like twenty pesetas a night. That was the equivalent of a shilling in old money. You could get in the pictures for a shilling back then. The next thing I needed to do was find a job until Vincent got back. That wasn't a problem. In Spain back then you didn't need a licence to sell booze, so there were bars everywhere. It really was a drinking city. There was a bar cum café on every corner; some of them, like Bar Bosch, are still around today.

The Majorcans were and still are great socializers, and these types of places were always packed, primarily so the customers could have a drink with the food they ate, unlike in Britain, where the culture is to drink to get hammered. Palma, the capital of Majorca, was a world away from the Salford of the 1960s. Salford was very *Saturday Night and Sunday Morning*: people worked until they dropped all week in a boring factory with no aim or ambition in life save for Saturday nights, when they could go out, get drunk, pull a girl and smoke a few fags before creeping back to work on a Monday morning with no money in their pockets. The Spaniards, and especially those in Majorca, didn't do that. They went out primarily to eat. And their working hours were totally different. They worked 8 a.m. until 1 p.m., then went back to work at 4 p.m. until 8 p.m. Two hours later they went out for food, primarily to have the *menu del dia*. This was a cheap three-course meal with a glass of wine and bread for about 100 pesetas, maybe less.

I found work in a small restaurant in Palma that was typical of the type of place that catered for the locals. This was a good job. Spain and the Balearics were poor back then, and working in a bar or restaurant was seen as a good profession by the locals and one that was highly desired. Every bloke aspired to be a head waiter. That was the job to have. The restaurant I worked in was more like a working-class café than some haven of gastronomy. It had no menu, only a chalkboard showing the dishes of the day, which could be fresh fish or other things like roast beef, a Spanish stew, or minced cod stuffed in giant green peppers which was a speciality of the island. Whatever they got fresh that day went up on the chalkboard. There was also the obligatory sawdust on the floor. I was in the back butchering the meat. In the kitchen worked a great big fat woman who was the pot washer. She was a monster who always dressed in black and only had one tooth. On my first day I needed her help and shouted, 'Maria, *te quiero*,' which basically meant 'Maria, I want you.' Unfortunately I'd got my Spanish terminology wrong. When you say '*te quiero*' in Spanish it basically translates to mean I love you. Her eyes lit up, and all the other kitchen staff were on the floor rolling with laughter and shouting: 'Frank fancies old Maria.'

But it got me in with them, they liked me for that, and they liked me even more for my butchering skills, which were far more advanced than any of theirs. But within a week they had me front of house working as a waiter. The waiting work helped my Spanish get better and better. The restaurant boss saw me as a novelty to be exploited for the good of his business. Rather than have me in the back working he wanted me out front, because many people were not used to seeing an Englishman working in Spain; most of them were just starting to come for their holidays. When the locals asked me what I was doing working in a bar I told them I wanted to be a bullfighter: '*Quiero ser torero*,' I said to them.

Their reaction to this was almost always the same: 'What!' they'd exclaim in disbelief, and then they'd start taking the Mickey. They would say things like: 'Show us how you are going to be a bullfighter. Make a pass.'

I used tablecloths or whatever I could lay my hands on to

show them, but I didn't have a clue what to do because I'd had no training. I was basing all my moves on what I'd seen and remembered in the bullfights I had been to in Malaga and Ibiza. What I was doing was obviously nothing like a pass, and they found it hilarious. I told them about Vincent Hitchcock, and they asked to see the book. When I brought it in they were very dismissive and said, 'These are two-year-old bulls he fights. They are not the proper ones, the big ones that are four and five years old.'

There was a bloke sitting in a corner alone listening to all this going on. As they took the Mickey out of Vincent and me he suddenly said to them, 'Who are you to mock this young man and his bullfighting friend? How many two-year-olds have you lot fought in the bullring?'

They suddenly looked very sheepish and uncomfortable. He called me over and said, 'I am Eduardo Ford, an ex-matador from Valencia. Take no notice of these idiots.'

Sometimes life deals you a great hand. I'd not really had much luck pursuing my bullfighting dreams so far. Eduardo Ford was the ace in my pack, and he said to me, 'What I want to say to you is your Englishman, the bullfighter, is not the right person to take you along the road of bullfighting. If you like I will give you a letter of introduction to be given to someone in Valencia who will teach you how to fight bulls. He is a proper bullfighting man.'

'OK,' I said. 'No problem. Bring me the letter and I'll go to Valencia.'

I was more inclined to listen to him than to Vincent, who hadn't and would never reach the status of fully fledged matador, and didn't have the experience this man had. He brought the letter to the restaurant the next day. It was an introduction to the bullfighting school in Valencia. That was it for me. This was what I'd been dreaming of for months. I quit my job on the spot and went to get all my gear together to catch the midnight ferry to Valencia.

I was going to miss my workmates. Although I'd only been at the restaurant two weeks I'd made friends with a good set of lads and lent them money while I was working there. I had taken £100 over with me from England, which was a lot of money back then, but I only had £10 to take with me to Valencia and didn't think I'd ever see the money I'd lent these lads again. After all, why should they pay me back? They were broke, and I was off, and I didn't have time to wait for them to get it together. But I did get it back. One of the lads came to my digs and dropped it off. He left the money in an envelope at the side of my bed with a note to say good luck.

Before I caught the ferry I went to this posh café which had a terrace overlooking a big square. I'd walked past it going to and from the restaurant and always saw people outside drinking wine and eating strawberries and cream. It was perhaps the most sophisticated place in Palma. I vowed to eat there before I ever left the island. So I walked in an hour before the ferry was due to leave, ordered my strawberries and cream with a glass of wine and sat daydreaming about fighting bulls and pondering how life had changed massively in just a few short weeks. What would have happened if I hadn't met Eduardo? If he didn't give me that invitation I would've probably hung on and met Vincent, I suppose. Whether I would've made it as a matador, who knows? When I met Eduardo rather than Vincent it was a defining moment in my life. I was so happy I went out and bought a cape to take with me to Valencia. After all, I'd need a cape if I was going to fight bulls.

I'd been voraciously reading up on bullfighting while I was there because I wanted to get a feel for why it evoked such passion among Spaniards. I was also fascinated by its history. Bullfighting is steeped in tradition and history and can trace its roots back to prehistoric bull worship and sacrifice. There are cave paintings that are thousands of years old in Spain depicting a man facing a bull. Bullfighting also has strong links to ancient Rome, where many human versus animal events were held as warm-ups for the gladiatorial combats to come. In one of its earliest forms the bull was fought from horseback using a lance. Picadors are the remnants of this tradition, but their role has now diminished to one of preparing the bull for the matador.

Bullfighting evolved into a tradition that was largely undertaken by the nobility. Religious festivities and royal weddings were celebrated by fights in the local plaza. The Spanish introduced the idea of fighting bulls on foot round about 1726 with a man called Pedro Romero, who is widely regarded as being the first to pioneer this new style. As it caught on men started using capes, which drew ever-larger audiences, and thus the modern *corrida*, or bullfight, began to take shape, and the riding noblemen were replaced by commoners on foot. The *corrida* encouraged the development of dedicated bullrings, initially square but later circular to discourage the cornering of the action.

The modern style of bullfighting is down to Juan Belmonte, who is seen as a great revolutionary. He introduced a daring and unique new method in which he stayed still throughout the pass. This new way of fighting was more dangerous, as seen in the number of times matadors got gored and killed, but it was also seen as the definitive way to fight bulls. The actual process itself has changed little since its introduction in 1726. Back then Romero, who was from Ronda in southern Spain, and was also the first man to write down the basic rules of bullfighting, used the *estoque*, which is a sword to kill the bull, and the *muleta*, which is a small cape for the last stage of the fight. This process generally still goes on today.

Modern-day bullfighting comes under an Act of Parliament administered by the Ministry of the Interior, so there's a whole list of things you have to fulfil to become a bullfighter and rules to follow during and after a fight. Failure to follow these rules could result in imprisonment. For example the basic rule is that the bullfighter is required to kill a virgin bull, and if he refuses to kill it in the ring he can be arrested. It's a criminal offence not to attempt to kill the bull after signing the contract. But there are other requirements a bullfighter must follow. A dress code is one of them. The entire garb worn by the matador is written down by law. He must follow the style laid down in statutes, from the shoes to the stockings, suit, waistcoat and tie.

The hardest part of getting dressed is wriggling into the skin-tight *taleguilla*, which are the famous figure-moulding breeches. As I would later discover, you literally have to be lifted off your feet and shaken into them. The lacing of the breeches is also of vital importance. They must be laced to just the right pressure: too tight and the circulation is cut off, too slack and the whole garb feels insecure and loose. Then there are shirts, a sash and a jacket which goes over the waistcoat, all made to specific rules and regulations. A matador must also sport a pigtail, and if he turns up at the bullring without his pigtail he can be fined.

On the day of the fight the bulls are selected at 12 noon. The bullfighters choose which bulls they are to fight by drawing lots: the matador's representative, usually the senior *banderillero*, goes down to the corrals of the bullring, and the bulls are separated as near as possible into three equal pairs. A big bull is normally paired with a small animal, for example, or one with large horns to one with a small pair. The numbers of each pair are then written down on pieces of Rizla cigarette paper which are screwed up into tiny balls and dropped in a hat to be drawn out by the representatives. Then for the next five or six hours the bullfighters rest. Most go and get some kip; others play cards or read a book. An hour before the fight the bullfighters get dressed. They're required to be at the bullring no later than fifteen minutes before the start of the fight.

Two policemen or women on horseback open the show. They go across the ring to where the President is sitting and literally ask for the keys to open the bull pen. The President is more often than not the Chief of Police or his delegate; sometimes it's the Mayor of the town. And he'll normally have two professional assessors either side of him to act as judges and advise him. The bullfighters are then paraded in the ring in their garb. They enter the ring accompanied by band music.

The senior bullfighter stands on the far left, the junior one in the middle, and the second in line on the right. When I talk about senior and junior it's all about when they got their licences granted. It does not necessarily go on ability. Often the best matadors, like the world number one in 2008, José Tomás, don't like to be placed on the far left because it means they'll open the fight. They prefer to go second and to be standing on the right. So José is always looking for someone who has been in bullfighting longer than him to act as the senior matador and open the fight.

To start the fight the President shows a white handkerchief, and a trumpet sounds to warn everybody the bull is coming into the ring. The bullfighter will then stand right opposite where the bull is coming out of the gate, and there will be a *banderillero* to his right and one to his left – the *banderilleros* are there to test the bull. When the bull comes into the ring the *banderillero* will flap his cape at the bull to check it can see it and react properly and that it doesn't have any problems with its eyesight. The other guy will then coax the bull into chasing him, and he'll deliberately run away when it charges. Tourists tend to laugh when this happens, but this is purely for the benefit of the matador, who can now check how it runs and how it gallops. In those first few yards the bull is showing the matador its traits. When it finally gets to the *banderillero*, who has now hidden behind a pen, the matador wants to see if the bull now puts its head right down or if it holds it high, because whether the bull's head is high or low tells the matador how he is going to use the cape.

The bullfighter observes all this and then attempts to make

a series of Veronicas, named after St Veronica, who offered a towel to Christ at the foot of Calvary. The matador offers the cape to the bull and is effectively teaching the bull how to charge and to stop so he has some control over it. In the later part of the fight, when the sword is used, the bull will be fully run to a standstill, because you can't put the sword in if the bull is running round willy-nilly. Ideally the bull will be standing still when the sword is applied.

The first act now begins when the two picadors come into the ring on horses which weigh a maximum of 600 kilos. The horses have sheet-metal padded armour so that when the bull charges the horse and hits it, the padding dissipates the blow, and the horse doesn't get injured. The bullfighter now watches the bull charge the horse, this gives him important clues as to how the bull is developing. As he does this the picador pierces the bull's shoulder with a lance. To put the sword in successfully the bull's head must be down.

By this stage the bull is tired and has realized this is serious, and its behaviour changes dramatically during this stage of the fight. If it didn't get picced it might have become bored of charging and simply retire to a corner of the ring and refuse to charge. But by piccing the bull it becomes focused, and its survival instincts come into play. Temperamentally these bulls differ from those bred for food. They are far more aggressive, so when they are threatened their neck bulges and they charge towards whatever has threatened them and attack. When a bull is alone it'll charge even its own shadow if disturbed. Now the bull is concentrating on the threat that presents itself.

The length of time a bull spends engaged with the picador

is only between five and fifteen seconds. Then the second act begins when the *banderilleros* run across the ring one at a time to place tiny barbed hooks, rather like fish hooks, into the back of the bull's shoulder and tossing muscle. The damage is minimal. This encounter causes the bull to run in a more measured manner and will assist in the lowering of the bull's head at the time of the kill.

The third act is the kill, when the bullfighter attracts the bull with his *muleta* into performing a series of passes. He is attempting to manoeuvre the bull into a position where he can place the sword between the shoulder blades and close to the heart. A clumsy thrust which doesn't result in a clean death will often result in loud protests from the audience, who want a quick and clean death. The final act is where everything comes together. This is where the really artistic element of bull-fighting comes into play: making the final passes with the cloth and crowning it with a kill.

If the bullfighter has done well, the crowd will wave white handkerchiefs to petition the President to give the matador an ear. Giving an ear is linked to a tradition dating back a couple of hundred years, when the dead bull's carcass was given to the successful matador as payment for his work. This tradition died out and instead was replaced with the awarding of an ear, which symbolized the bull's carcass. According to law, if the majority petition for an ear the President must give it, even if he didn't think the fighter was any good. But they don't always go along with this, and there have been instances of public disorder over the refusal to grant an ear. The awarding of a second ear is at the President's discretion. Generally, if a bullfighter has been very good and has pleased the crowd, he'll get two ears. In Madrid two ears is the maximum any bullfighter can receive. But out of Madrid in smaller rings two ears, a tail and even hooves may be awarded, which gets a bit ridiculous if you ask me. Whether a fighter gets ears generally depends on how well he has effected the sword thrust. The public will not stand for too many misses. Apart from the lack of elegance they hate to see an animal massacred. But they will forgive a fighter for striking the bone and not making a proper thrust providing he goes over the horns and exposes his body as he does so. But if, after the sword thrust, the animal doesn't drop straight away, a shorter sword is employed. The matador then has to lower the bull's head and sever the spinal cord with this sword by thrusting it between the back of the skull and the first or third vertebra. It's a spot dead in the centre of the neck. If it's done properly the bull instantly drops dead. Fail to administer it properly and the bullfighter faces the wrath of the crowd.

All this I was yet to learn as I sat in that Palma café, eating my strawberries and cream. I was simply desperate to get going. Ford had sent me to see Patricio Garrigos, and all Ford knew was that he lived somewhere in Valencia, which is a big place. I caught the midnight ferry in Palma and arrived in Valencia at 8 a.m., armed with my suitcase and this letter Ford had given me to take to Garrigos. Valencia was awe-inspiring. I had never seen anything like it. The first thing I noticed was a heavy police presence. They were everywhere. But under Franco Spain did live in a police state. There was no crime, though, that was for sure. And the streets were so wide, so clean and so bright. In Salford the predominant colour seemed to be grey. Everything was just dull and miserable back home. Here the magnificent wide streets were a magnet for light. The place seemed warmer, brighter and cleaner – but then an army of water trucks did come out every evening and hose down the city with water cannons.

As I strolled through the outskirts of Valencia, gazing in wonderment, I noticed there was only one make of car, the state-produced SEAT. Nobody could afford to buy foreign cars because the import taxes slapped on them made their price extortionate. So everybody drove round in SEATs. But in the absence of choice the Spaniards had loaded them with extras – jazzy wheel trims, posh wing mirrors, car radios, all sorts of things to differentiate them from the next vehicle.

I hopped on a tram to the centre of the city to begin my search for Garrigos. The great thing about the trams was if you could cling on to them from the outside rather than go inside you could get a free ride. Those who went inside had to pay. So the trams would always be loaded with bodies, all clinging on for dear life. When I got off I asked for the bullring. Valencia has a magnificent bullring, built in the mid-nineteenth century and modelled on the Roman amphitheatre in Nîmes. I walked in, and it just felt and looked fantastic. In the middle of the ring all these young kids were practising, and I asked them, 'Does anybody know Garrigos?'

They all knew him and said, 'He doesn't come here, but go to the Calle Sevilla, number two, that is where you'll find him.'

It was less than 100 yards from the arena. Garrigos ran a tailor's shop with his brother. I walked in, and he was standing there, not very tall at 5ft 2in, but very dapper, his clothes all cut to fit, and he was smoking a cigarette out of a silver cigarette holder, which suited his style. He spoke with a very gruff voice, which is quite common among bullfighters. Why this is so I have no idea. I approached him rather nervously, shook his hand and said, 'I want to be a bullfighter.'

I gave him the letter of introduction, which he took, read slowly, folded back up and gave back to me before looking straight in my eyes, frowning and saying, 'How old are you?'

'Twenty-one,' I replied.

'How much bullfighting have you done? Have you fought any cows or anything like that?'

'No,' I said, 'I've not done anything at all, nothing. But I have got a cape!'

I thought I needed to mention that, because the gear is expensive to get when you're just starting out, but he didn't look impressed and said to me, 'Have you got a family back home, and a job back home?' But he didn't give me time to answer before adding, 'Listen, the best thing you can do is get on the train now and go back home, because what you're talking about doing, becoming a bullfighter, is simply impossible.'

My heart sank, but he then used an expression that's quite famous in bullfighting circles and said, 'It's impossible, and besides that it's very difficult.'

There is genius in that saying because underneath it means nothing is impossible, so I saw a glimmer of hope, but he added, 'I have got here in my bullfighting school José Puerto,

Pepe Luis Diaz, Paco Pastor . . .' and he went on naming these bullfighters who were all terrific before saying, 'None of them can get fights. You need money, you need backing, you need to be very good, and all these things need to come together at the right time, and that's why only one in a million makes it. You have walked in from England aged twenty-one and you think you can just come in and do this?'

His look of utter disdain left me stunned. I couldn't believe I was being spoken to like that, but I was later to find that in the world of bullfighting people don't mess about, they come straight to the point. Everything is serious; there is nothing about bullfighting that's light-hearted. He told me very honestly that I was wasting my time, but I knew this could be my only chance so I said, 'I've not travelled 1,500 miles just to go back home.'

His reply made me want to kiss him: 'I'm not saying I won't let you come and join my school, I'm just telling you how it is, honestly and up-front. Get a tram to Patraix, which is near the cemetery. There's a cinema there which we use for practising on. Go and practise.'

The cinema was open-air. At night it filled up with cars to watch the latest movies but during the day it was packed with all these wannabe matadors practising. When I turned up an hour after meeting Garrigos they were there working out. I felt like had made it. At last I was about to make the breakthrough as a bullfighter.

I noticed immediately that this was something that demanded great technique, and this part of it is what I have battled with all my life – I have fought fight after fight to become proficient with the cape and *muleta* – and I watched all these boys, especially Pepe Luis Diaz, who I could tell was very good and had great balance and coordination, and knew I had my work cut out. Pepe eventually went all the way and looked like he was going to become a top-class matador, but he found he didn't have the courage to fight the bigger bulls. With the smaller two-year-old bulls he was fantastic and he was as good as the top stars, but the stars had to do it with five-year-olds, which are bigger and more intelligent. To be a top matador you have to triumph with them, and once you've triumphed you have to do it again and again, you can never drop back down to fighting two-year-olds in the main events. Pepe just couldn't make that final step up to become the one in a million that succeeds, but at this stage his career was just taking off, and mine was about to take its first tentative steps.

Paco Pastor befriended me; he was a fully fledged matador and started giving me lessons with my brand new cape. I looked a bit of a prat at first, to be honest. I was very conscious of having a brand new cape and not being a bullfighter. But you have to start somewhere, and I worked out with them for the week, and he showed me how to make a Veronica and how to hold the cape properly. It was all technical stuff. And I was picking up other bits from the other lads, all of whom I observed. At the end of the week Garrigos took me to one side and said, 'Listen, I'm not saying anything that I didn't tell you at the beginning; you're not going to make it as a bullfighter because nobody ever does, but you definitely have got some talent for it, and I'm happy for you to carry on here, and we'll teach you all you need to know about bullfighting.'

He then said, 'Have you got a job?'

I shook my head, and he added, 'Well, in that case I won't charge you any money.'

I couldn't believe it. I'd joined his school for nothing and I never ended up paying him a penny for the rest of my life. But I realize now that he did see something in me and was hopeful that I actually would make it. He just had a funny way of expressing it. But that was Garrigos through and through. His passion and his life were bullfighting, and if he saw some spark in a potential bullfighter he wouldn't let a lack of money ruin that lad's dreams, because Garrigos had lived the dream. His bullfighting name was Graneret. It was a diminutive of the great Valencian matador Manuel Granero, who was killed in 1920 in Madrid. His death was a famous goring that Ernest Hemingway wrote about in his book *Death in the Afternoon*. Granero got caught by the bull against the boards, and Hemingway described it as his head being broken like a plant pot. It was a nasty one. The bull gored Granero right through his eye. Garrigos was nicknamed after this legendary figure and was the most influential figure at the training school. He was thirty years older than me, and I learned very quickly to respect him and take his advice on board. Every morning Garrigos would be there at the school, watching his protégés and moving among us, saying, in the politest way possible, 'No, you put your leg there,' or 'No, your cloth is in the wrong position,' and what he used to say to me a lot during those early days: 'You have to have more reflexes.'

Every now and then he'd tell us to stop while he told us a bullfighting anecdote, or gave us a verbal lesson, or simply had a general chat about bullfighters and bullfighting.

His school was typical of a lot of training centres in Spain at that time. He had assistants who taught the kids how to do it. Anybody could join these schools from the age of eight, but twelve was generally the average age you started. I was twenty-one, so I was miles behind. Garrigos was right in a way, I was far too old. But I was naive and optimistic and at that age I thought I could do anything, whether it was rugby, football, boxing, cricket, golf, you name it, and so bullfighting wasn't going to be a major problem in my mind. I went to the school every day and became pally with Pepe and José Puerto, who lives in Brazil now.

José was a very, very brave, almost cold-blooded matador, who was flamboyant but seriously fearless. It was his personality that probably stopped him from becoming a star matador because he was certainly good enough to make it; he just did-n't have that winning charisma in the ring. Puerto soldiered on for donkey's years as a *novillero*, which is one step down from a matador and means you only fight two- and three-year-old bulls. But he was a great *novillero*. In the villages outside Valencia they had annual fiestas, where the local government would put on a bullfight, and at the end of it they'd put a cow in the ring for the locals to have a go at fighting. Puerto was often called to these villages to be on duty while the villagers played around with these cows. But if there was a dangerous bull in the corral, Puerto was the man they'd call on to deal with it. He'd fight and kill it, much to the delight of onlookers, and pocket upwards of 2,000 pesetas in the process. He made his living from doing this. Puerto did have several fights in Valencia, which is a first-class bullring, but he could never land a really big triumph and consequently never got his foot on the ladder.

He became a full matador by a stroke of fate. He was walking down the street in Valencia when he was befriended by Paco Peris, who supplied horses for the picadors. Paco asked him if he'd travel to Benidorm the next day, where a famous matador called Serranito was killing six bulls on his own but didn't have a reserve. Puerto packed his bags and went to Benidorm as reserve, got changed under the terracing of the ring and expected to pocket a few thousand pesetas for effectively doing nothing. But the second bull broke Serranito's back, putting him in a wheelchair for the rest of his life. As he was being taken out of the ring in agony the panic-stricken impresario asked, 'Who is the reserve? Quick, get him into the ring.'

Puerto stepped forward and declared, 'Right, this is my fight now. Step out of the way, I'll go at my own pace.'

He went out, killed the bull and faced the other four, one at a time, getting two ears and the tail for every bull he killed. He was tremendous with the cape and the *muleta* and one-arrowed (killed with a single sword-thrust) all of them. It was a masterful performance. Puerto was the complete matador. The next day his photograph was on the front page of the Spanish national newspaper *Levante* under the headline, 'Who Is This?', because he was relatively unknown outside bullfighting circles and he had caused a massive sensation. So Puerto became a matador, but he made a mistake: he went with the wrong manager, and, although he had a fight at the end of the season and one or two the next year, all the momentum he'd got after this sensational Benidorm fight had gone after about two seasons. With the right manager he'd have made it.

A couple of years later he was walking along the port in Valencia when he bumped into a friend of his who said to him, 'Fancy coming on a trip in a merchant ship?'

He ran home, packed his bags and was away travelling the open seas for six years, in which time he made enough money to buy himself and his parents a flat, and to invest in land which he later sold. He used the money to set himself up in Brazil, where he lives the life of a millionaire with a six-bed-roomed house on the beach and flats he rents out.

Pepe Luis and Puerto were my pals, and on our days off we'd sometimes travel together to one of the outlying villages where one of the relatives of the Rocarruig family lived. They'd always lay on paella for us. Valencia is the spiritual home of this dish. They invented it and are the only people that do it properly. There is an art to making good paella, so much so that at that time they had competitions, with inspectors going round the restaurants that specialized in it, testing it for quality. My only gripe was when we did have paella away from Valencia the things like chicken that went with it could be quite tough because the animals were killed and cooked straight away without being given any time to rest and hang. I saw how they were killed on one visit. The chickens were all running round, and this guy had a stick with a sharp protruding blade which he threw at them in such a way that the blade took their heads off. He had incredible skill in being able to do this, but it wasn't a pretty sight. We ended up eating these chickens in the paella an hour later, and the meat was tough.

I also saw them kill rabbits for the paella. I never want to see that again. The woman preparing the dish hung these two rabbits upside down on what looked like a clothes line before hitting them on the back of the head with a stick. It didn't knock them out. I could see they were still fully conscious. Then I watched in horror as she started gouging their eyes out. I couldn't stand it and said, 'What on earth are you doing?'

'I'm killing them,' she said. 'They don't feel any pain because I have hit them on the back of the head first.'

The poor buggers were fully conscious and in agony, and I was getting riled: 'Why are you taking their eyes out,' I shouted.

'That kills them,' she said.

So she gouged the eyes out of these two rabbits and then started skinning them. They were still alive! I was so upset and felt so sick at what I'd seen that I couldn't eat the food. The woman didn't think she'd done anything wrong. That is the way she'd been taught to prepare rabbits, and this method had been passed down to her. It was a dreadful experience.

But then the whole food scene back then was a bit odd when you'd been brought up on meat and two veg back in Salford. Back home Mam would make a meal from whatever hadn't been sold that day in the butcher's shop, be it chops, liver, mince or chicken. I was never short of protein. In Spain they ate every part of the animal. Nothing was wasted. They'd eat the necks of the chickens in paella; even the gall bladders got eaten. I ate paellas containing chickens' feet. You'd pick a foot up and suck the meat from between the claws. Pigs' knuckles were another favourite. They were fantastic. The fat mixed with the pork from between the knuckles was so sticky and flavoursome. What I couldn't get used to was a delicacy they ate which resembled somebody's finger. It was something they pulled from the sea bed, but it was as though you were eating a monkey's digit. I could never get used to this particular dish.

At weekends when we weren't eating paellas or monkey's fingers Pepe Luis, Puerto and I would walk round the centre of Valencia, which was and still is a very Spanish city that has escaped the worst excesses of tourism. Every evening the Spanish would come out with their families dressed in their finest clothes and walk the streets, chatting with their neighbours and occasionally stopping at a café for a drink and some tapas. It was a wonderfully civilized way of life.

We also went to the dogs, which was another great experience. I'd seen greyhounds run at the White City dog track in Manchester and watched all the lovely thoroughbreds there flying round. The first time I went to watch the dogs in Valencia I couldn't believe it. I nearly always chose the winner because I'd go for the one that looked the nearest to being a greyhound! There were dogs racing with big bushy tails, other dogs were mangy mongrels. It was a joke, but it won me some money.

And there was always the bullfighting to go and see at the main Valencia ring and also in Barcelona, though we could rarely afford to actually pay for tickets to get in. In Valencia if you hung around outside the main gate for long enough they would often let you in for free, and in Barcelona we simply climbed over the wall. For some bizarre reason the cops turned a blind eye to this and let us do it. But if the crowds wanting to get in for free became too big the Civil Guard shifted us, and if they said move everybody moved, otherwise they had a habit of tapping you on the funny bone with their truncheons, and that hurt.

To keep fit we'd also go for long walks along the beach. At the end of the beach was a long walkway that led out to the lighthouse. Round the back of this lighthouse, looking out to sea, was a six-inch ledge, and we'd sidle across this ledge until we were looking out over the rolling waves and at the ships on the horizon, feeling like we were the furthest men out to sea from Valencia and letting the spray wash over our faces and wet our clothes. We were healthy, we were fit, and there was no talk of women, no smoking, no drinking; we were all fully committed to our dream of becoming bullfighters. That was the sole focus of our existence, and as we stood on that ledge looking out over the Mediterranean we didn't talk to one another, we just daydreamed, and it was obvious what we were all thinking of: we were dreaming of fighting in the great bullrings of Barcelona and Madrid, dressed in a suit of lights. It felt good. It was where I wanted to be in life.

On weekdays it was all training, training, training. I'd found a room to rent through a *sereno*. But I was running out of money and needed a job. Fortunately I could say I had experience working as a waiter, albeit two weeks in Majorca. I got a job at a quality restaurant called La Luna, where everything was very high-end and spotless with white tablecloths and waiters dressed in white tails and dickie bows, apart, that is, from the head waiter, who wore a black dickie bow. I was his assistant. The only downside was my routine became horrendous, and I quickly ended up malnourished. When I got the job I explained to the owner that I was in Valencia to be a bullfighter and went every day to the outdoor cinema to train. He said, 'I can't just let you go off and pay you when you are not working here. It wouldn't look right to the rest of the staff. The best thing I can do for you is this: instead of coming in at 10 a.m. like everybody else to get the restaurant ready for opening, come in at 8 a.m. and clean all the windows and all the brasses and lay the tables and just make yourself busy, then at 10 a.m. go off and do your training. But come straight back afterwards to start work in the restaurant again.'

So I did. The trouble was there was no time to eat. I couldn't really have breakfast because the place I stayed at didn't cater for it, and I didn't have time for lunch because I was too busy working. I was meant to have a break at 3 p.m., but there was always some sod of a client who insisted on staying put and didn't leave until a couple of hours later, by which time I was desperate to get back to my digs to get a bit of kip before the evening service started at 7 p.m. That didn't finish until the early hours. If there was any food to be had at the restaurant it was generally barely edible. There was one staff meal at lunchtime, which generally consisted of fish scraps and cold soggy vegetables, leftovers basically. I couldn't eat it. Just the smell of it used to knock me sick. I had to steal leftover food from diners' plates to survive. When we collected the plates from the table we walked straight across the restaurant to the kitchen, passing a screen on the way between the diners and the pass. This screen gave me a chance to eat some food. More often than not it was a piece of leftover steak, but other times it could be a bit of veg or a potato, anything that would fill my empty belly. One day I was put on the line making flans. These caramel flans would come out of the oven in little metal pots, and the trick was you picked it up, gave the inside a little flick with a knife and tipped it onto the plate. There would be fifty of these to do, and their design meant they would fit into the mouth perfectly in one go. So I would get a couple on the plate and pop the third one into my mouth, until one day I made the fatal mistake of looking round as I did it, to see the boss's wife staring straight at me and shaking her head. I never did flans again. They took me off it.

But I did get 100 pesetas a week plus tips for the job, even though the tips didn't amount to much because the Spaniards were real tight sods who'd tip one peseta, if you were lucky! But I had enough money to pay for my digs and to just about survive, though dehydration was another problem I had to contend with. When I was practising in the outdoor cinema it was in the full glare of the sun. It was merciless, and I found I could never quite quench my thirst. The others bullfighters were fine. Eventually I acclimatized myself to it. It was wearying, but I could see the light at the end of the tunnel. I could start to see myself as a potential bullfighter.

After a couple of months I did go to a few village fights with Pepe and Puerto. I went as their reserve. They never got injured, so I was never asked to stand in for them, but I at least walked into the ring with them as one of their team and I was now very much part of the bullfighting scene in Valencia, even though I had as yet not seen any action. But after a few months of non-stop working and training I realized I had a problem. I was utterly exhausted, emaciated, dehydrated and in serious danger of becoming burnt out.

The season was coming to an end, and I was preparing to go back to England for the winter before returning to Valencia the next year. But I knew I couldn't return to the same ball-breaking routine. My mission back in England would be to save up and earn enough money so I didn't have to come back to work. With enough cash saved I could simply come to Valencia and train to be a bullfighter. Before I went back home, though, I had to fight a bull, for pride more than anything. I didn't want to go back to England without having had a bullfight. I didn't want to say to all my mates, who didn't know how difficult it was, that I hadn't fought anything, that I hadn't had any fight of any description. So, armed with my cape, I went to the annual fiesta in the village of Benimamet on the outskirts of Valencia, in which they were to hold a *capea*.

A *capea* is an unregulated fight where an animal is turned loose in the ring for villagers to chase and fight. There are no rules and regulations, and at the end the animal isn't killed. It's a tradition that dates back to 1560, when a Papal Decree banned bullfighting in Spain. Before the ban up to half a dozen bulls could be let loose in the ring for people to fight. When the ban was lifted a few years later a new rule was introduced that only allowed one bull in the ring to be fought by many people. This set the standard for modern bullfighting. When bullfighting was formalized it was one man against one bull. A *capea* is a throwback to the pre-modern days.

In Benimamet, the tradition is to turn a cow loose at the end of a fight, and about fifty locals come in the ring with it while it runs round and they try to make passes and fight it. The cow throws people all over the place; it's a bit of a barmy spectacle. Eventually it gets fed up of doing this and just stands there and won't charge. As soon as they let the cow loose I jumped into the ring with my cape, and it ran straight towards me and straight past. I had made my first pass with a live animal, only it grabbed my cape in its horns and ran off with it. Some kids managed to grab the cape and they ran off with it then, so there was the ridiculous spectacle of the bull trying to come after me and the kids, and me going after the kids to get my cape back. It was very Benny Hill. But at least I could say when I got back home that I had been in front of a bull, of sorts.

I left Valencia in the autumn of 1964, fully intending to go back the following season. But things don't always work out the way you expect them to!

Chapter Four

IS THERE AN ENGLISHMAN HERE?

When I arrived back in Salford from Spain Mam was delighted. She was convinced I was back for good and I'd got bullfighting out of my system. That was a view shared by a lot of people, including my friends. Dad was the only one who wasn't so sure. He could see I still had the hunger to become a bullfighter and was still very supportive of my ambition. Mam just didn't want to entertain thoughts of me going back for the obvious reason she was anti-bullfighting.

I started playing rugby again at Sale, to keep me fit while I was away from training. I enjoyed it this time. There was no weight of expectation on my shoulders. Now I was playing purely for fun and wasn't thinking in terms of having a career in rugby union. That made a massive difference to me. If they dropped me halfway through the season, so be it, I would play in the seconds to keep fit. But I ended up playing mainly for the first team, because they saw me as being quite versatile. I couldn't hold my place in any particular position, because they had some cracking players, but I was always in the first team to cover for those players who got injured or who were on representative duty.

I was picked in every position outside the pack over the course of the season: scrum half, full back, stand-off, centre, wing; and because there were no substitutes I always got a full game. This didn't always work to our advantage. When we played Waterloo away our centre, Roy Maddick, ran past their lad Jennings twice in the first fifteen minutes and left him for dead; he was a much better player than Jennings, who was the England centre. I could never understand why Roy was always overlooked at international level. He was an outstanding county player and in my opinion always outshone international opposition. I once saw him embarrass Ian McFaddyan, the Mosley centre who went on to become England captain. But against Waterloo Maddick eventually had to go off with a torn hamstring, so we were down to fourteen men. This was when our number eight, Richard Trickey, showed what a great player he was. Every time the opposition got away down the wing – and this happened several times – Trickey tackled whoever it was with the ball in the corner, and they never scored. We ended up winning the game with fourteen men.

It was a great level to play at, and I started to enjoy rugby again. I was mixing with healthy people, was in very good condition physically and was building my confidence up. I was also getting on with people who were very good in business. There was a great cross-section of people at that club, and I soon learned that just because you spoke with a plum in your mouth didn't mean you were soft. Some of the hardest and meanest bastards I knew back then spoke with a posh accent.

So I stayed and played the full season, when really I should've been planning to go back to Spain in the March of 1965. Instead I stayed in England for the rest of that year because I just couldn't face going back to that eight in the morning until midnight starvation regime at the restaurant. I wanted to go back to Spain as a bullfighter with money in my pocket and not having to wait on people to make ends meet.

But the Catch-22 position I later found myself in was that to have a licence to fight bulls in Spain you have to have a work permit, and to have a work permit you also have to have a job. So even when I went back again with enough money not to work I still had to get a job to get my work permit which permitted me to get my bullfighter's licence! But in 1965 I was working my backside off in England to save up enough money to live on in Spain. My dad had sacked the butchering game and got himself a driving school, so I worked round the clock doing that. As soon as I had turned seventeen I learned to drive. I took some lessons and passed first time. It was quite unusual for someone as young as me to be able to drive in those days. But there was a reason: it helped the butchering business. If I could drive I could pick up meat from the market and deliver it to clients. It was Dad who pushed for me to take my test. My plan was to go back to Spain on 1 January 1966, and until then I was a single man working as a driving instructor.

It was obvious what was going to happen next. The job came down to giving lessons and getting legovers wherever I could. And there were lots of bored housewives out there, all of them after one thing. I don't think you could get away with some of the things you got away with back in the 1960s because anybody now in a position of trust can soon get into trouble. But back then it was different. If a woman wanted lessons, and I fancied her, I chatted her up, and I reckon I was successful about a quarter of the time. I was twenty-two, and my antenna was up virtually all the time. It's never really stopped being up, as it so happens.

It was very much reminiscent of the *Confessions* films featuring Robin Askwith, which were popular during the 1970s. He got his end away while working in jobs such as a window cleaner or milkman, or a driving instructor like me. There were about forty learner drivers on the books at any one time, of which 75 per cent would be women, and 10 per cent would be game for it. The problem was I started to see every woman as a potential conquest. Everybody seemed available, but I got the drift very quickly if they were not. I'd feed them cheeky or suggestive questions and look for a certain reaction. One of the biggest giveaways was when these women started calling their husbands names and saying they no longer satisfied them in bed. Then I knew I was in. I ended up doing them in all sorts of places: in their family bed, in the kitchen, on the sofa, all over the place really. And because the lessons were during the day, their husbands would always be out at work.

But this fooling around soon stopped when I met Margaret. She was a year younger than me. After four lessons we were dating. I had to tell my dad then, and he took her for the remainder of her lessons, because we had an agreement that if I became romantically involved with any of the pupils I couldn't take them for lessons any more. It simply wouldn't have worked, and he was right. For the driving school to succeed there had to be a certain amount of discipline. So I passed her over to my dad and started going out with her properly. But I fell in love with Margaret the moment I clapped eyes on her. She had something magical about her personality. Although I'd been out with lots of other girls, younger as well as older than me, and had experiences most men wouldn't get in a lifetime, none of them had me nailed to the emotional mast as much as Margaret. I knew right away that I was crazy about her.

But we were like chalk and cheese. I was passionate and hot-headed and had this obsession to make it as a bullfighter. She was cool, calm and very much in control of her emotions. I got the message very quickly that bullfighting didn't really interest her. She could see the pros and cons of what I did and what I wanted to do and was happy to just let me get on with it. Margaret's outlook on bullfighting was very English, because I've seen it in other people. It didn't fit into her psyche and doesn't with many people in this country. They simply don't get it. They don't get the passion and the tradition and the sheer gut-wrenching exhilaration of both participating in and watching a bullfight. And it was because of this we pretty soon made it an unwritten pact not to discuss bullfighting, because her reticent attitude towards it started to wind me up.

But it didn't wind me up as much as I wound up her parents. They were horrified she was dating someone as common as I was perceived to be. It turned out she had recently been engaged to someone her parents really liked but had only recently split up from. When I came on the scene they saw it as her going out with me on the rebound. They could never accept that she actually liked me so they were desperate to stop me seeing her. Her father was very wealthy. He had built his own house in Salford and had another in Wales. I think he thought I was after the family money. He was also a mason and didn't want his daughter going out with a Catholic.

It was one thing after another until it got to the stage where I wasn't even allowed to knock at the door or go up the path. They banned me from their house and banned me from going out with her. In hindsight they may have had a point. She was well educated and worked as a teacher, then one day she walks in with me, who didn't really have a proper job but was a bull-fighter with something of a reputation with the women. I was their worst nightmare. I was probably anybody's nightmare at that time. But really it was just snobbery on their part.

As soon as we got married he stopped being nasty to me and just tolerated me as a son-in-law. I remember going round and asking them out of politeness if I could marry their daughter. They threw me out! I tried twice, and on the second occasion he looked at me and said, sweeping his hands, 'You think you're going to be able to provide all this?' He pointed to all the material wealth he had accrued over the years. What a sad thing to do! But in the end I should be grateful, because he did give me my wife.

That was not how it looked when 1966 dawned, though, because I had plans to go back to Spain, and Margaret just didn't seem to fit into those plans. I faced a heart-rending dilemma. I didn't want to lose this beautiful girl, but if I stayed with her in Salford it would've meant an end to my bullfighting dreams. When I weighed it up I came to the conclusion that over time I could get over Margaret but if I turned my back on bullfighting I'd always have to live with the thought of what might have been. So I chose bullfighting over her and broke the news: 'When I go, that's it. We're never going to see each other again.'

It was quite a brutal way of ending our relationship, but I wanted her to understand that nothing could come between bullfighting and me. But it was a decision that nearly broke my heart.

We split up quite amicably. Her parents were delighted. While I was in Spain she wrote me a letter asking how I was and telling me how she missed me. It brought all my feelings towards her flooding back. I almost wanted to pack my bags there and then and go back to her because I did still love her. But my head told me I had to be strong, and I wrote back and was quite brutal in my choice of words. I wrote: 'Don't write to me again because I don't want to know.'

My return to Spain was inspired by an article I saw on *Granada News* about a bullfighting club that had got together in Manchester. This was something of a rarity. It was made up of purely British members who held their meetings almost in secret. When the animal rights activists heard about them they initially tried to disrupt their meetings, so they ended up holding get-togethers in pubs under the guise of 'A Common Interest in Cultural Society'. Even pubs would turn them away if they advertised themselves as a bullfighting club. I found out who they were and that they met once a week in a pub in town. The club still flourishes today and is called Peña Fiesta Brava de Manchester. A guy called Ray Wood opened it on the back of London doing one. London's came about in 1959 and was founded by George Erik. Two years later Manchester's got set up. I got in touch with them, and we met. But when I had a chat with them and told them my aims and ambitions they only echoed what Garrigos had been telling me back in Valencia and said, 'You're trying to do something that is pretty much impossible,' because at this stage I hadn't even fought a bull, apart from my brief encounter with the cow. It was exactly like listening to Garrigos; I couldn't believe it. They added, 'You're wasting your time.'

But to say things like that to people like me is like waving the red *muleta* at the bull. I wasn't going to be put off by their words. Ray Wood could see I meant business and advised me to get in touch with George Erik, who was living in Spain and was the managing director of Subbuteo, the makers of the table football game, which was based in Barcelona. When I wrote to Erik he wrote back and simply told me to come and see him.

So shortly after New Year 1966 I was sitting on the station platform at Manchester Piccadilly, waiting for the train. It came, and I said goodbye to my mates, who had come to see me off, and hauled this great big massive trunk onto the carriage ready for my next adventure. I went down to London and caught another train to the coast to get on a boat to take me across the Channel and then on another train that took me to Barcelona. The Rocarruig family had given me the address of a member of their family in Barcelona who would put me up for a few days; it was in the village of Santa Coloma de Cervello on the outskirts of the city. To get there I got on another mad tram in Barcelona with everybody hanging on the sides and when I got off I hawked my case up a massive hill and back down again to the town, which was half a mile away, only to find the next stop on the tram journey was 100 yards from where I was meant to be staying. I knocked on the door, and they were expecting me. I was introduced to Francisco Rocarruig's mother, Roseta, and shown to my room. Roseta would become my mother in Spain. She was one of the kindest souls I have ever met. She was later killed in a tragic accident, and I will miss her for ever.

A couple of days later I was off to meet Erik in Barcelona. Meeting Erik was an experience in itself. He was 6ft 2in and very much larger than life in stature and in personality. He was an ex-Army man with piercing blue eyes and hair that was moulded by Brylcreem into a short back and sides style. He had a moustache with pointed ends and a goatee beard, and he always wore his black blazer with a bullfighting club badge sewn onto it. But then he'd go and wear a skull-and-crossbones ring, like a biker or someone who was into heavy metal would wear. I could never work that one out! It didn't quite go with his image. Like Garrigos, he was a chain smoker who smoked his fags through a cigarette holder.

As I walked through Barcelona to meet him I found myself in awe of Spain once more and enjoyed the warmth of the atmosphere and the people, and the fact that Barcelona never sleeps. It was like New York, a true twenty-four-hour city. I loved being there and meeting lunatics like George Erik. As soon as we met he sat me down and asked me what my plans were. I told him about Garrigos and said, 'I'm going back to Valencia to train with him.'

But Erik had different ideas. He weighed me up and said, 'Look, instead of going back to Valencia, stay here, and I'll manage you, and we'll take it from there.'

With hindsight he was OK for his bullfighting connections but he couldn't train me or put me in the hands of somebody who was better than, or even as good as, those training me in Valencia. By going with him I lacked the expert training and coaching I needed to bring me on. The only positive thing that happened was I became as fit as a butcher's dog playing rugby for Barcelona University as stand-off, where I got the worst injury I've ever had. I got punched on the back of the head off the ball and was out cold for about ten minutes. I came round in the shower. It could easily have killed me. I didn't bother going to hospital though to get it checked out; I just shook it off, got on with life and hoped there was no lasting damage. But despite everything I was doing fitness-wise and the fact I now had a manager I couldn't get really good bullfighting coaching and the experience needed to fight in a bullring. But I persevered and persevered.

I was only supposed to stay with the Spanish family for a couple of days. I ended up staying there for a year. But that is the Spanish for you. They are so generous, and this is epitomized in one of their famous sayings: 'The Spanish will lend you anything except their motor car and their wife.' But I have even almost received generosity from them on that score. The next-door neighbour of the family I stayed with was a big-shot director of the local factory. He lent me a Vespa motorbike, which was hugely generous. It wasn't a car, and I didn't fancy his wife anyway, but because of this kind act Spain opened up for me. I knew the streets of Barcelona like the back of my hand thanks to that bike, and it was the best way to get around the city.

I trained in the Monjuich Mountain area with a group of matadors and *novilleros* who included future stars such as Manolo Carra, Manolo Gallardo, Enrique Paton, Joaquín Miranda and Manolo Amaya, who was the nephew of the great Carmen Amaya, as well as other kids who were more on my level, in that they were beginners, learning from scratch. Manolo Carra was particularly kind to me and gave me encouragement and inspiration. He was a matador who got dreadfully battered by the bulls and suffered some horrendous injuries in his time. But although I was training on a patch of ground on the outskirts of the city with some fantastic people and living in such a great place I did have a question mark over the lack of proper tuition. Despite this every day I lived in hope that something would come up, whatever that may have been.

But at least I wasn't wasting away this time. I was eating, and eating well. There was a small rugby stadium next to where we trained, and occasionally a group of these matadors would pull the entrance gate off its hinges and lay it across a fire. One of the guys would buy some chops, another tomatoes and onions, some more had brought bottles of wine, and training would stop while they lit a barbecue and cooked the chops on this metal gate over the fire. Anybody who wanted to join the feast would put some money in a pot to cover the cost of the food. There was a real spirit of camaraderie here epitomized by a saying among the bullfighting community: 'I have eaten off the same plate as him.' Because in bullfighting you did tend to eat off the same plate before fights, and it was a sign of friendship and closeness. Everybody just tucked in, and it was very informal. That was shown by these impromptu barbecues. We were all a very happy band of people. I quickly got into a routine of doing a full day's training. After a couple of months of this, a matador called El Greco appeared at the camp. He had a look around and shouted, 'Is there an Englishman here?'

'Yes,' I said, being the only Englishman in the place.

'At the Bar Atlántico there is a guy called Paco Carbonero waiting with a contract for you to fight in France,' he told me.

I looked at him, hardly believing what I was hearing. 'Are you El Inglés?' he said seeing my astonishment.

'Yes,' I replied.

'Well there is a contract for you to sign.'

I simply couldn't believe it. My heart was ready for a fight but I was nowhere near qualified enough to go into a bullring and fight a bull. I hadn't even got to the stage where I'd practised with cows on a ranch. In bullfighting you start with shadow fighting, which was the stage I was at, before progressing to having fights with two-year-old cows on ranches. Only when you have built up enough experience of training with live animals will they let you anywhere near a bullring. But here he was offering me a contract to fight. It was baffling. I must have broken records running from the training ground to Erik's door. And when I got to his house I could hardly catch my breath through a mixture of excitement, exhilaration and sheer exhaustion.

'Calm down, calm down,' he said to me when he answered the knock.

'I can't calm down,' I said. 'El Greco has told me he has a contract for me to fight in France.'

Erik calmly invited me in while he washed his hands and face. Then he grabbed his coat and said, 'Come along Frank,' and we set off walking to the Bar Atlántico, which was on Las Ramblas, the heart of Barcelona.

Las Ramblas is still a bustling boulevard that runs from the Plaza Cataluña down to the waterfront, where Columbus's boat is moored. The Bar Atlántico was a bar within a cinema entrance. The guy who owned it was a bullfighting manager. I couldn't wait to get to this place, but Erik stopped at every bar on the way: 'Take your time, Frank,' he kept saying as we popped into yet another one.

He must have stopped at about ten, and I was absolutely bursting with excitement to get there. When we finally arrived, Carbonero, who was sat on a bar stool, pulled out the contract. He was representing the French impresario Pierre Pouly, who was putting on the fight. He said it was a contract for a fight on 26 July 1966, with six fighters all fighting one bull each; the one that was the best got the first prize, which was the equivalent of £70 cash in pesetas, a hell of a lot of money to me back then. The five runners-up would get £9 and all their expenses paid. We would be picked up in

Barcelona and taken by taxi to the fight in Pérols, which was near Montpellier. The whole thing just sounded too good to be true. I signed two copies of the contract and celebrated with a few drinks.

Later that night, as I lay in my bed, I couldn't sleep through sheer excitement. I couldn't believe what had happened. I'd made it. I was finally going to be a recognized bullfighter fighting in front of a crowd in a real bullring. It was just not real. I'd already penned a letter to my mates to tell them I had a fight. I wanted as many people as possible to come and see me. There was no point ringing anyone. You had to queue for about two hours at an exchange to ring someone back then, and even then, you weren't 100 per cent sure the call would get through. I wrote in the letter: 'I've cracked it. I'm going to fight a bull and I'm going to eat it for breakfast, I can't wait.' My exuberance had got the better of me, but I was that up and that positive. Then it all started going wrong.

Chapter Five

CROSS-BORDER DEBUT

Erik got a call from Carbonero a couple of weeks later, and he said to him, 'Bring your bullfighter to the Hotel Oriente on Las Ramblas. The impresario is coming from Madrid to Barcelona on his way to France and he wants to meet all the bullfighters contracted for the fight.'

So we went to the hotel, where another fighter, Juan Caparros, who was hoping to get on the bill, was waiting, together with two other *novilleros*. We hung about for ten minutes or so, and in walked the impresario, wearing a beret. He couldn't have looked more French if you had strung garlic around his neck. He shook hands with those he knew and then said, 'Where is El Inglés?'

Carbonero said, 'This is him here,' and pointed to me.

We shook hands, then he came up close, examined my face and said, 'Have I met you before?'

'No, we've never met before,' I replied.

'Have you fought in France?'

'No.'

'And you have never been to my house, have you?'

This was one of the strangest conversations I'd ever had. 'No,' I answered.

'This is not the one I wanted,' he said.

Suddenly I felt panic rising up inside me. They'd got me confused with another British bullfighter, Henry Higgins, who had fought a number of times in France. This impresario thought he was getting him. Higgins had been to this guy's house in France, and this impresario would have never believed there was more than one Englishman who fought bulls. And he wouldn't have remembered his name, because the Spanish and French are useless at remembering Anglo-Saxon names. They can't even say them, never mind spell them. The impresario had simply given the contract to his Spanish representative and told him, 'Get me El Inglés.'

So we all sat down and started having a bit of a chat. My heart was bouncing off my chest, I was anxious and I was getting all the wrong vibes, because suddenly this impresario's representative joined the conversation, and he was a real bully who thought he was a tough nut. 'How many fights have you had?' He snapped at me.

'I haven't had any.'

'Well have you had plenty of practice with cows?'

'No, I haven't fought anything,' I replied, wondering if I should have lied.

He bent over so he was close to my face, looked me straight in the eye and almost sneered as he said, 'You're thinking of fighting a bullfight and you haven't fought anything. It's not on, is it?'

Then he turned, had a bit of a chat with the impresario,

turned back to me and said, 'Listen, we'll scrap that contract and offer you something different when you're more ready for a fight. Go back and train. You're not ready yet.'

'Just hold on a minute,' Erik said and he led me to one side. 'Come over here, Frank, I want a word with you.'

He led me into a quiet corner and whispered, 'Are you sure you want to go through with this?'

I said, 'More sure than I have ever been about anything in the whole of my life.'

He smiled at me and patted me on the shoulder. 'I thought you'd say that, Frank.'

As he walked back the impresario said, 'Right, give us the contract back.'

'Oh, no, no, no,' Erik said. 'We'll see you on July 26th.'

And the impresario shook his head and snapped back, 'No, no, no, he is off the bill!'

Erik slowly pulled the contract out of his top blazer pocket and, waving it at them, said, 'Gentlemen, we will see you on July 26th. Come on, Frank, let's go.'

And with that we walked out. The contract was signed, sealed and sorted. There was nothing they could do about it. But then the skulduggery started.

My next job was to get myself measured up for the suit I'd need to fight. In Spain they have specialist bullfighting tailors, so I went to the one in Barcelona and got myself measured. I hired a suit, and the day before the fight went to pick it up. As I walked in the tailor said, 'Oh no, sorry, I haven't got any left. I've loaned them all out.'

I hadn't got a suit to fight in, and they wouldn't let me fight if I wasn't wearing the right clobber. Caparros sorted me out. When he found out what had happened he said, 'That tailor has been told not to give you a suit. They don't want you at that fight.'

He took me to Casa Pepita and convinced the woman tailor to fix me up with a suit. Sure enough, she sorted me out, only I had to wear a different-coloured top to the bottoms. It didn't bother me: as long as I met the regulations I would've gone out dressed as Coco the Clown if I had to. All I wanted to do was fight that bull. I hired the sword and the *muleta*, and the whole set up cost me 1,000 pesetas, which would be covered with my expenses.

Then the impresario's lot got in touch with me to say I'd need a Spanish licence to fight in France. It was a load of rubbish. The French don't ask for a Spanish licence. But I wasn't taking any chances so I got £50 together and took a train to Madrid and got a licence. Whatever they tried to do, however much they tried to stop me fighting, I found a way around it. There was no way they were going to get me off that bill no matter what they tried.

Henry Higgins also managed to get in touch with me while all this was going on. I don't know where he was living, but it was somewhere in Barcelona. Higgins was quite a decent fighter and he had great drive and ambition, so he was probably annoyed that I'd taken a fight from him. He has gone down in history as the first Englishman ever to become a *matador de toros*. He was born in Colombia in 1944. His dad worked for Shell, and when he was four he moved to Venezuela and lived in an oil camp. When he was eight he was sent to a boarding school in Kent called Holmewood House and three years later moved to the Isle of Man. Although his father is English, his mother is Mexican, and Henry never lost his South American accent, and his Spanish was much better than his English – he is about as English as Greg Rusedski, let's put it that way.

He went to Spain to learn to play the classical guitar. Shortly after arriving he visited a palm reader, who looked at his hand and told him he was going to be a bullfighter. I sometimes wish I had a story like that. So he went into bullfighting, and his great ability was to be able to sell himself. In that respect he managed to persuade Brian Epstein, the manager of the Beatles, to back him and become his agent. That was his way in, because when you are just starting out in bullfighting you need financial backing and you have to buy your way in to the fights you want to appear in. Then you have to buy the suits, practise with cattle and so forth, and suddenly it becomes very, very, expensive. To get on the first rung of the ladder today you would need about £50,000. Thanks to the backing of Epstein, Higgins fought about fifty times as a *novillero*, buying into as many fights as he could.

When Epstein died in 1968 he got Tito del Amo to back him. He was an American who had inherited a fortune. But when he withdrew his backing Higgins's career nosedived. The trouble was, good though he was with the cape and the *muleta*, he couldn't kill. Potentially he could've been huge, because when he took his alternative – that is, became a fully fledged matador who fought four- and five-year-old bulls – he got a good crowd to watch him and afterwards he got a lucrative contract from the great matador and impresario Antonio

Ordonez to fight the following season, 1971, in Málaga, Torremolinos, Fuengirola and a string of other bullrings in the Costa del Sol. His first fight was in Málaga, which is a first-class bullring, and he was a disaster with the sword. Both bulls he fought nearly went back alive because he couldn't place the sword. There are occasions when a matador fails to kill the bull swiftly. It seems that the more times you miss, the more difficult the placing of the sword becomes. It is a setback for any matador, but if it is a one-off the profession and the public won't hold it against you. So they gave him his next fight two weeks later in Torremolinos, but the same thing happened again. After that fight his contract was torn up. He did manage to fight again in Benidorm and Tenerife, but in Benidorm he was badly gored and in Tenerife he was again poor with the sword. After that his career just fizzled out.

He got an agency to manufacture parlour games and he became very successful as a businessman. But then he got an agency to market hang gliders, which were the new thing back in the early 1970s. In 1978 he gave a demonstration, taking the glider to 30 feet before coming to earth with a crash, breaking his neck as he landed and dying three days later.

His life seemed to be one of eccentricity, but I personally found him serious. When his fights dried up he got the British Consulate in Spain to complain to the powers that be that the reason he wasn't getting any fights was racial discrimination, because he held an English passport. The truth was he didn't get fights because he had a problem with the sword; if you're terrific with the cloth but don't put the sword in then you've failed. Alternatively, if you're only adequate with the cloth but you put the sword in successfully first time you've had a triumph. The last thing people want to see is the bull being massacred – they talk about the kill as being the 'moment of truth' because it is the ultimate test, not only of a bullfighter's technique, but of his bottle. This is what ends many a bullfighter's career. When you stand in front of a bull, they look massive, and their heads look even bigger. The law requires that you kill the bull from the front. You can't come from the side or the back; you have to go over the horns. It's the first time in a bullfight that you take your eyes off the horns. Before then you're timing the charge and focusing on the bull's horns. When you go for the kill you have to look at the target, which are the withers at the back of the bull's head. For a successful sword thrust you have to rely on the bull's head being down, otherwise you stand a very good chance of being gored, and that is where the previous stages of the fight come into play, they are all geared to lowering the bull's head and getting it under control.

At this time, however, Higgins's career was still on the up. He met me with his *banderillero*, Elio, and between them they tried to talk me out of the fight. He'd been told that I had his contract and he was going to get it back. We met in a bar, and, although he never came on aggressively towards me, he did ask if I really wanted to go through with this and gave me the opportunity to change my mind. He was hoping I'd offer him the contract back: after all, it was rightfully his. But I was having none of it, and eventually they gave up. I was in no mood to be gracious or kind. I was going to fight that bullfight no matter what. In my mind if I could just fight that one fight I'd be a bullfighter and a bullfighter for the rest of my life. Even if I never got another fight at least I'd have done it once, but I was sure the fights would come in thick and fast after I made my debut.

Higgins ended up coming to the fight and was quite nice with me, telling me to relax and everything would be OK. He said he always drank a cup of peppermint tea before every battle and produced some for me to drink. In a way I'm grateful to him because, if he had really kicked up a fuss over my stealing his fight, there's every chance I wouldn't have fought, and they would have simply torn up the contract and got his signature on a new one. I'll give him credit for that; he was a real gentleman about the whole thing. I walked out of that bar knowing I had the licence, the suit and the backing of the bullfighter I'd stolen the fight from. The impresario and his cronies simply ran out of ways to try and stop me and finally accepted less than twenty-four hours before I was due to fight that my name would go on the bill.

The arrangement was we'd meet in a place called the Plaza Real, in the centre of Barcelona, at 11 p.m. to be driven through the night to France. It was cheaper to do that. They didn't have to spend money on putting us up in hotels then. When I arrived in the Plaza it was buzzing with people, and there in the centre of the square was the biggest taxi I'd ever seen. It was like a stretch limo almost, but it was better than that: it was an old-fashioned Buick with running boards along the side. It could've been used by Al Capone, it was that type of vehicle. Seven people got in it; five bullfighters, the sword-handler and the driver. The kit was strapped to the roof.

We set off through the night, every one of us feeling we were in competition with each other, like a team of boxers who were going to fight. We couldn't really see what we were passing because it was dark; mostly it was scrubland until we got to the border. We told the border guards that we were bullfighters, and they didn't even bother looking at our passports. They just smiled at us, shook our hands and wished us luck, and we drove on to Pérols.

We arrived at 7 a.m. We'd been driving cross-country for eight hours. Close to the ring was a barn where we were told we could put our heads down for a few hours. But I was too nervous to sleep. The ring was quite a small one that could hold about a thousand people. I didn't really take much notice at the time but when I saw it years later it was very pretty. As I was new to bullfighting there were a lot of things happening then that I wasn't quite noticing. We went to the *sorteo*, where numbers are put into a hat and drawn out to see who gets which bull. When the *banderillero* came back, one of them said, 'Your Inglés has drawn the best bull.'

It was a beautiful brown bull with a lovely head on it, and the *banderillero* said, 'You're going to have a great time with this bull.'

At this point one of the other bullfighters on the bill, the one who didn't come in the taxi with us but instead had come from Zaragoza and whose name was Diego Francisco – he was a bit older than the rest of us and a bit more experienced – put his arm around me and said, in rough translation, 'This is a piece of shit, this. You'll piss it, no problem.'

It was the kind of language I spoke: not typical Spanish, but almost Salford Spanish, and we hit it off straight away. When we all sat together for lunch I was so nervous I couldn't eat a thing. Francisco could see I wasn't eating and kept saying, 'Get it down you.'

But I couldn't and fumbled about and played with it until he said, 'Over here, then, give it to me and I'll eat it.'

It was better food than what I'd been eating in Spain. We had pea soup followed by lamb with French fries and local freshly picked salad. It was very tasty, but I didn't want to know. After lunch we were taken to a barn near the bullring to get ready. I had a shave using a piece of broken glass from the barn window in which I could just see enough of myself to do it properly. To wash we all had a bucket of cold water each. The bullring was only about a hundred yards away, so when we were ready we walked down to the ring together. That was a great feeling. A band was playing, and all the locals came out to clap us to the ring, but as we walked into the ring the butterflies hit me and I suddenly became on edge. I looked round for my mates from England or my dad, someone I could recognize who would help calm my nerves, but nobody had turned up. Even my manager hadn't bothered to come. So I was alone with my frayed emotions. For the parade we all put a dress cape on, which gets wrapped around a fighter's left side and covers his left arm. I couldn't get mine on. My hands were shaking that much. Francisco had to help me out. And because I was making my debut tradition dictated that I carried my hat in my hand and didn't wear it on my head like the rest of them. Francisco could see my nerves were shredded and kept banging his fist into my chest and saying, 'You're going to get stuck in today, don't worry about it. You and I are going to murder all this lot.'

He was a tremendous help morally for me, and when we made our march across the bullring to be introduced to the President I'd managed to regain some of my composure. Then the skulduggery began again. The cartel had all six of us listed in order, and the order was put down on a list rather like the grid line-up of Formula One cars and pinned on a wall. The lad in sixth place was a French kid also making his debut. I was fifth to go, and my bull, this blinding little thing, was in the fifth pen. My mate Francisco had killed the second bull, and the third one was due to come out now when one of the organizers said to me, 'Right, you're on now, Frank.'

I said, 'I'm not due to go out yet. I'm on fifth.'

'No, no, no. You are third,' he said, and he went down the list vertically rather than across to show I was third.

'You're reading it wrong,' I said. 'The order goes across from left to right not down in rows.'

Now we were having a full-blown argument over who was on next, and while this was going on the pen was opened and this black bull came into the ring. 'That is not my bull,' I shouted, 'and I am not going to fight it.'

I then pointed to whose bull it was. The kid I was pointing at was a called Mariano Borlitas, who was managed by Carbonero. Carbonero was with the President, watching the fight and helping to decide who won the £70 first prize. The next thing I knew there was a *gendarme* next to me, who said, 'I don't know about all this bullfighting business but I have to say to you if you won't step into the ring now I'm going to have to arrest you.'

I put my hat on and simply said, 'All right,' and off I went. I wasn't going to fall out with the Old Bill.

I'd never fought a bull before and I got slung all over the place. The first time I made a pass at a bull was then, on my debut, in full view of the paying public. It was a performance of utter incompetence with the cape. But beforehand I was sure I could do it, and all the arguing prior to me going out into the ring did help in a way because it took my mind off what was about to happen. At first I made some attempts at passing with the cape and managed to stay on my feet. But then they put the *banderillas* in and I swapped the cape for the *muleta* and got permission from the President to start the work with the *muleta* and to kill the bull. From that moment on I got caught a lot. The bull was constantly throwing me to the ground. But I always got up, and that got the crowd on my side, because they liked to see someone having a go.

At one stage towards the end of the fight I actually got a bit riled because I couldn't get this bull past and I was sick of it flinging me around. I was also gutted that my suit was getting ripped. The bull didn't injure me, which was something of a miracle, but I had some nasty bruises and scratches afterwards. I was just no good and I shouldn't have been in there really. But the crowd was with me all the way because they expect a *novillero* making his debut to get tossed around a bit. Then disaster turned to success, I got the sword and went whack, straight between the shoulder blades, and with that mortal sword thrust the bull went down. So even though I'd been thrown, in the end it was a triumph. It's funny, but with all the action and the drama, the emotion of the moment seemed to pass me by. The whole thing seemed to be over as soon as it started, and I was left standing in the middle of the ring, overwhelmed by a feeling of shock and disbelief. It was traumatic, because really I didn't know what I was doing, and yet brilliant at the same time. I'd had a go and I'd done it. The *banderilleros* came over to me, and one of them said, 'You're definitely going to get an ear now,' and the entire crowd were petitioning for an ear by waving their white handkerchiefs.

It was a magical moment. But the President refused to give me an ear, and that set the crowd off booing; they were furious. The bull was dragged from the ring, and I was left standing there. This tosser didn't want to give me an ear because he didn't want me to win the £70 prize money. If you don't get an ear the next thing down from that is to have a lap of honour as the crowd clap you and show their appreciation. To give you an idea of the crowd's anger with the President they made me take four laps of honour. How can you not give someone an ear on his debut? Nearly all *novilleros* get an ear in their first fight, unless they are really bad. It just wasn't on. Then this other lad managed by Carbonero came out with my bull, got awarded two ears and took the prize money. But frankly I didn't care. I'd made my debut, I was now a bullfighter. I'd killed the bull with one sword thrust, and it was hailed a triumph. That was beyond my wildest dreams. It was much more than I should've deserved or got. I'd only been training for about six months, and even that was the equivalent of shadow boxing. Most bullfighters have to train for eighteen months minimum before they get their first fight. But in fairness to the people who didn't want me to fight they were right really, because if someone came up to me now and said, 'I'm going to fight next week, I've been training for a year but I've never made any passes with any animal anywhere,' I'd say to them: 'You're mad, you're completely barmy.'

But there was no way I was going to let go once I had the chance. I felt terrific after that fight and was in a real party mood. Caparros was hoping to have got on the bill. He'd had a couple of fights. But he didn't make it on, so instead I gave him a thousand pesetas to come and see me fight. He got there before we did! After the fight I had a bit of a wash from a bucket in the barn and as I was getting changed he came up to me and said, 'I've got a couple of girls here from out of the crowd. They are Austrian girls. They've got a taxi waiting outside and they're going to give us a lift to Barcelona.'

That was lucky really because I didn't get my 1,500 pesetas expenses. When I went for the money after the fight everybody had scarpered. This happens a lot in the bullfighting world, as experience would later teach me. The profession has its fair share of spivs and thieves. Then I didn't care. I was a bullfighter. Nothing else mattered any more. And to make it even better these Austrian girls were stunning. They were touring Europe and had stopped off at the fight purely by chance on their way to Barcelona. All I could think at this point was: this must be the life of a bullfighter; you get women now as well. So we all got in the back of the taxi and started kissing these girls and had a bit of a fiddle and a play around. It was party time. When we got to Barcelona we did a tour of a few bars and ended up in Monjuich. I couldn't take mine back to where I lived, because the family I stayed with wouldn't have allowed it, and I don't know why we didn't end up staying in a hotel. Instead we all ended up sleeping in woods near the area where we trained. It was quite romantic really, and I ended up having sex with this Austrian girl before we both fell asleep under the stars wrapped up in my cape.

When we woke at dawn I found to my horror that my swords had been pinched. Some little sod had crept up in the night and nicked them. They were my hired swords from Casa Pepita! I had to take my gear back without them and was wondering how I could explain away their disappearance. Added to that was the fact that I'd been sleeping rough and looked like hell. As we stumbled out of those woods, I bumped into bullfighting trainer Pepe Ordonez, who trained with us. He looked at me in disgust and said, 'You don't really want to be a bullfighter, do you? This is not how you become a bullfighter.'

He didn't know I was celebrating my debut in the ring twenty-four hours earlier and had no idea of my situation. I wanted to say, 'It's not like that.'

But he'd caught me with girls as though I'd been on the town all night. I had, but I had good reason to be there. Nonetheless it was highly embarrassing. To make matters worse I was worried because I had to go into Barcelona and take back the ripped suit minus the swords. As I walked down I thought: stuff it all, I'm a bullfighter, and that's all that matters. Caparros took the kit back to Pepita and told her the swords had been pinched at the bullring, and with a shrug of the shoulders he walked out. We later got a few pesetas together and sorted her out, and there were no hard feelings.

My only regret was there are no photographs of my first fight. There was a small newspaper report printed, but I wish I had a photo. There was nobody there to take one, though. Not even my manager, George Erik, turned up. People later told me he didn't want to go because he truly believed there was going to be a serious disaster involving me and the bull and he didn't want to be associated with it. He was supposed to be there to collect my expenses and make sure I got what was owed me. No wonder I was ripped off. But when I went back to training all the young lads shook my hand and congratulated me on my success. One of them said to me, 'Nobody expected you to kill that bull, Frank.' Neither did I, but here I was: a bullfighter.

Chapter Six

FAILURE IN ARLES

I was quickly into the routine again, but this time I expected Erik to get me more contracts. Naively I didn't realize that I needed money to buy into fights at such an early stage in my career because, unlike Spain, in France nobody asked for anything and everything was taken care of by the organizers. It was a good arrangement up there. But in Spain there was so much competition to fight that organizers often asked the bullfighters to pay for their own team or provide their own bulls, which costs money. I didn't have any money to stump up, and Erik didn't have the right level of experience. Although he had formed the bullfighting club in Britain he didn't have the knowledge and contacts within the profession itself to get me fights. So I decided I should go back to Valencia to train under Garrigos and let Erik continue to be my manager.

I got them both to meet in Barcelona to try and agree to share me. But they couldn't agree, and because they couldn't agree I suffered. I ended up going back to Britain at the end of August 1966 to work because I'd run out of money. But in

October I went back to Spain, only this time I went to Salamanca in the northwest, which is one of the biggest bull-breeding areas of Spain. Erik was friendly with some important people in Salamanca during the Franco period and managed to get me on the ranch of a breeder who let me train with his cows. I fought the cows after the senior matador, who was also there to practise, had finished. I was making passes with small animals almost every day; it was fabulous.

I loved it in Salamanca; it was a great spell for me. Every morning. I got up early at about 5 a.m. and ran 4 miles to liven me up before driving out to the ranch, which was a lovely place to go to. I'd drive by the side of rolling fields where bulls had been put out to pasture among giant oak trees. They were very wealthy people who ran this ranch, and there was a small bullring on it where the cows were tested. They say the fighting bull gets its spirit from his mother, so usually at two years of age the cows are tested by going through a sort of mini-bullfight. If they pass the test they're put out to breed. The ranchers who oversaw this were very similar to the British upper classes in style in that they all wore tweed and boots and were quite dressed down. Whereas the Yanks wear things like chaps, the Spanish ranchers dress quite conservatively.

Very occasionally the ranch played host to coaches filled with tourists who came down for the day to see the bulls in the fields. And the tourists watched us training with the cows. At lunchtime we'd all have a break and sit down to a giant stew, very similar to Lancashire hot pot but with different types of herbs put in them. They were better than hot pots to be honest; the herbs gave it a much better flavour. Then it was back to training for the afternoon. To see the herd running across this sprawling field of thousands of acres was a sight to behold. You knew they were coming because you'd hear the sound of rumbling from their hooves as they approached. It was a great experience. But I did wonder where my next fight would come from.

Fortunately for me my debut had been such a success that when the impresario of that fight was organizing his next one the following year in 1967 he offered me a fight at a major *feria* in Arles. This was a first-class bullring in France, where they were planning to stage three fights over the Easter weekend. On Easter Saturday they had three matadors, including El Cordobés, the great Cordobés; on the Sunday there was a *novillada*, which included me; and on the Monday was another cartel of top matadors. The biggest stars in bullfighting were on the bill, and I was in the middle of all this. But this time I was going prepared because I'd been practising on animals at the ranch in Salamanca, where, during a six-week spell, I'd fought cattle every single day.

When I arrived in Arles on the day of the fight I was a completely different person to the one who had made his debut a year earlier. This time I had some idea of what I was doing, but I still had a nagging doubt that I was slightly short of proper coaching experience. Nonetheless I was much better prepared and I had a matching suit. A pal from England, Eddie Hindle, came with me for this fight, but he said he didn't want to sit in the crowd; he wanted to be with the pros in the corridor between the ring and the spectators which is called the *callejon*. So I said to him, 'You be my sword-handler.

You can pass me the sword and make yourself useful.' Big mistake!

The impresario putting on the show said we all had to share the sword-handler he'd be providing, to cut costs. I thought it'd be easier to bring Hindle instead. This time my father came along with my brother and some of my friends for the fight, so I had some support in the crowd. We arrived in Arles and went to the hotel where we were staying, and I met the usual suspects from the year before. Carbonero was there as well as the bullfighter who had nicked my bull and won all the pesetas. I was the last one to arrive so I came in and shook hands with the bullfighters and when I got to this bull thief he pretended not to know me. As he shook my hand, I thought: are you taking the piss?

I simply snapped; something just went inside me. I grabbed his hand and said, 'You will remember me, you little idiot, and if you steal my bull today I'll shove you up the bull's arse sideways.'

I let go of his hand, grabbed him by the neck and flung him backwards before turning to Carbonero and saying, 'And you, you twat, you nicked my expenses.'

I'd completely lost it at this point and screamed at them both, 'I'll see you two arseholes at the bullring,' before storming off.

We were all to have a meal together at the hotel, but I couldn't face eating with them. I didn't get paid for that fight either. But that was probably my fault for having the row. At midday the bulls were picked, and I didn't get the chance to see my bull. But when it was time to get dressed I was focused on the job in hand. I put on my leotard, then the stockings and finally the breeches, which I needed help to get into. Because they are designed to fit perfectly tight I had to wriggle into them and while doing so manoeuvre my bollocks to the left so they didn't get squashed. Hindle was helping me get into these and had a thing where he always went on about men with big balls. In his eyes the bigger the bollocks the more of a man you were. When he saw mine he said: 'Fucking hell, Frank, that's not very good, is it?'

'What do you mean?' I said, 'They're not that small. This suit squashes them.'

The next thing I knew he'd left me there with these breeches hanging off me and gone into a side room, coming back with a handful of paper. He pulled my breeches up and began shoving this scrunched-up paper down my pants to create a lump where my balls were.

I started laughing and said, 'Stop it, you daft sod, get that out of there.'

But when I looked in the mirror I did start to think: well, it does look all right actually. So I told him to leave it there and carried on getting dressed.

The ring itself is an old Roman amphitheatre, so it wasn't like a traditional bullring; it was oval, whereas normal rings are perfectly round, and there were lots of little coves and crannies. When I walked out into the ring for the parade before the fight started the first thing that happened was my trousers came undone. Hindle had failed to tie them properly. So the parade had to be stopped for a second while the real sword-handler came to fasten them. It was mildly embarrassing.

But he tied them properly, and we all continued to walk across the ring. As we got to the end where we saluted the President there was a bloke standing next to him pointing directly at me and whispering something. Unbeknown to me the paper stuffed down my pants had worked its way down my leg. I looked down and just closed my eyes in embarrassment. It was a horrible feeling, made worse because there was nothing I could do about it. I just had to carry on the parade with this lump halfway between my knee and the top of my thigh. When I arrived in front of the President it simply became one long comedy of errors. Hindle was supposed to be there to remove my dress cape, but he had gone missing. I didn't have a clue where he was but managed to pass my dress cape to a ring official before exiting the ring. Erik, who had seen what had gone on, came down and got the paper from out of my breeches. As he pulled it out he said, 'Where's your kit?'

'Hindle has got it,' I said.

'Well he's not here,' Erik said, 'and neither is your kit!'

I couldn't go on without my kit, and my turn was about to come. In panic a search party was sent out. When they eventually found Hindle and brought him to me I said, 'Where's my cape and my swords?'

'I've put them in one of those coves,' he said pointing in no particular direction.

'Which one?' I asked, because there were hundreds.

'Er, I've forgotten.'

For the next ten minutes there was complete pandemonium as a dozen of us went on a search for my kit. Eventually we found it, but Hindle had managed to reduce me to a bundle of nerves.

Fortunately I was fifth on, and the four bullfighters before me were terrible. They were running scared of the bulls and were awful with the sword. France has a reputation for sending out big, well-armed cattle, and I think they were unnerved by this. When I came on, everything went brilliantly. I let the bull run the cape and felt totally in control. I had been taught from very early on to keep very still when the bull charges. If you can keep still there's less chance of the bull catching you because it goes for movement, and that's where the cape comes in. You move the cape, keep still, and the bull goes for the cape. It's not quite as black and white as that, but that is the general idea. Some beginners flinch during the bull's charge, and that's it, the bull sees them move, ignores the cape and goes for them instead. But I was doing well. There were five bands in the place all playing their trumpets as I made my passes, and the place was rocking. Hindle was running up and down the corridor shouting, 'That is how you do it. That's how you fucking fight bulls,' which I could have done without.

But I'd set the crowd alight. Everything had gone brilliantly, and if it had come off that day I don't know where I'd be today; maybe my career would've taken a different path. But this was the day when I picked the sword up, and with the crowd alive and awaiting a triumph in eager anticipation, I couldn't kill the bull. I simply couldn't get the sword in and had half a dozen attempts. It was embarrassing. But my technique was all wrong, and if that's wrong the art of the sword thrust doesn't work for you. Effectively you're killing by chance, and I ended up having a disaster. I did finally manage to kill the bull, but unfortunately for me it was at the end furthest away from the President, and when you kill it you have to walk back towards him for his dispensation. As I took the long walk towards the President the crowd were booing and whistling and throwing food, drink, cushions – anything they could lay their hands on, really. (Although throwing things into the ring had been banned, it didn't mean people didn't do it.) But for some reason when I got halfway across they must have felt some sympathy for me, because they started clapping. The French crowd are different from the Spanish. They seem more English to me. A Spanish crowd would have never started clapping. I would have got booed all the way out of the ring. They knew I had failed, though, and failed miserably.

I was devastated and knew that, if I'd had a proper triumph that day, there was every chance I'd have got more fights with this impresario. But I didn't and I made a big jump backwards. To make matters worse my right leg was in a mess because I'd been gored, so I had to go back to Barcelona to have a small operation on it – I had no idea I'd been gored during the fight because the endorphins had kicked in and I didn't feel anything.

I knew I had messed up, though, and spent the next few weeks having a good long think about what to do next. Things were not going well. I'd failed in a major fight and I knew I couldn't really carry on with the set-up that was in place so I wrote Erik a letter from Salamanca, thanking him for all that he'd done for me and telling him that I was going back to Valencia to get some proper training. I was back with Garrigos. But I knew deep down that the fights would never come, because Garrigos and Erik couldn't really get them. Garrigos did get me something in August of that year in a small holiday resort called Benicasim, near where they filmed *El Cid*, but it was a total nonentity. The fight was in the back of beyond, and there were maybe a dozen or so people turned up to watch it. It was a depressing sight to walk out into that ring and see it empty. But I had been practising with the sword since my disaster and did fight a blinder, killing the bull with one thrust.

Some fighters just cannot follow the sword in, because for a successful sword thrust to penetrate the heart area and kill the bull first time the bullfighter has to stand behind the sword line and follow it in. A bullfighter cannot place it from the side, because it won't go in properly. Some fighters are scared of the bull's horns and fear a goring. For a successful sword thrust you have to be consistent in your technique and determined at what you're doing. It was my salvation, because I concentrated more than anything during training on the kill. I was determined to get that right, more so after my second fight in a place called Morella, where I was quite reasonable in the *faena* but failed with the sword. I simply couldn't understand why. An ex-fighter, Pedro Ruiz Soro, the father of the star from Valencia 'El Soro', who had been a comic bullfighter, had been watching me and collared me after the fight and said, 'Come with me, we're going to cure you with the sword.'

That was music to my ears. He explained to me that when he was a bullfighter he fought in villages in comic bullfights where you fight cows aged between twelve and fifteen years old. They're very thin, almost skeleton-like in appearance; therefore he had to be very accurate when putting the sword in. He showed me his technique, which involved putting the hand forward that held the *muleta* so it was ahead of his body and by simply advancing forward the cloth arrived at the bull before he did and the bull's head went down to meet the cloth, making it easier to hit the target with the sword. We went into his barn and I practised on bales of hay. I just put sword after sword after sword in until I had cracked it. Thanks to Pedro I now have a reputation in Spain of being able to kill the bull first time with the sword, and that's the best reputation I could have.

Unfortunately there was no interest generated from the fight in Benicasim and no spin-off from it. It was a bit pointless really and was real bottom-rung-of-the-ladder stuff. At the top were places like Madrid and Valencia, where, when you fight there, the whole bullfighting world gets to know about it. But where I fought was like fighting in the equivalent of Slattocks near Rochdale. Not many people have heard of it. I was starting to get the drift now that to make it I'd need a bit of backing. This is where Higgins got it spot on with Brian Epstein, and what a coup that was. But I didn't get that sort of backing. My modus operandi was to go back to England at the end of the season and get a few quid together to return to Salamanca, really to try and get someone to take an interest in me or find somebody who'd back me. Erik just didn't have the contacts. Erik knew about bullfighting from what he had read and seen, but he wasn't a professional in the game and effectively he'd over-reached himself in taking me on. I went back in 1968 and trained at Salamanca and Valencia. But I was backwards and forwards, always looking for opportunities; unfortunately for me I couldn't get a single fight anywhere. I didn't have enough money and I had no one to be my manager. My mate José Puerto was fighting a lot, and I did go as reserve to him for a couple of fights but I never got to make any passes.

The only difference when I went back to Spain in 1968 was that I went as a married man. When I returned to Spain in 1966 and finished with Margaret the idea was we would never see each other again. But when I came back to Salford I bumped into her, because Hindle had kept pally with her. As soon as I saw her all the old feelings came flooding back. I was in love again, it was that simple. And part of me did suspect I was going to spend the rest of my life with this woman because no other girl seemed to affect me emotionally the way she did. Inevitably we ended up meeting, and little by little we started going out again. And I came to the conclusion that, rather than cut her off when I went back to Spain, I'd have to juggle bullfighting with seeing her. I couldn't go through the emotional torment of parting again. That's when thoughts of marriage entered my mind. I was convinced I wasn't going to meet anybody like her, so marriage was the inevitable outcome of this. It was just a question of when. I'd asked her parents twice if I could marry their daughter, out of politeness, before I proposed to her. Each time they went ballistic. So I reasoned I'd wait before trying again. Maybe give it a year or so to see if their attitude towards me softened.

I was getting some money together to go back to Spain and

was working at a place called Moors Bakery doing the night shift. Moors was a great big bakery in Salford, and when the lads came out of prison after doing a stretch they could get work there doing nights packing bread and loading vans. Hindle and I got a job there for the month and were paid £30 a week, no tax, which worked out quite well for us. When I wasn't at work I took Margaret out. But when her mam and dad found out she was back with me they were furious. The atmosphere was horrific until one night in December when she left my parents' home to go back to her house, and half an hour later I got a telephone call. It was Margaret in tears, saying, 'You better come and pick me up. I've got a bit of a problem with my father.'

When I picked her up, it all came pouring out. She'd gone in and a row had gone off about me. He'd slapped her, and in retaliation she'd thrown a cup of coffee over him. I said, 'Sit in the car,' and went to knock on her parents' door.

I'd not seen them for months because they'd banned me from coming anywhere near their house, but Margaret's mam came to the door, and I said, 'I'd like to speak to your husband.'

He half appeared in the background so I shouted, 'Come here, you!'

As he walked towards me, I pointed at him and said, 'I'll tell you one thing, if you put your hands on her again, I'll break every fucking bone in your body. Keep your hands to yourself, you fucking tosser,' and I turned and walked back to the car.

Margaret came to stay at my house that night, and, as I lay in bed, staring at the ceiling, I knew I couldn't carry on like this, with this constant battle with her mam and dad. By morning I'd found a solution. We got up, had breakfast and went for a walk. As we were walking I took hold of her hands and said, 'Let's get married right away. It's the only way we can sort this problem out.'

It wasn't the most romantic way to propose to a girl, but the situation demanded it. 'OK,' she said, a bit stunned.

I don't think it had really sunk in with her. God knows what I'd have done if she'd said no, but we immediately went to Police Street in Manchester to get a marriage licence – I paid £2.50 extra to do without banns. The wedding was the day after – I'd got married two days after proposing! We invited her parents. I never expected them to turn up, but they did! We had the reception in the main restaurant at the Midland Hotel in Manchester. Twenty-one people turned up. I can't say it's how I wanted to plan my marriage, but I had to do it. We just couldn't carry on the way things were. We stayed at the Midland Hotel on the Saturday night, and that was where we had our honeymoon. On Monday we went back to work. It was all rushed. But I couldn't believe her parents had the nerve to come. The last time I spoke to her father was to threaten him, but he must have had balls of brass, because shortly after the wedding he came over to me, shook hands and said, 'Let's forget everything that has gone on in the past between us and get on with our lives.'

My jaw nearly hit the ground. Why couldn't he have said that before the wedding, the barmy sod? We wouldn't have had to get married so quickly and could have planned a proper bash.

After the wedding the atmosphere of total war subsided somewhat. We rented a flat and lived together in Ellesmere Park in Salford, and Margaret, who was a teacher, came out with me to Spain during the school holidays. Financially the reason I could go back there had a lot to do with her. I begged, borrowed and stole and lived in a little dump in Valencia, just about managing to get by on what I had got and going to the open-air cinema every day to practise.

But my career as a bullfighter was effectively finished. And it took me a full year to realize this. Between 1964 and 1968 I'd had three fights. I'd had my little chance in Arles and failed miserably, so that was it. At the end of 1968 I knew I'd had it. I knew I wasn't going to be a bullfighter unless something really drastic happened, and there seemed to be zero prospect of that. That was a horrible year, shocking, the most depressing year of my life.

So at the beginning of 1969 I packed my belongings and left Valencia for Salford. Something in my mind told me maybe I would fight again, but I knew I had to get back and make a living rather than stay in Spain getting nowhere. It was soul-destroying. But I quickly came to the opinion that, if you can't do something and it's not available to you, then get on with things, forget about it and move on. As I came back to England to work I had a nagging suspicion Spain hadn't seen the back of me and that I would be back. If I could make a lot of money quickly, I thought, I could even go over and back myself. During 1969 I still went over there to watch my mates fight and still kept in touch with the bullfighting community, so I was still sort of involved with it, without actually being there doing it myself. Twice during 1969 I spent a few days in Valencia, making passes in the open-air cinema. Even though I thought my bullfighting days were over I still kept myself sharp. Never say never, as the saying goes.

I was now living the life of a family man. My first son, Matthew, was born in December 1969, and my second son, Jim, two years later. It was all business, business, business. I took over part of my dad's driving school, though it wasn't doing so well, and in 1969 I had become a nine-to-five man working in a travel agency. At night I'd go out and do three driving lessons and do lessons all day Sunday. I was making a decent living out of this, but the fun seemed to be over for me. Little did I know that the real fun was just about to begin.

Chapter Seven

THE GEORGE BEST YEARS

Eddie Hindle was a guy who was both a pleasure to know and an absolute nightmare at times. Together we were thick as thieves. When we weren't having a laugh we were getting into trouble, and this went on throughout the 1960s, the 1970s and into the 1980s, when really by that time we should've known better. Trouble seemed to follow us everywhere. In the late 1960s he came with me and a mate called Ken Hildrew on a beano to the Salamanca Feria, stopping off at Madrid on the way. I drove, and when we got to the centre of Madrid it was 10 p.m. on a Saturday night, and the place was packed with people all eating and drinking and generally having a good time. We wanted a room for the night, so began walking around the Puerta del Sol area, trying to find a place. It was buzzing, and we walked past the main police station, which was opposite a great big plaza – the traffic police were out in force corralling the traffic – when suddenly disaster struck. There was a shop opposite the police station, and I stopped to look in the window because they had some great leather jackets. Eddie and Ken walked on. Seconds later they walked back to me, fuming. Two Spanish blokes – one was built like a prop forward, the other slightly fatter – were out with their wives and had wolf-whistled at Eddie and started calling him a girl because of how he looked – Eddie was wearing pink cords, with a red neckerchief and a Paisley fitted shirt; he also sported a hippy-style beard; this was the era of Flower Power after all. Eddie flipped and said to me, 'Come on, we're having these two.'

'Hang on a minute. We're in Madrid; you can't just start fighting in the street. This is Franco's patch. We won't see daylight for years if the police catch us,' I said, and I pointed to the cop shop across the road.

'They're a pair of arseholes,' he said, 'and I'm going to do them.'

I needed to do something quick to calm the situation down so said to him, 'Leave it with me a minute,' and I got these two lads over and began talking to them in Spanish. I said very politely, 'Listen, you gentlemen have been out for the evening with your ladies, and we are foreigners in your country. We don't want any trouble, so why don't you carry on walking that way and we'll go the other way?'

But then, and this is where I couldn't help myself, I made the big mistake of saying, 'And you're lucky we didn't take exception to what you said.'

The next thing I knew one of them had hold of Eddie's neckerchief and he dragged him towards him and went smack, smack, smack. He was punching Eddie backwards down the street. I started throwing punches at the other

Spanish lad and noticed that a crowd had gathered to watch, and this was right in front of the police station of all places. I really needed to end this quickly and drew off the biggest right hand I could muster and missed him by about a yard. But because I missed him he turned and ran towards Eddie, who was still fighting the other Spaniard. We were now running up and down the street chasing each other backwards and forwards. If the police had joined in it would've looked like something out of the Keystone Cops.

Suddenly Eddie turned and began running away from one of the Spaniards. I couldn't believe it. Eddie never ran, it wasn't his game, but he wasn't actually running away out of panic, he was just giving himself some room, and he came back at this guy and smacked him flush on the nose. He sent him sprawling into some railings, where he rained blows on him until the tosser was out of it. I managed to land one on the other Spaniard, and he went down screaming like a coward. Suddenly two other Spaniards got hold of us and dragged us down a side street. I panicked for a moment because I thought these two lads wanted to do us. But they were actually helping us get away from the police. Eddie had a cut on his eye, and we could hear the horns of the black Marias. The cops were out looking for us. These two Spanish lads had saved us. They told us to run, and we did, through shops, side streets anywhere to get away from the sound of the sirens. If they'd have caught us we'd have been taken back to the police station and given a good beating before being hauled in front of a magistrate and jailed. And the Spanish jails were tough. That's why nobody committed many offences under Franco.

But that was what life was like with Eddie. It was one long drama, not all of it good. It was thanks to Eddie that I had some of the wildest and most exciting years of my life, because when I came back from Spain in 1969 Eddie had befriended one of the greatest footballers that ever lived, Manchester United legend George Best. Eddie ended up moving in with George at his house in Blossom Lane, Manchester, which was known as the public toilet because it was all tiled on the outside; it was a very nice house actually and cost him £30,000 to build it. He sold it years later for £25,000. The 1970s were an era where house prices weren't really moving, and you couldn't necessarily make lots of money by investing in the property market.

I don't think George really wanted a lodger, but, George being George, he found it very hard to say no. In later years I'd go back with him to that house after a night out, and he'd have a group of women in tow. The fun often started in his huge, deep bath that was as big as a room. It was like a football bath and it was tiled red; it was massive and could easily hold a soccer team. It was through Eddie that I was introduced to George. They drank in the Brown Bull pub in Salford. George invited me to play for his charity team, the George Best XI, in a game at Bellevue. It was a fantastic experience because I played in the same team as the great Stan Mortensen. I was in awe of him and harboured memories of watching him become the first and only player to score a hat-trick in an FA Cup final when his team, Blackpool, beat Bolton 4–3 after being 3–1 down in a game that became known as the Matthews Final after the part played by Stanley Matthews.

It was through this game that my friendship with George was cemented, and not long after this I was given the opportunity to work for him. Eddie had persuaded George that I had enough business acumen to run part of the George Best empire, and I'm eternally grateful to Eddie for that, because the next few years were an experience I will never forget for the rest of my life. George had opened two clothes shops in Manchester in the late 1960s, George Best Edwardia on Bridge Street and another on New Brown Street, just off Market Street, with a guy called Malcolm Mooney as his partner. They later sold out to the Saville Row tailors Lincroft, who were a huge and ambitious outfit. But George kept a vested interest in the business. They paid him to be the face of the shops and do any promotion they needed, so George, although he had sold out, was still heavily involved.

While all this was going on I had my head down, working hard in the travel agency and the driving school and doing anything that would earn me a few bob. I was earning £20 a week, which was poor pay even back then. Eddie came to me with a proposition. George had agreed to me working for him, and it was left to Eddie to ask me if I wanted to give up what I was doing and go and work for George Best Enterprises on the clothing side of the business for £40 a week plus expenses, which was more than double what I was on. It was a dream offer. I accepted and found myself working in the clothes shops under Lincroft but paid through George Best Enterprises. I had to manage the shops under a guy called Harold Tillman – the owner of Lincroft who is now estimated to be worth £350 million and who went on to take over the Jaeger brand of designer clothing. The designer who worked at the shop also went on to achieve fame and fortune. He was Paul Smith, and he helped put up the window displays. There were no airs and graces, it was very hands-on in those shops, and a pecking order as such didn't really exist.

Looking back, we were all star struck because George was as big as the Beatles at that time. Everybody wanted a piece of him. Working there was one of those rare jobs in life where you couldn't wait to get dressed and get to work in the morning. It was one long series of incidents after another and it was marvellous. There was lots of money floating about and loads of beautiful women. I wasn't involved with the women because I was recently married but I noticed everybody else around George getting the crumbs. George didn't stay with a girl for very long, and those hanging around him would often move in after him. George's leftovers went round quite a few people. George had a prolific sex drive, and our offices became useful to him for his casual encounters. George would take good-looking girls, sometimes after just picking them up outside the shop, upstairs to our first-floor office and have sex with them. The only problem was there were no curtains or blinds; I don't know if George was ever aware, but there were often sightseers peering in watching George get up to mischief with these girls. It wasn't uncommon for George to take girls into the dressing room and have sex with them in there. The dressing-room doors were louvred, so we had them turned upside down and put a shoe mirror close to the door so that we could see everything that was going on inside. They got up to all sorts of things. He was unbelievable and seemed to be able to pull any girl he wanted during the years I knew him. George could never say no to girls, and I noticed when he was with a girl he generally thought she was the most beautiful woman in the world. He'd be madly in love with her and he'd tell her that. He made girls feel that they were the only thing he lived for. The next minute he had walked out of the door and forgotten them and he was on to the next one. But he was completely sincere when he was with them.

After a few months of working for George my job role had changed beyond recognition. I ended up effectively managing George rather than the clothes shop and acted almost as his unofficial agent. This is where the craziness kicked in, because George needed managing to save him from himself. But George was virtually unmanageable. A great example of this was in the early 1970s, when United played up at Middlesbrough in an FA Cup replay on a Tuesday night. The following day George was due to appear in London at the International Clothes Show. This is what Lincroft paid him all the money for, because George was going to represent the company on the catwalk. United had drawn the first game against Middlesbrough at Old Trafford on the Saturday, and when the show's organizers realized the replay was only twenty-four hours before he was due to make his London appearance they were on the phone to me in a panic. Harold Tillman implored me: 'Frank, for Christ's sake go with him to Middlesbrough and follow him if you need to even into the toilet. We've got to have him here on Wednesday for the show.'

They knew through bitter experience that there was no way he'd turn up on his own if he had to travel from

Middlesbrough because he was so unreliable. Malcolm Wagner, his best friend and business associate, whom we nicknamed Waggy, and I went up to Teesside. George travelled with the team. Before kick-off and at half time a crazy situation developed in which Waggy and I were standing in the doorway of the dressing room watching the then United manager Frank O'Farrell give a team talk – can you imagine that happening today under Fergie? We looked like a pair of heavies. While the second half was going on I got hold of a policeman and said to him, 'George has got to get to the airport quite urgently after the match. Is there anything you can do?'

Experience had taught me that coppers loved this sort of drama, and as soon as the game finished and George was ready we got a police escort straight to the airport. Now call me naive, but I'd known George a couple of years and only now did I start to get the drift that he might have a drink problem. Before, because I'd never been much of a drinker, I didn't take much notice of other people's boozing habits so I never noticed George knocking them back, but as soon as we got to the airport he went straight to the lounge bar and started hitting the vodka and lemonades. Waggy was on Scotch and coke. I had half a bitter! We got on a small aeroplane to take us back to Manchester, and George carried on drinking on the plane. At Manchester airport George hit the vodkas again in the hospitality bar there. And then on the plane to London there was more boozing. By this time I was quite impressed – I shouldn't have been in hindsight. George, despite drinking prodigious amounts, didn't appear any different to how he'd been when he was sober, and that amazed me. I'd have been on the floor if I'd downed as much as he had.

At Heathrow airport Tillman picked us up in his chauffeur-driven Rolls Royce and took us to Franco's Italian Restaurant, which was then one of the showbiz places to be seen in and was open well into the early hours – the place was the equivalent of the Ivy or the Wolsey today. Lord Snowdon was in there having a meal with friends when we arrived. As we sat there everyone in the place was making a fuss of George. We had a bite to eat, and George had his usual, which was Steak Diane, which is a bit of a showy dish in itself. The beef tenderloin is flamed at the table using brandy and a sauce made from the pan juices of butter, shallots, beef stock and Worcestershire Sauce. He had it with a bottle of wine and a bottle of sambuca.

Then off we went again into the night to Tramp nightclub, where we bumped into Ringo Starr and all sorts of different celebrities. I wouldn't have been able to get into any of these places if I wasn't with George. George just walked in; he didn't have to pay to get in anywhere. Nightclubs would have paid him just to turn up. We met Tillman there and one of his Lincroft cronies, who was with a beautiful girl. After about five minutes it became apparent this girl only had eyes for George, and George fancied her as well, so they spent most of the night together in the club. Suddenly, when George had his back turned, this girl had disappeared and so had the Lincroft bloke. George was gutted because he'd lost the girl, and the club was almost empty, so there was no one else he could go for. He basically felt he'd had a wasted night, and this put him in the foulest of moods. Tillman put us up in a glorious penthouse suite on the tenth floor of a block of apartments in Mayfair. But when we got there the bedroom where George was supposed to sleep was locked, and inside was George's girl with the Lincroft fella. By now it was about 5 a.m. So the world's greatest footballer simply said, 'Fuck this, I'm going to sleep.'

He dossed down on the lounge floor fully clothed and with no sheets or a pillow to make it comfortable for him. But he was quietly fuming at what had happened. George could tramp it. He was tough like that and he was quite content to sleep rough. His rough-and-ready lifestyle even extended to the clothes he wore. He was never into clothes, despite having a vested interest in the boutiques. But he always seemed to have the right clothes on. Whatever he wore just seemed to suit him. He wasn't like David Beckham; George really couldn't care less how he looked, despite the fact that he always looked stunning.

When he woke up a few hours later he was still steaming and annoyed. The Lincroft bloke had gone by then, and eventually this girl crept out of what was meant to have been George's bedroom, only to be confronted by George, who went for her. She had to run out of the apartment because George had lost it. In a rage he threw all of her belongings out of the apartment window. I went down to help the poor girl pick her stuff up off the pavement. He did that quite often with girls because he didn't like it when they let him down. It was quite a selfish way to behave really. With one girl the police charged him with stealing her fur coat. George didn't steal it; he threw it onto a fire in a rage and burnt it. But this girl I was with on the pavement just got away with having her things thrown onto the street. She picked them up and scarpered. I went back in to make breakfast. George didn't want the fry-up I was making; he found a bottle of Scotch and had a drink instead! How anyone could drink like that at that time of the morning was beyond me. An hour later we went back to Franco's, and I said to George, 'We better start thinking about this show.'

'I don't want to know about it,' he said. 'I'm not going to the show. They can all fuck off.'

He was that fed up with everything that had happened at the apartment he wasn't prepared to have any communication with any Lincroft employee, and that also included Tillman. I phoned Harold and told him to come down to the restaurant, which he did, and he began kissing George and hugging him and eventually, when that didn't work, begging him to turn up for the show.

George just sat there and said, 'I'm not fucking talking to you, go away, fuck off.'

But eventually, after much begging and cajoling by all of us, he finally and rather reluctantly agreed to go, and it was panic over. But he'd had a monumental amount to drink. Even so, as we walked into Earl's Court, where the show was being held, they put a new jacket on him and slipped a drink into his hand, and he strolled out onto the show stand looking like a film star. I couldn't believe it. He'd been drinking, he hadn't had a bath, wash or shower and yet he looked better and more striking than any of the models, male or female, who had appeared, and he was fully composed. He looked perfect as he turned on the charm. Leaving the show stand he began smiling and chatting to people, and as soon as he felt he'd done enough he turned to me and said, 'Come on, let's go.'

We got driven straight to the airport, where George carried on drinking, flew up to Manchester, with more drinks on the plane, and got a taxi to drop us off at the Brown Bull, which often stayed open after hours. I went home, and Waggy stayed with him. I'd had enough and was shattered, plus I wanted to see my wife and two kids. George stayed in the Brown Bull until closing time and in the early hours went to a place called Phyllis's, which was an all-night drinking den. In there he met a girl who was a very well-spoken woman from south Manchester. But at 6 a.m. the telephone went in my house. I picked it up, and there was a copper on the other end who said, 'I have somebody down here at the station who is saying some very nasty things about your mate. You should get down here and get her out of the way.'

George was in trouble again. Luckily the copper was friendly and was prepared to tip me off about this girl making a complaint about George assaulting her before any further action was taken. I got my car and went to pick her up from the cop shop. Then I got the story. She told me that she fancied going somewhere else with George after Phyllis's, but George fobbed her off. He was shattered and probably didn't want to get involved with her because he was too exhausted after the two-day bender. She was getting nowhere so in desperation she threatened him and said, 'I'm going to ring the newspapers and tell them where you are.'

George was supposed to be tucked up in bed because he

had training a few hours later and, when he looked round, she was already on the pub's phone talking to a newspaperman. George walked up to her, grabbed the receiver off her and hit her over the head with it before slamming the phone down. That was her complaint, that he had hit her over the head with a telephone. I phoned George and said, 'You daft sod, what did you do that for?'

'I didn't hit her hard, but she screamed and ran off,' he implored.

Luckily this friendly copper just wanted to get rid of her. He wouldn't have got away with it today but back then he was doing what he thought best and was probably a fan of George and a supporter of Manchester United. I picked her up and took her home and tried my best to smooth things over. When she got home she had calmed down, and it looked as if she wasn't going to pursue it any further. A day later I got a call. She was in hospital with suspected brain damage. George was already waiting to go to court on a charge of assaulting another woman. He needed this like a hole in the head. I went to the hospital with a load of flowers and clothes from the boutique all signed by George to try and smooth her out and basically tell her whatever she wanted to hear. George couldn't go because as soon as he showed his face at hospital the papers would have been tipped off and would be round there like a shot. So I saw her alone and just started saying whatever came into my head first. I told her, 'George can't believe what has happened. He really likes you and wants to go to Majorca with you for a week to see if you both can try to get your lives back on track and maybe have a future together.' It was quite cynical really and something I'm not really proud to have done in hindsight.

Fortunately she didn't make any more complaints. But when she finally did come out of the hospital after getting the all-clear I did start to feel sorry for her, because George had no intention of ever taking her to Majorca. She came into our travel agency. George and I spotted her walking up the street, and he shot out of the back door as she approached and ran off, leaving me and Waggy to deal with her. I had to bite the bullet and said to her, 'Look, your arrangement with George is your own business, but this is my business, and I have to make a living here, and your relationship with him is impinging on my business, so I don't want you to take this the wrong way but don't ever come here again. Please leave and don't ever come near this place any more.'

She left in tears. It was a dreadful thing to do really, but I couldn't leave her hanging on in hope, because that would've been even crueller. So I was brutal and to the point. As well as sorting out problems like that I also had to contend with the fact that he never turned anyone down who asked him for help, but then never wanted to go through with the commitment. He would promise to go to so many dinners and functions and then on the night simply not turn up. I'd say to him, 'George, all you have to do when people say will you come to this or that is tell them, "Yes, I'd love to do it, but speak to Frank first." And I'll then ask you if you really do want to do it or not, and if you say no I'll find a way of letting them down gently. If you do want to do it then everything will be fine.'

'OK, Frank, I'll do that in future,' he'd say to me, but he never did.

George did do a lot of favours for people. But he only did things that he really wanted to do. After he left Manchester United he helped out Southport FC, which was being run by Alan Ball's dad, and he'd always turn out for lower-league clubs as a favour, and they could guarantee capacity crowds because of him. But often he said yes when he meant no, and things could turn our rather sticky for me, because I had to sort out the mess if he said yes to something he had no intention of doing. One of the people he let down was Ivan Mauger, who was the world champion speedway rider. He walked into the shop one day and said to me, 'I've come to pick up Mr Best.'

I looked at him puzzled and said, 'What have you come to pick him up for?'

'He's opening a new track in Barrow tonight.'

When he said that I knew there was no way George would slog up to Barrow for that, he just wouldn't.

So I said, 'Oh, all right, who've you made the arrangements with?'

'Oh, I've made them directly with George Best himself.'

'Right, OK, just take a seat, and I'm sure he'll be with you shortly,' and I went into the back room where George was now hiding, his ear glued to the door, listening to my conversation.

'What's all this about a race night you're opening in Barrow?' I said.

'Oh for fuck's sake, I forgot to tell you about that.'

I looked him in the eye and said, 'George, you can't let these people down. He has come all the way from Barrow for you and he is waiting to take you up there. There's a huge crowd of people going to turn up, and they're all expecting you to open this track.'

'Well, you'll have to get rid of him,' George said.

I just didn't know how I was going to get him out of this one. But there was no way he was going to do it, so I had to think of something.

As I walked out I didn't have a clue what I was going to say so I bluffed it as best I could and told him, 'I've just had a telephone call from Mr Best, and unfortunately he is not very well.'

Ivan looked at me and, smiling, said, 'That's OK. As long as he shows his face that's all he needs to do. If he lets them down you see it'll affect the future of the speedway track. The local council will not fund it if they feel we've let them down, and the people who turn up for Mr Best won't come to the race nights if he doesn't show his face. It is vital that he comes.'

'Right,' I said, my head spinning, 'I'll see what I can do.'

Then we all saw George go across the road. I think he was trying to sneak past them and escape. Ivan, the moment he clapped eyes on him, ran over, and they were all smiles and handshakes, and George walked back into the shop looking directly at me, and I was wondering what the hell he was going to do next. Ivan was happy now; he'd got George with him and he wasn't going to let him out of his sight. So George said to Ivan, 'Right, I'm just going to go next door and get my hair done for tonight,' and he popped next door to the hairdresser's that Waggy owned.

He was up to something; I knew he was planning his getaway. Before he went he sidled over to me and said what he always said to me in this sort of situation which was 'O.T.W.' That meant 'over the wall'. But how, I thought, how was he going to do it? Ivan wasn't going to let him out of his sight. He followed George into the hairdresser's and sat opposite him while he had his hair done. I walked in after about five minutes, and Waggy was blowing his hair. He had got an inkling of what was going on and looked at me ever so slightly shaking his head. I just shrugged. He brushed him down and he was finished: 'Smashing,' he told him, 'I'll just pop for a wee.'

And he went through the back of the barber shop, into the toilet and straight out of the toilet window. As soon as he went into the toilet I left the place because I knew what was going to happen. It was going to go off big time. Ivan was left on his own waiting and after about twenty minutes he came back into the shop and shouted, 'Where is he?'

'He was with you last time I saw him,' I said looking up, my face a picture of innocence.

'Are you sure he wasn't with you?' I said. 'Because I definitely saw him with you when I left.'

'Well he's not with me now. He went for a piss, and that was the last I saw of him.'

I really didn't know whether to laugh or to sympathize with him, and then the telephone rang. We had offices in nearby St John Street about 200 yards away, and George had gone in there: 'Tell him I'm ill and I've had to go and see the specialist,' George said to me. 'Tell him I have an ear infection.'

'Right,' I said to him and I whispered, 'I will try and say it with my face straight.'

I put the phone down and said to Ivan, 'He's been taken ill.'

The whole scenario had descended into a farce. I said to him, 'He's been taken ill with a serious ear infection and he's had to go and see the specialist in St John Street.'

Ivan left, possibly to look for him in St John Street. I didn't wait for him to return. I shut the shop and got out of there. George did one as well, and we never saw or heard from Ivan again. But that was George. If he didn't want to do something he simply would not do it, and I learned very quickly never to pressurize him, because it wouldn't and couldn't make him change his mind. And even if he did agree to do something he tended to work in his own time zone and would often be late. He was due to go on *Parkinson* in the early-1970s and he arrived late to Manchester airport and missed the flight to London. It was left to me to phone the show's producer, Richard Drewitt, and say, 'Look, he's missed the flight and won't be able to make it. We'll have to cancel.'

'Oh, we can't have that,' he said. 'I'd better get a private aircraft for him.'

The BBC rang a firm at Manchester airport that chartered private planes, and we flew down to London, where Parky's lot met us, and he made it on to the show – just. The poet John Betjemen was on with George, and I remember the barmy old sod saying to him, 'When are you going to sort your life out, George?' He just didn't get it. George was never going to change. In George's mind his life was sorted; what messed it up was the football, because he didn't enjoy doing it, and that was what made him so fascinating. His life was a constant battle against the one thing that had made him great and allowed him so many other opportunities. The rest of the interview went without a hitch because in those days there was no booze backstage, so George was sober, unlike on his infamous *Wogan* appearance some years later. But I was a bit annoyed about the *Parkinson* show. George had basically gone on to do his mate Parky a favour, because the pay was only 100 guineas! Worthless really, and then they had the audacity to send us the bill for the private plane! What a cheek! Although of course Parky had nothing to do with that side of things.

Working for George meant every day was different. No day was ever the same, and each one was always incident-packed. Henry Higgins came into the boutique one day completely out of the blue. I'd been out of bullfighting for a couple of years, but he'd managed to track me down: 'Hello, Frank,' he said. 'What's happened to the bullfighting? Have you given it up?'

'No,' I said, 'I've got a family now so I needed to sort myself out financially. But I'll be back,' though I was not certain how I'd get back in without a lorryload of money to back myself.

It turned out that a lorryload of money was exactly what Higgins was after, and the reason he'd come to see me. He wanted to raise money to buy Ibiza bullring for £15,000 and wondered if George Best Enterprises wanted to invest. I invited him to stay with me for a couple of days, and we met George in the Brown Bull. But when Higgins put his proposition to George, his answer was straight and to the point: 'Sorry, we're not going to get involved in bullfighting in any way, shape or form.'

That was that. Bullfighting just didn't interest George, and if something didn't interest him there was no way he was going to get involved in it. I just shrugged, turned to Higgins and said, 'Sorry.'

I then introduced him to Manchester nightclub owner Les Simms and boxing promoter Jack Trickett to see if he could persuade them to loan him some money. But they said no. Bullfighting just didn't seem to appeal to anyone connected to business in Manchester. I was as disappointed as Higgins about this because I always wanted to compete with him as a bullfighter and looked forward to a day when I could get on the same bill as him. If his dream had come off it could've been a way for us to fight together. But it wasn't to be. We ended up drowning our sorrows on a pub crawl round the city with Higgins getting very drunk and telling me, 'I just can't get a fight any more. They won't put me on because I'm not Spanish. They think just because I'm British I'm no good.'

I didn't have the heart to tell him the real reason was because he couldn't kill the bull. I just listened to him sympathetically and gave him my drunken reasons for not fighting any more: 'I had no money and no contracts. I just had to come back home and get on with life.'

The next day I took Higgins to Piccadilly station to get his train back to London. As he left I shouted, 'Don't worry, Henry, one day I'll be back.'

He smiled, waved and got on the train. That was the last time I ever saw him. I walked through Manchester back to the office, and it was raining. It was depressing. Everything seemed to be conspiring to stop me from ever appearing as a bullfighter again. But when I got to the office my mood changed because I was back at the heart of the hurricane that was George Best's life. And that was the perfect tonic.

George was no more interested in bullfighting than the rest of Manchester. In all the years I knew him he only asked me about bullfighting once and said, 'Are you any good at bull-fighting?'

I just said, 'Maybe not as good as you are at football,' and that was it.

Although George wasn't interested in bullfighting, we did have Spain in common. He loved Spain. Whenever he ran away from his problems and his demons he'd run to Marbella; everybody knew him down there. The chasing press pack would always find him on the beach surrounded by lots of lovely young ladies. And the hotels would always send complimentary tickets to his room for the bullfights. He never went. I, if I was down there with him, went to them instead, and on one occasion Waggy came with me. George didn't look beyond the beach by day and the clubs at night. I took Waggy to a fight at Torremolinos. It wasn't very good. It's never good if the matador can't kill the bull, and this guy was cutting the bull to pieces. Waggy was sat watching this massacre and clearly wasn't enjoying it, when suddenly he piped up: 'Frank, I hope that bull stakes him to the fucking floor.'

I cringed. You can't say anything worse than that in Spain. It's a terrible thing to say. To a Spaniard that is putting the life of an animal above that of a human being, which again shows the cultural differences and outlook between the British and Spanish on matters like bullfighting. But I had to agree with him in a way, because it was a shocking spectacle. After the fight we'd invariably go back and hunt down George. He wouldn't be hard to find because he never went anywhere really apart from nightclubs and pubs, and even if you were standing drinking with him at the bar he wasn't a great conversationalist. He didn't go in for long and meaningful chats and he was actually quite shy and introverted. But the rebellious streak was always there, even in the early days when he came to Manchester United from Northern Ireland as an apprentice. He went back to Ireland after a month, he was homesick. But he was persuaded back to United, and to keep his mind off home they gave him a job at a woodyard near Old Trafford. George said to me, 'I was walking across the yard with a load of fucking wood in my hands and I just thought: I haven't come here to do this. So I dropped the wood on the floor and walked out. I never went back to that place.'

I had the same feeling when I was in Valencia doing the waiting job. I wasn't there to be a waiter, I was there to be a bullfighter, but I didn't have the rebelliousness to just drop everything and walk out of the place, unlike George. But if you don't have some discipline in your life then eventually you'll fail. It catches up with you in the end.

Chapter Eight

CATCH A FALLING STAR

Everything with George seemed to build to one huge climax in 1973 when I became involved in one of the most famous incidents in his career. He came into the shop one morning when he should have been training with Manchester United. 'What are you doing, George?' I said. 'Why aren't you at training?'

George looked a bit down and said, 'Are you busy? Have you got anything to do right now?'

I said no I hadn't, and he told me to lock the shop, and we went to sit in a place called Mr Strones, a café across the road, where we ordered a coffee and found a quiet place to sit. George leaned over to me and whispered, 'I don't want you to tell anybody about this for the time being, but just read that.'

He handed me a handwritten letter. It was a resignation letter. He was quitting Manchester United and he was running it past me first. 'I want the club to know before the newspapers do,' he said, and he added: 'What do you think?'

I was stunned and said, 'George, I don't know what to think. This is like an earthquake. What's the problem?'

'I've had it,' he said, 'I don't want to go near football or have anything more to do with it any more.'

He was having a mini-breakdown. The weight of having to carry a team that had clearly been in decline since its heyday of the 1968 European Cup win had become too much of a burden for him. Now he'd come to a mental block where he just couldn't do it any more. He'd had his run and felt he just couldn't face kicking a football. If the success on the pitch had continued I believe he could have coped. But things were going wrong, badly wrong, and his heart wasn't in it. Matt Busby hadn't had the wisdom to do what Alex Ferguson has done, which is ditch players who showed signs of deterioration or dissent. Fergie has always done it right. Even if he has paid £30 million for a player it becomes irrelevant if they prove not to be good enough or cause trouble. In that case he gets rid of them. In Ferguson's eyes no player is bigger than the club. But in the early 1970s George had become bigger than Manchester United, and without him it seemed obvious they'd plummet down the league, as indeed they did do when he finally left in 1974. United were still winning games but only because of the genius of George, who was in his prime. When he wasn't scoring goals he was creating them, and he also did his bit in defence. It was not that far from the truth to say that United almost became a one-man show with him making up for the deficiencies of the other ten. It had been a slow period of disillusionment for George that started with Busby moving upstairs at the club to be replaced by Wilf McGuinness, who was given the job without any proper preparation for the huge task in hand. There was little investment in new players; Wilf's arrival was when it all began to go wrong for George.

There was a little sequence of games in the 1969/70 season where it was obvious Wilf wasn't getting it right, and George certainly wasn't himself. His form dipped and he rapidly lost interest. I remember them playing an FA cup semi-final against Leeds which went to two replays, at Villa Park and Bolton. Two things stick in my mind. Paul Reaney was playing for Leeds in the first replay and he was a very good full back, but not much better than other good full backs around at the time, and the day after the match I read reports in newspapers that said Reaney was a cracking defender who had got the better of George Best. I wasn't going to give George any advice about soccer. He was the greatest footballer of his era and he rarely spoke about football for the simple reason the game appeared so easy for him to play he never had much to say about it. But I couldn't let this lie and I showed him one of the articles and said, 'Listen, George, don't let these idiots write all this rubbish about you being unable to play. Let's get fit. I'll come out with you every day, and we'll get fit together. Let's get up in the morning, do a run, get super fit, and you show them who's boss.'

It was a pep talk more than anything. But he just said, 'Nah, I'm the greatest footballer that ever lived. Let them say what the fuck they want because I know I'm the best. Let Reaney have his moment,' and he broke into a big smile.

He was ultra-confident. So confident in fact that he couldn't care less if a newspaper said so-and-so was better than him. George had no chip on his shoulder in that respect. But all this talk of George being in decline had been in a few newspapers right up until the replay at Aston Villa. So George really should have been mindful of this and put on a display that would've had the newspapermen eating their words. But that was not the way he operated. George had gone down to the team hotel in Birmingham with the team for the game. The game was an evening kick-off, but they arrived at the hotel at midday, and George, from the moment he walked in, spotted a beautiful girl at the bar, pulled her and took her to his room for sex. Ten minutes after they'd gone up Wilf called a team meeting, but no one knew where George had disappeared to. When Wilf went up to George's room the door was unlocked. He walked in, opened the bedroom door and George was on the bed with this girl. They were both naked and getting down to it. 'Downstairs, George,' Wilf said, and he left George to get dressed.

Wilf still picked him, and during the game the unthinkable happened. George got the ball behind the defence and only had the goalkeeper to beat. For George that was never a chance, that was always a goal, and he was always able to dribble the ball past the goalkeeper with a body swerve and walk it into the net. You very rarely saw George shoot from any distance, even though he had a terrific shot. But this time he didn't even reach the goalkeeper. He stood on the ball as he ran and fell over. His legs had gone. And that was what was starting to happen post-Busby. He was behaving in a wayward manner, the inexperienced manager was making all the wrong decisions, and little by little it was all falling to pieces. So they ditched Wilf, Busby did another six months as manager in which things did actually improve a little, and then they brought in Frank O'Farrell, who did an eighteen-month spell.

George hated this period even more than the Wilf McGuinness era. Frank was a bit distant with the players, and really George, to play well, needed a manager who understood him. So he regularly turned up late for training because basically he didn't want to do it any more: he'd well and truly had it. Then things started to happen off the pitch. George got in trouble with the law for being a bit rough with people, and I was the one Frank always rang to ask for cooperation in trying to get George back on track. I'd have to try and tell George to calm it down a little, but George didn't listen to anybody.

Despite this, under Frank they got off to a blinding start and were top by Christmas. All the young players like Ian Storey-Moore and Ted McDougall would come into the shop for clothes and confidential chats. I felt like a sodding father figure to them. They were all young lads and very good footballers, but without that life experience, and that's what footballers maybe lack even to this day. It's certainly what George missed out on.

Under Frank, despite the excesses of George, things were going swimmingly, and the place was buzzing. Then, after Christmas, it all fell apart, and it coincided with George becoming seriously uninterested. Outrageous things were happening that, if they'd happened today, would've almost certainly seen him sacked from any football club, be it Premier League or Football Conference. George had an assault case pending where a girl accused him of attacking her in a nightclub – George pleaded guilty to this, but as the case was due

George went on the missing list, failed to turn up for training, and everybody was frantically trying to find him.

Not only that but the cops were now looking for him for something else he had done. I always tried to keep sweet with the law when it came to George, because they had tremendous respect for him. They would always say things like: 'We don't want to get involved but we need to have a word with him,' and there was a certain affection shown towards him by the police, despite what he had or hadn't done. They were as much in awe of him as everybody else. But now that they wanted to question him he was missing, and it was a real headache. It was Waggy who found him. He was at a house in the Chorlton area of Manchester, in bed with two sisters. He rang me up and said, 'Frank, I've got him.'

'Well keep him there until I've worked out how to play this,' I told him.

Twenty-four hours before this he'd gone one better and bedded the girlfriend of George Carman, QC. Carman, who died of prostate cancer in 2001, was one of the most famous English barristers of his generation. He rose to fame in 1979 when he successfully defended the former Liberal leader Jeremy Thorpe after he was charged with conspiracy to murder. But he was also quite a womanizer who had three wives and many girlfriends. Unfortunately for George, Carman, who was practising on the Northern Circuit in Manchester at the time doing mostly criminal and personal injury work, found out about George and his girlfriend and was so furious he got in touch with a local gangster and offered him money if he'd break George's legs. Unluckily for Carman this gangster was a friend of George and said, 'I don't sort out domestic disputes and I'm not going to harm George. So you can take your money and go somewhere else. But I'll tell you this, if any harm comes to George I'll know who did it and I'll come after you.'

No harm ever did come to George, and when Waggy found him after his wild forty-eight hours, it was left to me to phone Frank O'Farrell at Manchester United. I said: 'Frank, there's a problem. I've got him in Chorlton with my partner, but the police are looking for him, so I'd like to bring him straight to the club so that your lawyers can be there with him and I can arrange for him to meet the policeman at the club. That way nothing untoward will go on.'

'Don't bring him anywhere near me,' Frank said.

I snapped and said, 'You shithouse. I've helped you all these times and I'm asking you to help me now by letting me bring George to the club and you're telling me basically to piss off. He is your player and your responsibility.'

'I want nothing to do with it,' he said and he put the telephone down on me. I found out later that he was about to be sacked, and a meeting was taking place at the club while I was on the phone to him to discuss his position. In hindsight I can understand why he didn't want to be drawn into this at a time when he knew the prospect of his sacking was imminent. He was given his marching orders shortly afterwards.

When Frank went Tommy Docherty was brought in. But by this time George was getting it from all sides and he'd had enough. It was hard for him to go anywhere or walk along the street because people, especially Manchester City fans, would have a go at him, and this tended to give him a short fuse. So, male or female, if they had a go, he'd have a go back and try to smack them. He was a bit too quick to snap sometimes, and because of this he had very few friends, because there were few people he felt he could trust. This pressure had been building up over many years and finally led to the explosion and George's decision to resign from Manchester United. The resignation letter was published in full on the front page of the *Daily Mirror* on the day he retired. I'd taken his letter to my dad, and he typed it out using one finger because he wasn't very good at typing. I couldn't give it to anyone else because it would've probably leaked out before Manchester United knew. He mistyped one word near the end. But rather than start all over again he just crossed it out and wrote over it. The trouble was nobody actually believed he wanted to retire from football, and everybody, from the moment that letter appeared, wanted to sign him. One of the most persistent was Doug Ellis, who was then chairman of Aston Villa. He came up in person, and we entertained him at the offices in St John Street. But Doug didn't know George at all and didn't really say the right things to tempt him back. He told him, 'Come on, George, I know you don't really want to retire. You love playing football.'

I remember sitting there knowing he didn't love football and he really did not want to play any more and was sick of the game. But Doug, through no fault of his own, didn't understand the type of person George was and said to him, 'Listen, what I'd like you to do is come to my club and come and have a look at some of the other facilities I've got.' He owned racing stables, had a big property portfolio and really was an immensely wealthy man and he added, 'See if you like our set-up and then make a decision. I'll pay you double the wages you are on at Manchester United and I'm building a block of apartments in Fuengirola, which you can have the agency for selling.'

This would have been a major coup for the estate agency we'd set up and could've earned it and us a lot of money. We were just dipping our toes into everything and every type of business at that time and being a bit daft about it all really.

But as soon as he left I got a call to say Real Madrid were interested in signing George. When I told George about this I could see him half think: hmm, I wonder if I might fancy playing for them in Spain. He half wobbled when the words Real Madrid came up because they were the most successful side of the period, having six European Cups under their belt and are today considered to be the greatest European club side of the twentieth century. I had to speak to Alfredo di Stefano, who in my opinion is the greatest footballer ever to have lived – he was Real Madrid's all-time leading goalscorer at the time, with 266 goals in 342 games between 1953 and 1964. Alfredo, despite being manager of Valencia at the time, was acting as go-between, and I had arranged to meet representatives of Real Madrid in Valencia with George. On the way we'd see Doug Ellis. The idea was we would go to Birmingham to have a look around Aston Villa's ground, and then Doug would fly George out to Majorca on one of his private jets. We were desperate for the press not to get wind of this so we wanted to disguise the trail. From Majorca we'd fly to Valencia and meet

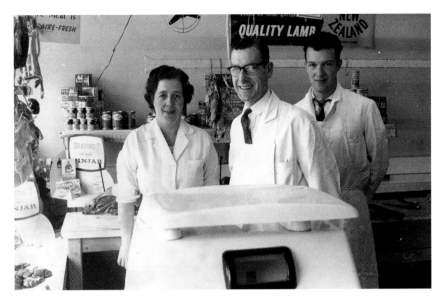

In the butchers shop with my mam and dad in 1956.

St. James' RC School rugby trophy winners in 1957.
I'm on the front left.

Waiting to begin. Arles 1967, with my friend Eddie Hindle
and my manager George Erik.

And in action! My second bullfight in Arles, 1967.

With George Best in happier times.

Making a lap of honour with the bull's ear on my reappearance in Alboraya in 1979.

When I reappeared in 1979 I was at last able to have a clean shave!

Salamanca 1984. Pedro Ruiz is about to open the door to release this animal into the fields. Moments later its horn was buried in my backside.

Left to Right: Ortega Cano, Curro Vazquez, Corbelle, Antoñete, me.
Front row: Soro II, El Jaro, El Soro.

I had the great pleasure to turn out for Sale F.C. 4th team with my two sons Matthew (left) and Jim in 1986.

With Manolo Montoliu before my alternative in 1991, where I would be formally made a matador. Manolo was killed by a bull in Seville nine months later.

This bull from Joaquin Barral, Sevilla, was the best I ever faced. You can see the hole he smashed in the fence when he came out.

Don't try this at home!
A 'Porta Gayola' in Benalmadena, 2003.

A right handed pass ('derechazo'). Benalmadena 2003.

Jiquilpan, Mexico 2003. I was well on top with this excellent bull from 'San Maximiano' and was awarded an ear before the bull put me in hospital. Here I am performing a right-handed 'pase de pecho'.

Juan Caparros cuts off my pigtail in the ring at Benalmadena to symbolize my retirement on 14 August 2005; I would reappear in a bullring in 2008.

di Stefano. There was already a deal on the table. He told me that Real Madrid wanted to pay him £250,000 a year tax free, a huge amount at that time, and they would buy his registration off Manchester United. This would've probably swung it, and there was every chance George would've signed for Real Madrid on the spot.

But on the Monday we were due to go I went with Waggy to pick George up. He was staying at Mary Fullaway's house in Chorlton, where he lodged when he first came to Manchester United – he sometimes stayed there if he'd had a night out in Manchester to save going back to his gaff. I got out of the car in this small cul-de-sac and knocked on Mrs Fullaway's door. When I went into her living room it was full of people including Paddy Crerand, a great midfielder for Manchester United who had retired the season before and was a great friend of George. He was possibly the only person George ever listened to in his life. Paddy said to me, 'Frank, I don't know what you've arranged, but George is going to meet Matt Busby and Louis Edwards at Mr Edwards's house to discuss the situation, and we'll see what happens after that.'

What happened after that was simple: I left in a huff and rang Doug Ellis to tell him, 'It's off. The whole deal is dead. George has been kidnapped by Manchester United.'

Later that day George came out of club chairman Louis Edwards's home flanked by both Edwards and Busby to meet the press who had camped on the doorstep. A sheepish George told them, 'I'm going to carry on playing for Manchester United, because this is the club I have only ever really wanted to play for.'

I watched it on the news and could tell George was gutted. He had his head down as he said this, and I muttered to myself, 'Oh George, what have you done?'

His love of football had gone. Things that should've been quite simple for him had become an enormous problem; like just turning up for training and playing the game on the pitch. He couldn't cope with it. He played on for a couple of months and walked out again, this time for good. It was just madness. The way Manchester United had got him back was not the way to treat him. They should've just let him go where he wanted to go because once George made his mind up there was no going back.

His last game for them was on 1 January 1974 against QPR. But yet again nobody would believe that he didn't want to play football any more, and I got a call from an entrepreneur called Joe Martin, proposing a move to Canada. Martin was a Hungarian referee turned businessman who was based in Ontario. He had an idea for a new type of soccer in which speed and constant action were the key and incorporated some aspects of ice hockey into it. The pitch would be ringed with a 3-foot-high wall to stop the ball going out, and other elements of play had also been modified. Corner kicks were replaced by penalties taken from 23 yards out, goals were made bigger, and the offside law was scrapped. Martin called his new game the American Soccer System, and his ambition was to see teams compete for millions of dollars in prize money. But meagre ticket sales meant the sport never really took off, so his last gamble was to try and persuade George to front an indoor league with similar rules in which he'd get paid £2,000 a game.

The moment I put the phone down on him it rang again with a New York Cosmos representative on the line wanting to sign him up. As I relayed this information to George, he kept saying to me, 'I don't want all this. I'm never going to play football again.'

I said, 'What do you want me to do? Shall I tell them all it's a no, then? Here's the deal, Joey Martin wants to send us return tickets and put us up in a five-star hotel and pay all our expenses. All we have to do is listen to what he's got to say, and so do the New York Cosmos. They want us to go and meet them in New York. They just want to put offers on the table, that's all. Let's at least listen to what they have to say.'

George thought about it and said, 'I tell you what, Frank, I fancy going to San Francisco for a holiday just to get away from all the madness for a bit, so let's go and see these guys on the way.'

I booked the flights, and off we went to Ontario. I was just planning to go on the business end of this trip, while George was going to carry on to San Francisco with Waggy. It never worked out that way, of course. These sorts of things never went to plan when George was at the centre. When we flew in to Ontario we were met at the airport by the world's press. They were all there. That was not supposed to happen. Then he got pulled by Immigration who asked him, 'Have you come here to work?'

He spent a good hour trying to persuade them he was here for a holiday and not on business, despite the fact that the press were buzzing around the place. Eventually they let him go, and we were taken to a lovely five-star hotel, where representatives of Joey Martin gave us all £1,000 each in spending money.

We went to the hotel in stretch limousines and were told to have a quick shower, because Joe wanted to meet us for a meal in a flash restaurant. We didn't argue, because the guys assigned to look after us looked a bit heavy and a little bit too threatening for my liking. At the restaurant all the talk was of contracts and how much George would get paid and what he'd have to do for the money. Joe then took us all to a nightclub, knowing George liked nightclubs, and in the club he handed me the proposed contract for George, which he wanted him to sign pronto. I said, 'Joe, I'm going to have to have a good look at this, because there are one or two little bits that might need changing.'

'Fine,' said Joe. 'Let's discuss the changes in the morning and hopefully get George to sign.'

We left the club at about 4 a.m., and George came back to my room, where I showed him the contract and said to him, 'Right, we'll have the meeting later this morning, and then I'm off to see the Niagara Falls and one or two other sights.'

George didn't say a word. Instead he stood up and went over to the phone in my room and started dialling a number. Someone answered, and he said: 'When is the next flight to New York? What about a taxi?'

I said: 'What's going on now?'

'O.T.W.'

I was gobsmacked. 'Well, what about this gang who want to meet you in a few hours, and all the money they've given us to spend? These people are quite heavy. They won't like being messed about.'

'You deal with them.'

I looked at Waggy and said, 'Are you staying with me or what?'

I could always tell when Waggy was in a bit of trouble because he started pushing his glasses up the bridge of his nose. Whenever he did this I knew he was going to wriggle out of the situation, and this was no exception: 'I've had it for here, Frank,' he said to me. 'I'm with George on this one.'

So they left me with their bags and went down the hotel fire escape and got in a taxi to take them to the airport and onwards to New York. As soon as they left I hit the phone and rang the *Mirror*, the *Sun*, the *Mail*, the whole of the British national press and told them: 'Press conference at 9 a.m. today in the hotel foyer.'

I wanted plenty of people round me because I was worried what Joe's lot would do if they found out George had done one. I also had a few bob in my pocket and didn't want to give it back. So the press conference went ahead as scheduled and they were all there when I made an announcement. I told them: 'Mr Best has left for New York because he had a very important meeting and wanted to be there early so he could be fresh for this meeting. But he was very impressed with Mr Martin's offer and very impressed with the whole set-up, so he is going to discuss it with me over the course of the week, and he will be making a decision in the very near future.'

I managed to get away with it and made plans to meet George and Waggy in New York, only for Joe to send one of his men with me who was built like two double-decker buses. I decided I had to come clean with him and said, 'Listen, I've got to be straight with you, there's no way on earth he's going to play football for your man Martin, or anybody else come to that. He's had it with football. He's finished.'

And this man mountain laughed and said, 'Don't worry, I know that. I'm just coming along for the ride.'

'As long as you do know that,' I said.

We flew into La Guardia and then got a transfer to Kennedy airport, where George and Waggy were waiting to meet us. I had to walk through the airport with this hulk as well as all the bags. I could see George and Waggy looking at this bloke and thinking: what the hell is he doing down here?

But I said to them, 'Don't worry, he knows the score,' and added, 'Right, where are you staying in New York because this lad knows a few good hotels?'

George said, 'We're not staying anywhere. We're off to San Francisco right now!'

'You can't! We're meeting the New York Cosmos,' I spluttered.

You didn't mess with these people. The Cosmos were owned by Warner Brothers, which even then was one of the world's largest companies: 'We have to meet these people,' I added.

But George very calmly said, 'You go and sort it out, you go and do it. You like all that sort of thing, you like talking to business people.'

'No I don't!'

'You do, you go and talk to them. I'm off to San Francisco.'

Waggy was nervously smiling and pushing his glasses up his nose, and off they went to San Francisco. I was left to meet

Clive Toye, one of the world's most successful businessmen, at his Park Avenue office, alone. This wasn't necessarily a bad thing in hindsight, because George hated business meetings. He'd fall asleep during them. If the meeting lasted longer than two minutes George would start fidgeting, and his mind would wander, so he decided he wasn't going to do them. He would leave it up to others, like me, to negotiate his business matters, and he got to trust me in this, simply because I was reliable. If I'd agreed to meet him at a certain time I'd be there, regardless of whether George was there or not. So I met Clive Toye alone, and the first thing he said when I walked in was: 'Well, where is he?'

I had to think on my feet and told him: 'Actually, George is not feeling very well.'

He wasn't very happy and told me in no uncertain terms: 'This is a serious proposition we're making him here. We're talking about giving him a million dollars to play soccer, as well as buying his contract off Manchester United.'

This was well up on Real Madrid's offer, and I had a feeling George might just be tempted. But there was more: he added: 'As well as the million we are also looking at turning him into a major singing star and film star. We want to do a film of his life. There are all sorts of deals on the table.'

They were a blinding outfit to get into, and this was just too good to turn down. He added: 'We own Elvis, and Elvis gets a million dollars a film. We could turn George into the next Elvis. But really we need to speak to George and we have to speak to Manchester United.'

I walked out of that room buzzing. It was a great deal and

one that George would be barmy to reject. When I told him I really couldn't control my excitement, but he simply said, 'I've told you, Frank, I can't be bothered with that shit any more,' and that killed it stone dead.

They ended up getting Pelé instead. The contract Pelé got was the same one they offered George. But George had other ideas. On his return to England he decided he wanted to open a nightclub, and Waggy and I decided to go in with him. We appealed to the magistrates several times for a licence to open a club but every time we hit a brick wall. There was a precedent that had been set in Manchester when the businessman and philanthropist Selwyn Demmy opened a club called Blinkers. When he was granted the licence for the club magistrates put a regulation into position to say that there were now enough licences in town and there should be no more until a club closes. Only then could a new licence for a nightclub be approved. So even though we put up a rock-solid case we could only get an existing licence, and because no clubs were closing no licences would be granted. It was a diabolical ruling, really, but fortunately the rule has been changed since then.

We got knocked back about three times, but each time it didn't really bother me because I wasn't too hot on the nightclub idea. I had a family, and George and Waggy were both single, so it suited them more than me. Plus they were prepared to take a chance on borrowing a fortune. I could have lost everything in this venture. For George it was an ambition, so Waggy brought in a couple of his uncles as backers to spread the risk. One was called Barry Joseph and the other

Maurice Sakalov. They were two Jewish businessmen from Manchester who were cracking lads but from the lunatic fringe, like most of us were in Manchester during that time. So everything was in place to launch a club in town, but we couldn't get a licence, and then, completely out of the blue, Colin Burn, a nightclub owner, told us the Del Sol Club was available just off Deansgate and we could have it for £10,000 plus £500 for the piano. Maurice said, 'Five hundred pounds for a fucking piano? You can fuck off. It's not worth a fucking tenner, that thing.'

Waggy said, 'Maurice, don't think of it that way. Just think of it as you're buying the place for £10,500.'

But Maurice wouldn't have it and he didn't go in on the deal because of the piano, which was madness. Then Mr Strone approached me and said he wanted to sell his café, the one where George first gave me the letter of resignation. It was on the corner of the street opposite Kendall's. The location was spot on. He offered it to me for £30,000. We agreed on £29,500. Then I fronted the lads, including George, and said, 'Look, we have the possibility of buying the Del Sol Club, but I fancy buying Strone's. Who is in with me?'

Despite the huge risk I ended up going in with the two Jewish lads to buy Strone's. I couldn't really afford to do it, but the reckless streak in my nature just came out, and I went in feet first. George, Waggy and Colin went ahead and bought the Del Sol Club. Strone backed out on the deal in the end, and we never bought it. Instead we opened a restaurant on Bridge Street. It cost us £30,000 to convert the premises, and we had an overdraft at the bank five weeks later of £33,000. But it was a disaster. There were no customers coming in, and we couldn't even pay off the interest on the overdraft. We ended up selling the place for £10,500. It nearly put me on my back for good, but I got into the property game soon afterwards and recovered from the loss after about three years.

George called his nightclub Slack Alice, and it took off like a bomb. It was making a fortune. The place was always heaving because it belonged to George. He was always in there along with every famous person who came to Manchester, and subsequently the whole city wanted to go so they could hang out with the stars. Where they went wrong was that hubris took hold. A great big old establishment called the Waldorf came up for sale on Princess Street, and, high on the euphoria of having this successful club, George and his gang then bought that. They thought they had the Midas touch. They opened a nightclub in the basement called Oscar's, a restaurant on the first floor, and a conference room on the next floor for weddings and other functions. It didn't take off and instead ate all the profits Slack Alice was making.

In the end George got bored with the nightclub game and bailed out. He reminded me of the people who go to Spain on holiday and decide they want to live there. When they eventually do move they find it's not the same as being on holiday and they can't wait to get back home again. George got fed up with the routine of playing soccer and fancied the life of being a nightclub owner. When it happened he actually discovered it was a miserable, boring, hard-working and stressful job. In the end the whole business empire collapsed, and George moved on and eventually went back to what he did enjoy doing right at the very beginning of his career: playing football.

But he was a different player when he joined Fulham in 1976 to the one that had played for Manchester United two years before. With United he'd been a great individual, a great dribbler of the ball and a fantastic goalscorer; it was all him, and the other players played the game around him. When he came back he'd put on a bit of weight and lost half a yard of pace, and only then did you see his true genius in that he could actually play football within a team structure and could release players with 50-yard passes and could see passes that nobody else could spot. He would split defences with through balls of pinpoint accuracy. George was like a great boxer who goes from beating everybody up to beating people psychologically and mentally when some of the physical strength has waned.

When we split up and the business went belly-up, George and Waggy gave me their shares in the estate agency, and I went alone with that and moved to Eccles to get back on my feet. But I still saw George. I went in his nightclub quite often and saw him in there because really he was never out of the place. But he never spoke much because he never really had a lot to say, and I was quite surprised in later years at how good he was on Sky Sports as a pundit with Jeff Stelling on Saturday afternoons.

I felt dismayed, though, when I saw him on chat shows, and they asked him about the women and the drinking and the things he did wrong. He should've just said, 'Yes, I've done that, I hold my hands up, that is me and that is who I am.' Instead he always tried to shift the blame. If George had put his mind to cracking the deficiencies he had in his behaviour to the same extent that he put into mitigating it and explaining it and justifying it then he would've been a lot more successful and maybe happier. Instead he became very clever at doing things that weren't right, like the unreliability, and he became a master at explaining away his demons, so much so that he could completely justify what he did and make it appear normal and right, when in fact it wasn't. He became dysfunctional and ended up believing what he was doing and how he was behaving was the right way. But it destroyed him in the end, and only at the end, when he was on his death bed, did the penny finally drop, and he warned others: don't do what I did, don't end up like me.

But that was what made him so fascinating a personality, and we all loved him to bits. If he had been a straight type of businessman, life wouldn't have been the same. He was the antithesis of his team-mate Bobby Charlton, in my opinion one of the greatest footballers that has ever lived, who conforms and behaves as you should in society and is a good family man. When George walked into a room he turned heads. He was sheer brilliance, but he was a villain, a self-destructive, indulgent shocker who behaved dreadfully, if truth be told. But in a funny way you admire people who are prepared to do the things you sometimes are frightened to do, people who don't fear the consequences. They do destroy themselves in the end, though, as George did through his drinking, but I absolutely loved working with him and I was really sorry that we didn't in some way carry on together. I would really have liked to have been his full-time agent, not because of the money, but because I felt I could've done it well and negotiated the type of contracts that needed to be negotiated. And I felt I could've at least got him to turn up for things I knew he would've liked to have gone to. He might not have been as unreliable with me around. But he was already contracted to an agent. Even so the whole experience was as exciting as it could get, and I can't say anything bad about my period with George because it was such a wonderful experience.

Although George left Manchester in about 1976, he did come back regularly. The place held too many good memories for him to turn his back on it. I bumped into him occasionally. He didn't really take an interest in anybody, though, and never had what you would describe as close friends. Nobody could tell George he was doing wrong because George was the archetypal loner. He didn't need anybody and he didn't particularly want anybody, and that extended even to the girls he went out with. With girls he was a Casanova. He'd give them all of his time and tell them they were the only thing in his world that mattered. But as soon as he left them that was it, and this happened not only to girls, but to his friends and even his family. He didn't even turn up for his own father's ninetieth birthday party. In a funny sort of way, it attracted people towards him, including myself, because we'd all want to penetrate that hard outer shell and see if there was a soft centre inside. He'd do things like arrange to borrow £50,000 off the bank for an important business deal and not bother turning up to meet the bank manager. The lad just didn't give a toss and would let down the most famous and important people and not bat an eyelid. He didn't live by the rules and was to football what El Cordobés was to bullfighting, a true maverick. He was due to go to court over a motoring offence some years after we split and didn't bother going. There was a warrant out for his arrest, and the cops finally found him in some girl's house, and like the daft sod that he was he tried to do a runner through the back door. They managed to catch him but they said in doing so he tried to push them away. So the charge of not turning up at court for a motoring offence suddenly became one of resisting arrest and police assault. He was sent down as a lesson to him and others, but it wouldn't have taught George anything apart from don't let the bastards catch you next time. He reminds me of Maradona in a way. Everybody loves a rebel, nobody remembers a conformist.

The last time we were together was in the mid-1990s, when I bumped into him in Harper's shortly after he'd married Alex Best. I was with my son Matthew and we ended up having lunch together. Alex was a smashing lass and very good for him. His life really did fall apart after they got divorced. She was different from his first wife Angie whom he married in 1978 and later divorced. Angie was wary of the people around George, fearing the majority of them were hangers-on. In many respects she was right. But some of us did have George's best interests at heart. During our few years together I never actually felt I was hands-on with George. I worked for him and I went into business with him but I was never a pal as such. We were friendly because of it all. But I didn't go boozing or anything like that and I didn't hang around with him in bars and nightclubs. Every now and again I'd go to a club, but more often than not at the day's close it was home time.

The last time I met George was when I'd gone to a black-tie bash at the Midland Hotel in Manchester round about 2002. I was sitting in the foyer lounge with my dickie bow on and done up to the nines waiting for the party to start in one of the function rooms. I didn't know he was in the place and I just happened to turn around and he was sitting about 10 yards away. We just caught sight of each other and had a lovely big embrace. I wish I'd had just one more night out with him because that was it after that. George had gone, for ever.

Chapter Nine

FROM BULLRING
TO BOXING RING

Bullfighting was never far from my mind during the George Best years, but I simply had to make money and get on my feet financially so I could provide for my family. And having such a young family meant that in the short term there was no way I could really justify going back to Spain and spending the time that I needed there to get me back into the swing of fighting bulls again. For a start I'd miss my lads growing up, and I also didn't really have the cash to support not only myself once I was over there but my family back home. But bullfighting was always nagging away at me like a devil in my ear. Fortunately, because I was in the travel game, I was able to at least go to Spain with my family for holidays, and we always went to either Valencia or Barcelona, where my bullfighting connections were. But even that became a strain because after a few years of this my wife said, 'Can we start going to places where you don't actually know anyone!'

I didn't blame her, really. We'd always get tied up with meeting people in bars or have to go for meals with my contacts and generally spent a lot of time hanging around people connected to bullfighting. My wife, on the other hand, wanted some quality family time. But it did keep me in with the bullfighting fraternity, and thoughts of making a comeback did start to creep into my mind during the mid to late 1970s. I was lucky I was able to think like that, really, because after the George Best years I really had landed on my feet business-wise. I ended up with a property portfolio of twenty-seven flats, which I rented out, and I also had student bedsits. Over a ten-year spell beginning in 1969 I got lucky and successful. I also bought a new driving school, got three cars on the road and generally had a go at lots of different things

The only disaster was the restaurant. I was a bit lucky there, because my bank manager was homosexual and fancied the pants off me, so he was quite lenient with my repayments. But this could be highly embarrassing at times. He collared me one day and, grabbing my arm, told me, 'You're daft, if you had me as your boyfriend you could take me anywhere, and we could be seen in any place together and no one would suspect. But if you had a girl on the side everyone would suspect and you'd get found out.'

He was right in a way, but I wasn't gay and I'd have to constantly ward off his advances and say, 'Look, thanks for the offer but I just don't fancy men.'

Unfortunately, he could never accept that, but he was marvellous to do business with. If I had a business proposal that required funding he'd say, you need this, that, this, that, bring me the plans, bring me the estimates, done. He always gave me the money I needed and then said, 'Right, let's go and have a bite to eat.'

I was with George and Waggy during one such deal. And, true to form, after we shook hands my bank manager said, 'Right, let's go for a meal.' George and Waggy got in one car and left me on my own with him, the sods. As they drove off I could see them laughing and giggling. I had an XJ6 Jag, so we got in that. The gear lever was four inches tall with a crossbar at the top, and as I drove into the pub for some lunch and parked up my bank manager said to me, 'Have you ever eaten here before? It's a great little pub.'

As I was about to tell him I had he got his little finger and wrapped it round mine; my hand was on the gear stick. I looked at him in bewilderment and mounting panic. I didn't know what to do. Should I get my hand out? Should I tell him to get lost? He was lending me some money, a lot of money, and I wanted it so badly that in the end I simply carried on talking while we linked pinkies. But I was going bright red as I spoke, and when I got out sweat was running down the back of my neck and I could feel my blood pressure rocketing because the veins in my neck seemed about to burst. This all felt like every silly 1970s smutty sitcom. When we got into the pub I went straight to the toilet and the next thing I knew he was standing right next to me at the pot, looking down and trying to check me out! I just couldn't do it and ended up leaving the toilet still bursting to go. I had to go back five minutes later and blame it on a weak bladder!

But despite all this, he was great to do business with.

Away from bullfighting, when I was not building up my small business empire I was also involved in boxing, which came about through Freddie Griffiths. I knew if I ever was to get back into bullfighting I'd want to go back to Spain fully fit and raring to go. Boxing training was one of the best ways to maintain my fitness levels. I trained and kept fit with Freddie at the YMCA, and in there was a trainer called Brian Robinson, who was in charge of the boxing section. Brian was one of the toughest people I have ever met. He was totally driven – his whole life was keep-fit and the boxing world. A lot of people think Frank Warren is responsible for bringing boxing back to Manchester, but it was Brian who started it all. He rented a nightclub called Rotters and put fighters like Chris Coady on there. The place would be packed. He then did other small shows before putting on a big one at Bellevue. When the big-time London fight promoters heard about this they moved in around him and gradually took over. But Brian was the first one to bring boxing back to the city, and it's massive now all over the Greater Manchester area thanks to him.

I'd done a bit of boxing in my youth, and Brian was running the amateur section, but he had a professional licence as a manager and welcomed me wanting to get involved. I got a licence as a trainer and worked as his second, and we had a great stable of fighters, including Neville Manderson, who was the English amateur champion, John Malone, John O'Hare, Peter Freeman, Coady, the Commonwealth light-middleweight champion Steve Foster, and Billy 'The Preacher' Graham, who went on to train Ricky Hatton. Billy was a great example of someone who didn't have a formal education but whose knowledge, acumen and intelligence in boxing should have justified him getting a Masters degree. I had a great time with all of them, keeping myself fit and doing a bit of boxing as well. And it was boxing that saved my life. If it wasn't for boxing I would probably not be here today.

The night in question was in 1977, when I took John Malone to Stafford to a fight where Dennis Andries topped the bill. He was virtually unknown then but went on to become world light-heavyweight champion – he fought Tommy Hearns and lost in a dramatic bout in which there were something like eleven knockdowns. I took Malone to Stafford on a miserable night when the rain was pelting down. We got there just in time for the weigh-in. There was only John and me in the room, and a doctor came in and gave John his medical check. It was the usual routine for just before a fight, and for some reason I fancied having my blood pressure taken and said to him, 'Do you want to give me a go on that?'

He put the blood pressure machine on my arm, checked it and very casually told me, 'There's nothing to worry about, but go and see your GP tomorrow.'

What! That certainly got my heart pumping. But there was something to worry about. My blood pressure was through the roof, and if I hadn't asked for that check I would have gone through life thinking everything was fine, and a heart attack would have floored me. I ended up having to take blood-pressure tablets for the rest of my life. The boxing in many ways saved my life. I simply took the tablets and continued to work with Brian.

Life just carried on fortunately. Brian was a fantastic bloke. He was the only manager/trainer I knew who fought his own boxers. I've never seen Frank Warren and Don King go into the ring with their lads. But Brian used to get in there and give them a hell of a hard time. He said to me, 'If they can't beat me, Frank, there's no point in them getting in the ring.'

He was no pushover, though, because he was a big, strong bull of a man. His biggest success was steering Steve Foster to a Commonwealth title, but they ended up falling out, and Steve wanted to drop him as a manager. The only problem was they had a watertight contract that needed honouring. So this mad situation developed where I was still pals with them both, and at a fight involving Steve at Everton's ground, Goodison Park, I went with him and was ringside while Brian stood at the back. I got Brian's 33 per cent off the promoter, paid him and then he left. Then I gave Steve the rest of the cash. They weren't talking to each other, and it was a barmy situation. But I always remember Mickey Duff when he fell out with Lloyd Honeygan but carried on managing him saying, 'There's nothing in the contract that says I've got to like him.'

And this was the same with Brian and Steve. It was quite embarrassing. Brian was more outspoken than Mickey Duff and before the Goodison fight said to me, 'I may not be speaking to the fucker, but I still want the money.'

It was a strange night at Everton because the boxing world seemed to collide with bullfighting. I was in the dressing room with Steve when the ref called me over and said, 'You speak Spanish, don't you?'

I told him I did and he said, 'Come over here and explain to this lad what the rules are in England. Tell him about punches below the belt and all that.'

This boxer was on the undercard. He was sat quietly when I walked up to him and said, 'Where are you from?'

'Venezuela,' he replied. 'My name is Crisanto España.'

'There's a world champion bullfighter with your surname.'

'That's my brother,' he said.

So we talked bullfighting for a bit before I said: 'How many fights have you had?'

'Seven,' he replied.

'And how's it gone for you?'

'Oh, I've won them all. I've knocked out all my opponents in the first round.'

That simply doesn't happen in boxing. This kid was either lying or he was potentially the next fight sensation. As it transpired, he was the latter. He looked like a typical Indian kid with very high cheekbones; he was barrel-chested, had no weight on him but had very strong arms. He looked quite a handful to me. Then the ref called me over again and asked if I'd go and be the second to his opponent, whose second was stuck in traffic due to the awful weather and wouldn't make it in time. Boxing is quite strict in that respect. A boxer has to go into the ring with a licensed second. So I turned up in the corner with this other lad, and the Venezuelan boxer was looking at me as though I had been a spy in his camp and was now passing on information; it was mildly embarrassing to say the least. But they both went into the ring. The ref got the pair together eyeball to eyeball and said this, that and the other, and the bell went. I walked down the steps by the side of the ring and as I got down the third step I turned to see my lad spark out on the canvas. The ref didn't bother counting; he just called in the medics straight away. España had won another fight on a first-round knockout in about five seconds.

I collared him in the dressing room later and said, 'What was all that about?'

'That's just the way it is. I saw an opening, gave him a left, and he went down.'

I kept my eye on him after that fight. He went on to become the world welterweight champion, only to lose his title in France. A mate of mine saw him years later in Venezuela and said he was broke. I only wish I could have managed him. I could have shown him how to invest his money and build for the future. He would have been in a better position with me looking after him. But I did manage one fighter, John Stone, who between the ages of fourteen and twenty-one had spent something like three weeks to a month outside prison. He was wild as a youngster but later said, 'I'm proof that the prison system works,' because at twenty-one, after yet another sentence, he walked out of jail and said to a pal who was waiting for him outside, 'I'm not doing this any more.'

He never committed an offence after that and became a

successful businessman. It was Eddie Hindle who introduced him to me. Eddie had gone into the fitted bedrooms trade with Stoney, who was a master joiner. Eddie was a great salesman. They had a business in Broughton and started doing very well. But they fell out like a lot of people do in partnerships. I had a few quid at the time, and Stoney said for £2,000 we could set up our own business, and he'd come in with me on a fifty-fifty share. I ended up going with Stoney in 1978.

He was another personality born from the same mould as George Best. I could never decide if he was a genius or a madman. He had these daft theories about life which he'd put to the test, one of which was humans should be able to run quicker on all fours. To prove it he began practising and would run down the street like a dog to the bewilderment of passers-by. This lad was a gymnast and had a lot of physical ability, and it got to the stage where he did start really motoring on all fours to the point where he beat me in a 100-yard sprint. I was amazed. He'd use his gymnastic ability to do the barmiest things. We were driving to a job in a Bedford van along the M62, and Stoney was in the driver's seat, I was on the left and Stuart, our fitter, was in the middle. Stoney suddenly told Stuart to get hold of the steering wheel and he got out of the van while we were still travelling down the motorway, climbed across the front window and got back in this time sitting next to me on the left.

It seems such a mad and dangerous thing to do, but everything was calculated with him: he didn't really take risks because he weighed up the pros and cons of his actions before he did them. I went on a rugby trip to Spain with him, and he dived off his hotel balcony into the swimming pool 40 feet below. He'd checked the depth of the pool and everything. It was a dangerous thing to do, but he knew how to do it and knew he was safe. As I watched this dive I looked back up towards the balcony, and another rugby lad was standing there. He'd had one too many and decided to follow Stoney. As he dived his head missed the concrete side of the pool by two inches. My heart almost stopped. Two minutes later he was back on the balcony doing it again! I had to walk off. I couldn't bear to watch. Every time he dived he was within an inch of dashing his brains out.

Stoney was and still is a great bloke, but his Achilles' heel came if he was ever confronted by a policeman or a figure of authority. Because he had been in prison and arrested so many times he had no respect for the police. They were always 'pigs' to him. He got pulled by a cop while he was driving me somewhere. The traffic cop pulled him over and said: 'Wait there for a minute.'

Stoney wasn't one for hanging around and got so steamed up he ended up saying to the copper, 'Are you fucking nicking us or what?'

'Just wait there,' the cop spat back.

'Fuck off,' said Stoney, and he drove off. The traffic cop didn't follow him; I was amazed.

It used to scare me to death when I was with him because of all the barmy things he did. The craziest thing he ever did was decide he wanted to be a boxer. He knew I was in the boxing game, so I got him a licence to fight. We told lies and said he'd had twelve amateur fights when in fact he'd had none. When the licence came through Brian got him a bout in Cleethorpes. Brian was a bit miffed during the weigh-in because when Stoney had first come to the club he weighed 12st 10lbs, which made him a light-heavyweight, give or take a few pounds, and Brian put him in this division, but when he was being weighed in Stoney had trained like he had never trained before in his life. He'd also dieted and starved himself and at the weigh-in came in at just over 11 stone. I looked at his weight on the scales and said to Brian, 'What's going on here? Why is he in the light-heavyweight division when he only weighs 11 stone?'

I didn't know what his original weight had been and thought the whole thing was ludicrous. Brian looked at the scales, shook his head and said, 'We'll have to just put his weight down as 12 stone.'

Joe Frater, an ex-amateur star who he was fighting, was quite handy, but Brian and I had given Stoney instructions, and I said, 'If you do get in any trouble, get on one knee, look for me and I'll tell you when to get up and what to do.'

Then I gave him the usual boxing lingo: 'Keep your hands up, always go off towards your left, lead with the left,' all sorts of little things you tell people before they go on.

Frater has become a promoter now in Yorkshire, and before we went out I said to his second, 'What's this lad like?'

He said: 'He's done all right. He has got to an ABA final and has had seventy amateur fights and won over sixty.'

All I could think was: Oh Christ!

Brian was a bit daft putting him into this one on his debut because his opponent was way out of his league. It was almost like pitting Rochdale against Manchester United at football and only letting Rochdale play with nine men. But there was no turning back, and when the bell went I simply closed my eyes and hoped for the best. After the fight I said two things to him. The first thing I said was: 'Until the ref stopped it we were ahead on points.' The trouble was he stopped it after only a minute and 59 seconds. The second thing I said to him was: 'What the hell did you do that for?'

When the bell went they both walked round the ring, and Frater threw little jabs, he was just reaching and finding his range. Stoney didn't know this and thought he was soft. He said to me after the fight, 'I thought he was a coward. He was throwing punches and not really hitting me, he was just pretending to hit me, so I tried to go for him.'

And he did fly at him; I saw some of the film of the fight, some of it from behind my hands because it was a bit of a horror show. When somebody can't really box it does look hilarious. Stoney attacked this lad like he'd go for someone in the street. The next thing he knew was Frater had landed one on him and knocked him to the canvas. But he knocked him down right in my corner. I knew he was looking round, and I was banging my hand trying to get him to look at me so I could say something to him. But he didn't see me, got up and flew at him again, and he was up and down, up and down, and at one stage he had Frater by the neck. It ended up with a funny little scene where there was the ref, Stoney and Frater all looking in one direction, and Frater punched Stoney in the back of the head. I don't know if he meant to do it, but the ref stopped it there and then because it was obviously going badly wrong for Stoney, and he was going to get seriously hurt. He'd lost his first fight in the first round in a horrendous way but he ended up having six more fights, winning two, losing two and getting disqualified in two. The disqualifications were both against the same fighter, a lad called Jerry Golden. He was doing all right in the first fight against him but then got caught and was staggering about. Because he was not really an experienced boxer and he knew he was going to get done he head-butted Golden and was disqualified. He faced him again in Bolton and again seemed to be doing all right until again he got caught, and afterwards he said to me: 'I didn't mean to butt him this time, Frank, I just did it. It was a survival thing. I just wasn't thinking when I did it,' and once more he got disqualified.

His way was to always land one with the head when he was in trouble. It was the way of the street; unfortunately those rules didn't apply in the ring. His last fight was at a place called Blighty's, and Jimmy Swords was the promoter. Jimmy was a legendary ex-middleweight boxer who fought five British champions before turning his attention to promotion and other ventures. Stoney turned up late for the weigh-in, and I'd been thinking he was never going to turn up at all. 'Where the hell have you been?' I said when he finally arrived.

I couldn't get hold of him anywhere, and I could see by the state he was in that he'd been up all night. It later transpired that he'd been with two women in bed and hadn't had any sleep. He was due to fight a northwest area champion who had a great knockout record. This was not the best preparation. He had to get through six rounds, and this place was packed to the rafters with blokes all done up in dinner suits ready for a close fight. But my worrying was in vain because after the fight the organizers said to me, 'If you can get him on again we'll pay him double.'

For entertainment value he had the place rocking, and before he went into the ring I said, 'Just weigh him up at first and don't go charging in. Have a good look at him.'

He took absolutely no notice of me. To give him credit he knew he hadn't been training and couldn't go the six rounds, so he wanted to get it over with quickly, and this is what was inside his head as he stepped into the ring. He went to the middle, the bell went, and he simply went for it and butted his opponent, which he luckily got away with. Then he ran him down the ropes holding his elbow to this lad's throat, and at one stage he picked him up and threw him like a wrestler. These are things that you never see at a boxing match. At one point they both ended up on the floor in the middle of the ring on their knees, and Stoney hit him and tried to carry on boxing from a kneeling position. The thing was hilarious to watch. When the fight was stopped and Stoney had lost I got in the ring, and the other lad, looking quite bewildered, had gone to his corner, shaking his head. The ref quickly collared me and said, 'Frank, get hold of your fighter before he does anything silly.'

But Stoney went to his corner, ignored the lad he'd been fighting, climbed through the ropes and got out of the ring. At the back of the hall was a big green 'exit' sign. He walked up the aisle, drenched in sweat and out of the stadium into the night, dressed in his boxing shorts, boots and gloves. It's a serious business, boxing, and you have to do things by the book. At the end of the fight you come to the middle whether you've won or lost. Not Stoney. He left me standing alone in the ring with a towel in my hand. All I could do was smile because the crowd was going absolutely wild. They were cheering him, clapping him, patting him on the back and shaking his hand as he headed towards the exit. It was as though he'd just beaten Muhammad Ali to become the heavyweight champion of the world. But he'd had enough, and to everyone's dismay he called it a day shortly after that.

Fortunately he bowed out knowing he was the most popular fighter in the northwest who had at least one good win under his belt against a lad called Paul Burk, who was a proper big hardcase. Brian had Burk, and I had Stoney, so there was added rivalry. I trained Stoney to beat him because I knew this other lad's weaknesses. Stoney listened this time and won in the sixth round of an eight-round fight. But we had to leave by the back door because Burk's supporters were out to get us. It was a great period with Stoney. What he could've been was Rocky: no talent, no real chance, but a great, great character. You need people like that in life. He gave up in the summer of 1978. I was enjoying the boxing and the life I had. It was fun. I hadn't been in a bullring for nearly ten years and, although the dream of returning had never really died, I couldn't see where an opportunity was going to arise. But I had the hunger to get back like never before. It was a deep, gnawing hunger coupled with the feeling I had been drifting. But it took a monumental shock to the system to persuade me I had to launch my bullfighting comeback or be miserable for the rest of my life.

Chapter Ten

DEATH IN THE AFTERNOON

Although I'd had the opportunity of working with George Best and had some wonderful moments with boxing, my life by the mid-1970s had begun to drift. I wanted to get back into bullfighting, but I wasn't making any effort to do so. I'd effectively taken my eye off the ball. So much so that I failed to take much notice of dramatic events that were unfolding right before my eyes. Dad's background had always been one of toil. He was delivering papers and smoking by the age of six; in later years he lived a life of bad business stress and he never ate regular meals or at the right times of the day. All this was coupled with the fact that he never exercised and, from the driving school days onwards, had a very sedentary job. It caught up with him in 1972, when he suffered a heart attack. I was quite ignorant and naive about the whole situation and simply thought he'd get over it and would come out of hospital feeling OK, which he seemed to do. He left hospital with pills to take, and that was that. But medical knowledge of heart problems wasn't as advanced as it is now, and unbeknown to me his days were marked.

He soldiered on, though, and continued working. Every now and then he'd have a little setback in the form of a minor heart attack, but nobody in the family had the knowledge or foresight to say stop working, retire and put your feet up because none of us realized the hectic business lifestyle he led was killing him. Three years after his first attack he came to a shop I had in Eccles selling bedroom furniture and helped me to decorate it. I'd gone out when he began painting but when I came back I didn't like the colour and told Dad we'd have to do it in a different shade. Dad was a bit put out by this, and we ended up having an argument. In the end he downed tools and walked out. Mam came into the shop two days later.

'Has dad fallen out with me,' I asked her.

'No,' she said, 'he's not very well.'

Dad had been admitted to hospital. His heart was playing up again. His own doctor had gone on holiday, and a different doctor was treating him. This new doctor changed his medication, and as Dad sat on a chair in the hospital ward he said to the doctor, 'I have to say thanks because whatever it is you've given me has made me feel marvellous.'

The doctor turned round, smiled and said, 'Well that's good news Ralph . . . Ralph . . . Ralph are you OK?'

Dad's eyes were open but he'd gone, he'd passed away. They tried to revive him, but this time he'd had a massive heart attack. It was Mam who told me he'd died. She was inconsolable. I remember the shock almost taking my breath away. It really was too much for me to take in. I almost refused to believe her. One day he was fine and fit and working with me, a couple of days later he was dead.

Only when he'd gone did I realize just how close we had been. I'd worked with him all my life: he brought me up working next to him in the butcher's shop, and in later life we ran the driving school together. He even helped out on the odd day I was with George and came on property-selling trips to Spain. He was fifty-nine when he died. I kept thinking he was way too young. That he hadn't really enjoyed his life and could still have had so many more years ahead of him. It shocked me into thinking I was wasting my life. All right I was working and making a few quid, but really there was no point to what I was doing. At Dad's funeral I sat and thought I had to start doing what I really wanted to do, and that was fight bulls again. I made a pledge that I would never clean shave again until I got back in the ring. My hunger was back and so, once again, was my drive and determination to make it. I missed Dad, but I had to carry on, and every morning when I got up and went to the bathroom to wash my face my beard reminded me of what my goal had been since he'd died. I began getting in touch with my old bullfighting contacts and I made it known that I wanted to launch a comeback. Nothing happened for quite a long time, but then I got a call from Garrigos. He said, 'I'm training a young lad who is just starting out. He's going to be good. Do you want to come and train with us?' That lad was Vicente Ruiz 'El Soro', who would go on to become a great star as a matador but at that time was just a *novillero*.

I looked at my situation; I'd got successful businesses that I could place in the hands of others to run while I was away, I had plenty of money, and my family could be looked after. Sod it, I thought, I'm going for it, and I arrived back in Valencia after ten years much leaner and fitter through my training regime at the YMCA, and also a lot wiser and just as keen. I began training with Vicente, and all the hunger came back. That call was one of the best things that has ever happened to me because it paired me with a great friend. Like me, Vicente was fit as a butcher's dog and would always be running, sprinting and doing other things to keep fit. He loved training with me. Because I came from a rugby background I showed him new training methods and boxing routines and got him on light weights and did all sorts of different things with him. We got on with each other massively, and there was history behind our meeting as well.

His dad was the ex-comic bullfighter who taught me how to kill bulls after my disaster in my second fight at Arles. He knew someone putting on a fight at a festival in Alboraya, which is a lovely little village just outside Valencia where they make Lladro porcelain, and got me on the bill. The fight was scheduled for August 1979. Ten years after quitting the game I was back in business

As I stood at the gate waiting to go out I was euphoric because I was so happy to be back. It could have been the smallest fight in the world, or the biggest, it really didn't matter. What mattered was I was back in action again. I was almost on a high that day. There were no nerves. Maybe that's part of my personality. I just didn't feel nervous any more and I was itching to get out there. When I stood in the middle of the ring and the bull came out it was the best feeling in the world. Life was suddenly good again. I felt older, wiser and more confident. I'd been practising. This time, unlike ten years ago, I knew I could do it.

I got to fight one bull on my comeback, but it was a shocking animal. I was convinced it had been fought before, and I was thrown about all over the place. But this time it wasn't because I didn't know what to do, it was because no matter what I did, the bull was going to lift me off my feet. As I have pointed out previously, the bull goes for movement: during its life the bull never sees a man on foot, only on horseback. Because it goes for movement, theoretically if you keep still in the ring the bull should always go for the moving cloth. But once they realize it's the fighter they should be going for they wise up and ignore the cloth and go for the man on foot. If they've been out before, even if it's just for ten minutes, they know what's going on. These creatures are intelligent, they don't forget, and if you bring them out for a second time it's very, very hard to get a pass with the cloth because the bull will only go for the bullfighter.

It's a nightmare when this happens, and it happened to me in Alboraya. But I killed the bull with one sword thrust. Even so, as I went for the kill I knew there was no way the bull was going to follow the cloth so I deliberately let it toss me as I stuck the sword between its shoulder blades. It was the only way it could be done. There was a big crowd watching, and I knew that after being tossed repeatedly I wasn't going to get away with not being able to kill the damn thing. So I had the cloth ready; the bull put its head down, charged and went for me. As the sword went in it lifted me off my feet and over its head. The bull died instantly, and I breathed a sigh of relief. I had my triumph and I was unharmed, bar a few minor bumps and bruises. The problem was that in this kind of situation the public aren't always aware that the animal is not fightable. Some of them will whistle and boo, thinking you're rubbish. This is what happened in Alboraya. I could hear the crowd as I was washing my hands in the ring and I was seriously annoyed. Garrigos was by my side and he said, 'Frank, let's get out of the way, because the crowd are going to lynch you.'

But Vicente's dad was having none of it. Pushing him out of the way, he said to me, 'Go and get your ear and do your lap of honour.'

I took the ear, saluted the President and did my lap of honour as told. As I walked round, acknowledging the crowd, I noticed some of them were now clapping, but a few were still whistling and booing me. The odd one or two were even jumping out of their seats to get closer to me and shout things at me. So I wasn't as calm and collected as I'd normally be; in fact, I was in a bit of a state. I was halfway round when a bloke came towards me in the stand, shouting and waving his arms in the air. I snapped and screamed at him in Spanish, 'Listen, you get outside the fucking dressing room and we'll see what you're really made of. I'm going to do you. And bring the rest of your twats who are booing and I'll do them as well.'

Jaime, who was Vicente's younger brother and would later go on to become one of Spain's leading picadors, collared me and said, 'Frank, what did you say that to him for?'

'Because he's a tosser, and I'm sick of these idiots.'

'But he said you did very well and he was running down to congratulate you.'

As soon as he said that I turned to this bloke, smiled, waved at him and shouted, 'Thank you, thank you very much,' and bowed in his direction as a sign of respect.

But I could see by the look on his face that he definitely thought I was mental. And that was the highlight of my reappearance, calling the crowd a bunch of twats! But I had reappeared now and officially I was back on the scene as a fighter; even so, I had no idea in my mind what was going to happen next. What worked in my favour was that, unlike in the 1960s, I was now in a position where I could go over whenever I wanted to. I was living with my family in Salford in a big Victorian semi-detached house, my businesses were doing well, and I could afford to visit Spain about ten times that year, staying there for ten days at a time. I was getting lots of practice on ranches and making huge strides in terms of my bullfighting prowess. I knew people in the profession and I could put money up to fight. So I renewed my licence and in the next ten years fought between two and six fights a year and in 1984 I spent most of the summer out there.

Spain had changed. Franco had gone, the country was now under a democratic government, and I immediately noticed there wasn't the same level of security on the streets. With freedom had come quite a bit of lawlessness. Women were having gold chains ripped from their necks in the streets. I left my belongings in my car for five minutes in a car park before a fight and when I came back the whole lot had been stolen. Despite these changes I was moving forward at last in the bullfighting world, and at that time my only aim was to carry on fighting. I didn't really aspire to be a major star or want to go to Madrid. I just wanted to make sure I kept getting the fights, and I'd take anything anywhere as a straightforward *novillero*.

The response to my comeback was rather like when I first appeared. The Spanish press treated me with huge curiosity. They didn't report it as a comeback. The reports almost had an amused take about them – that here was this eccentric Englishman having a go at something perceived as alien to 99 per cent of his compatriots back home. But they were tinged with gratitude. The general feeling in Spain was many people in Britain were anti-bullfighting, and yet here was someone from Salford flying the flag for the pro-bullfighting lobby. I also got covered in the English press. And what I found was these initial reports were always factually correct and very straightforward, but they attracted follow up articles that were not so positive. That was when questions would be asked in terms of whether what I was doing could be perceived as cruel, and all those sorts of things. There was definitely a split in how I was being reported in Spain and in Britain. The Spanish lot treated me with respect, possibly more respect than I actually deserved, whereas the British press would sometimes go on the offensive and have a go at me.

Again my mind was on bullfighting, but as with my dad, it should've been on events that were happening back home. Horrible, tragic events that I basically failed to comprehend fully.

Mam had been hit badly by Dad's death. She was never the same when he'd gone and felt embittered that they'd had this struggle throughout their thirty-nine years of marriage;

through all the financial turmoil of trying to run a successful business and bringing up two boys, one of whom was disabled, and then, just when they could see retirement opening up for them, Dad died. Mam lost the love of her life, because Dad was the only man who had ever really been in her life. When he went she started to cut people off who she'd put up with for so many years. She'd put up with them because of Dad and was always the one who kept the peace, but now she wanted nothing more to do with them. Emotionally she became very brutal. She bought a flat in Eccles and moved there with Bob. Again a certain number of people weren't given her new address, and when they tried to get in touch she told them not to contact her any more. From the moment Dad died she refused to suffer fools. Her attitude to my going back to bullfighting hardened as well. She became vehemently opposed to what I was doing. At its worst she would say to me, 'You're the IRA to animals,' and that really hurt.

But there was no way I was going to get involved with my mother on the rights and wrongs of bullfighting, because we would've been arguing all night and then into the next day. I just left it alone. But she never went to a single one of my fights; she felt that strongly about it. In 1983 I went to Spain for a family holiday and had a fight at Benicasim, where I fought two bulls. But I'd primarily gone for a family break and didn't mention to Mam I was fighting. She came to our house to look after it while we were away for the fortnight. I had no idea the papers would report the fight and it'd appear in press reports back home. When Mam read about my exploits she went spare. She thought I'd used her to look after the house while I went and fought bulls. When we came home the house was all nice and tidy, but Mam wasn't there. Normally she waited for us to return from our holidays. I went round to her flat because I was worried. But she wouldn't answer the door to me.

It took weeks for me to make it up. If Dad was alive I would've got a quick bollocking off her, and life would have returned to normal almost straight away. Without Dad she tended to harbour resentment, and arguments and fall-outs tended to drag on. Mam was a Gemini and like many Geminis was either all nice or all nasty, only the nastier side of her personality seemed to come out more when Dad died. Anything that upset her she was no longer prepared just to put up with. She wouldn't tolerate anything she perceived to be nonsense. Her attitude became rock-like. and her emotions were kept firmly in check. In a way she no longer enjoyed life apart from the periods in which she was helping to bring up Matthew and Jim. I felt sorry for her at times and was always wary of upsetting her.

But a year after our row everything had been settled, and she phoned me up to say she wasn't feeling very well. She went to the doctor, and he told her to go to a nearby hospital, Ladywell, for a diagnosis. This was worrying for me because she came from a generation that never complained about being ill unless there was something seriously wrong with them. But she went, and they did tests on her. I knew the consultant cardiologist, Alan Bernstien, and when I went to hospital to pick her up and bring her home he took me into a private room for a chat. I thought he was going to say, 'Your mother is under the weather, but give her some tablets and she'll be OK.'

Instead he said, 'You mother has serious lung cancer, and it is advanced.'

I was mildly shocked at that. I wasn't devastated at the beginning of the conversation and said, 'Well, they're going to have to operate on her, aren't they? Will she be going to Christies?'

I was sitting there thinking: right, let's get going!

'Your mother's not going to survive,' he said.

I could see her sitting on a bed from the window. All the family were sitting with her, because it was her birthday. She looked OK, she looked relaxed and she looked well. I could feel myself losing it emotionally. I swallowed and said, 'Well how long do you think she has got?'

'Three weeks,' he said. I was stunned. 'It's very advanced,' he said, 'and your mother is not going to survive. She could go at any minute.'

Again I looked at her, and she didn't look like she was going to die at any minute. They sent her home, and she came to stay at my house while Margaret and I looked after her. I'd been told to make the most of what little time she had left, but June went into July, and the weeks passed, and she hung on in there. By the time October came I'd got over the worry and thought she was going to battle through it. And through ignorance and naivety I booked a family holiday for October half-term. I asked Mum if she'd like to go into hospital for a week to rest. Unbeknown to me she was really ill by this stage. But there I was trying to get her into hospital so I could go on holiday. Mam had bad days and good days, but because I had no experience of seeing anybody with terminal cancer I didn't appreciate what was really going on. The week before we were due to go away Mam complained of feeling unwell, so I drove her to hospital to be checked out. She could hardly breathe, and as I walked her through the hospital doors she had to stop to catch her breath. I dropped her off with a nurse and said, 'See you later, Mam.' I had a driving lesson to take.

One hour later she was dead. I had no idea how poorly she was. The only person who was with her when she died was the priest, and that's something that haunts me to this day. But Mam was tough and she was a battler. That's why I thought she was going to be OK. If I'd known the seriousness I would've stayed with her to the end. But in a way her death wasn't as devastating as when Dad died because I was ready for it. I'd already moved my life in a different direction when Dad died, so my mother's death only made me more determined to fulfil my dream. Bullfighting proved to be cathartic in a way. It was an escape from these realities of life.

Despite my thirst for bullfighting, the loss of my parents high-lighted the importance of family to me. The first time I took them to a bullfight was when Jim was three and Matthew five. It was during a holiday to Lloret de Mar. During the fight Matthew was on the edge of his seat and enjoying it. I could see he had been affected by the danger and the scent of emotion that was going on. But afterwards Jim made a comment that typified his attitude towards it for the rest of his life when he said, 'I think it's tight on the bull,' which was a great little comment for a kid to make.

And he has never really gone to bullfights since, apart from on the odd occasion. He has always been supportive of me but underneath he thinks the way the bull is treated is a bit too severe. Matthew doesn't get affected by any of that.

In the 1980s if I could get them over to Spain with me I would. They were growing lads who were learning to appreciate the culture of the place. And there was also the sense that things were starting to happen for me, which gave them a bigger buzz, because a son always likes to look up to his father.

But it was still a learning curve for me. I was still effectively a novice and, in getting fights, I soon discovered that I was not just fighting bulls, but also the spivs and thieves who still infested the profession like a disease. There's a lot of cash about in the bullfighting business and it's populated by people with no formal qualifications in bullfighting, because there simply aren't any qualifications to pick up. Anyone with a bit of nous can just walk in and get involved in it. So it does attract some of the wrong sort of people, and there is a lot of skulduggery going on. The organizers know all the fighters want to do is get in the ring and that they're desperate to fight. So at the end of the fight these spivs simply disappear with the money, and more often than not the fighters end up not being paid. But there's never any real trouble, because the fighters know that, if they kicked up a fuss, they probably wouldn't get booked again. And if you were appearing for an agreed fee you often didn't see your money. It happened to me. During the 1980s I got to locations and found there was no fight on. The organizers had simply taken the money and scarpered. I'd had enough of this. Nobody was going to rip me off. I'd get my money by hook or by crook, even if I had to hold up the bullfighting arena to get it, which I did!

By this time I'd met a small-time impresario who owned a bar in Valencia. A few years previously he'd managed to get in with some town mayors who paid him to put on fights. He'd get the bulls, contract the bullfighter, put on a show, and everything would be all right. I got quite a few fights thanks to him. Then he lost his bar. That was when it became a bit dodgy. When his bar went he started asking people, including myself, to lend him money to get the bulls, but instead of using the money for what it was intended for he'd spend it. And then when fights did get put on nobody would get paid because he'd run off with the till money. So this bizarre situation developed in which I was appearing in 1985 at a place called Maella in Zaragoza, in a fight organized by this impresario. I was on the bill with José Pacheco, who has gone on to become a star under the title 'El Califa'. He was hopeless with the sword but a very handy practitioner in the *faena*. The idea was that the winner would get a place on the cartel for the major *feria* in August, where there was a few quid to fight for. I fought my bull and killed it with one sword and was awarded two ears. My opponent was excellent but didn't kill it as well as I did and lost the trophies.

Amazingly I'd beaten this star of the future and I went back in the August, this time with my two lads, Matthew and Jim, for the major *feria*, which was packed with 1,000 people in the arena. There were three of us fighting there, and I was on a fee for the day as well as getting the money back that I'd paid out for my team in wages. But it got to midday on the day of the fight, and we were all there at the ring – the vets as well as the matadors and their teams – but there was no sign of this former bar-owning impresario, or the bulls he was supposed to bring. It looked like another rip-off, so all the *banderilleros* went home, and the police talked of finding this dodgy Arthur Daley figure and arresting him – if they could ever find him, that is. Suddenly he appeared in the distance, driving in front of a truck with a load of bulls inside. But they weren't the bulls that had originally been announced for the fight. So a policeman took me and the other matadors to one side and said, 'Look, these aren't the bulls that have been advertised. Are you prepared to fight them, because you have the right to say no? It's not in your contract to fight these bulls.'

'Yes, I'll fight them.' I was prepared to fight anything; I just wanted to get in the ring, that was my buzz.

The other two were just as eager. Then the haggling began. The other fighters were the Carrion brothers, Manolo and José, and their dad said his lads would only fight them if they got paid up front, at least to cover the cost of the teams. They agreed to pay us 150,000 pesetas each, which covered the teams, and we agreed to put the sticks in ourselves, effectively taking on the role normally performed by the *banderillos*. We were all capable of doing it, and that's what we did. It was a full house, and we'd all agreed with this impresario to get the rest of the money after the fight. I killed the first bull, and the others did well, but halfway through the show I noticed the impresario had gone missing from his seat. I got hold of my son Matthew and said, 'Quick, get to the office near the turnstile and take all the money that's in there, get all of it.' He's a big lad, Matthew, so I added, 'And don't take no for an answer.'

They were blowing the trumpet now, and I had to go back

in the ring or I would've done it myself. I went out into the ring fighting my second bull while my son took the till. Halfway through the fight he appeared in the *callejon* and, as I fought, he shouted to me, 'I've got the dough!'

He'd counted it and got 600,000 pesetas. There was no time to lose, I had to kill the bull quickly and get out of the place. As I got back to the changing room, Matthew was there: 'Do you want all the loose change as well?'

'Listen,' I said, 'count half a million and put the rest back,' because that was what he owed me. 'I don't want to be stealing money that isn't mine,'

I was happy. I'd killed two bulls successfully and I'd got the money owed to me, but as I was getting changed this impresario appeared with the chief of the civil guard. Matthew was in the background. I thrust the money in his hand and said, 'Go, now, run!'

I turned to the captain policeman and said, 'Listen, I'm the senior matador here. All the money is mine. It is what this man owed me,' and I pointed to the impresario.

But this policeman just looked at me and said, 'What are you talking about?' He added, 'You're the senior matador and I want to know why you didn't appear with your *cuadrilla* today.' He seemed to have no knowledge of the till money. So I changed tack and addressed the complaint about the team.

'Because when it was twelve noon the impresario should've been here with the bulls and he wasn't. My team went because they knew they wouldn't get paid.'

'Can you verify to me, then, that you didn't get paid for your team?'

We did manage to get the money but only after threatening to pull out of the fight, so I said to him, 'Well, as it happens, he did give us the money.'

The policeman looked at me, shook his head and said, 'Therefore that's defrauding the public, because you advertised that you would be appearing with a full team, so you're under arrest for defrauding the public.'

Matthew had hung back to hear all this, and I said to him in English, 'Why are you still here? Quick, you've got the dough, get out of here now. Get in the car and wait for me outside the village. Go, go, go.' He jumped into the car, and Jim drove out of town.

I was hauled off with the other two bullfighters to a civil government office. They even wanted to put handcuffs on us, but I wasn't having that and resisted. This barmy captain then said, 'You'll have to appear before a magistrate at some stage so you'll have to be bailed.'

I wasn't handing over any money. I knew I'd never see it again.

The Mayor then appeared in the office and said, 'This is ridiculous. If these lads hadn't agreed to fight without the cuadrillas there would've been no fight. Instead of vilifying them you should be praising them. I'll pay the bail money for them.' And he got his cheque book out.

But the police captain said, 'I'm not taking a cheque off you!'

'Of course you are. I'm the Mayor.'

The whole thing got more and more surreal as the captain said, 'I don't care who you are, it might bounce.'

So the Mayor's wife had to get cash. She came back with the money, and we were finally released. Outside the office the whole village had gathered to see what was going on, and when we came out we were greeted as heroes. But all I wanted to do was get out of the place. I found Matthew and Jim on the outskirts of the village and said to Jim, who was driving, despite being only fourteen, 'Head north, not Valencia. I don't trust the coppers. They'll have that money for themselves if they catch us.'

I related the story to an English news agency based in Madrid and couldn't believe what happened. The story went worldwide and was in every paper. The trouble was it portrayed us as though we were in the Hole in the Wall gang and I was the mastermind of this robbery and had used my two burly sons to terrorize the organizers into handing over the cash. In all honesty it wasn't that far from the truth, but desperate means required even more desperate measures, and I was sick of getting ripped off. I also got a bit of stick for allowing my sons to become involved at such a young age, and I agree that's possibly not the right way to have brought them up. In hindsight there are plenty of things I wouldn't have done, like swearing in front of them and getting them involved in incidents such as holding up bullrings.

It may seem odd to some that I let my kids watch bullfighting, but it doesn't seem to have damaged them. I believe all the exposure they have had has made them more rounded personalities. Matthew was destined to get involved in things like that anyway, because he's a bit reckless like me and enjoys taking risks in life. Jim is the complete opposite. He's careful and more cautious. But both of them have benefited in some ways from the things my father taught me, which I have passed on to them. I have taught them never to quit anything halfway through. Whenever they've started something I have never let them give it up. Rugby has been a great discipline for them. They went through the rigours and enjoyment of playing mini-rugby as six-year-olds, and both of them went on to play student rugby at international level. Matthew represented Ireland in the 1992 World Cup in Australia, and Jim was in the England side that won the Four Nations championship in 1994. In the end James showed more talent than Matthew or myself ever had. James had balance, timing and great courage. If he possessed my pace over ten yards he would have been test match material. It's all in the genes. I hope I live to see it. They both went on to enjoy several years as professional rugby league players. Jim played for Swinton when they were in the old First Division. He was an excellent footballer with a rock-solid defence. Matt played for a number of different clubs. There is where the similarity between them ends, especially in their attitude to bullfighting.

Life was good. I was fighting regularly and training with a lad who went on bit by bit to become a top matador. I was going with him to ranches and fighting cows and accompanying him to places like Bilbao, Valencia and Madrid, which were top-class rings where I mixed with the elite of the profession and made a lot of contacts. I was in the swing of things and just where I wanted to be. But 1984 was a real horror year, one of the most sensational years ever in the history of bullfighting; sensational only in the sense that it was a year that triggered a series of horrible gorings and some traumatic deaths.

One of the dangers of bullfighting is if you get nailed outside a major city you can die of complications due to haemorrhage if they can't get you to hospital. In the early 1980s I made the decision to always carry litres of plasma with me wherever I went and I learned how to put it in my vein if I ever got in any trouble. The trouble was I was fighting all the time in the sticks, well away from a major hospital. And I'd known horrific tales of fighters like Pepe Mata, who got gored three hours from Madrid. He was still awake and alive when they got him to Madrid but he died a couple of days later because of the traumatic shock to his body caused by the massive internal haemorrhage he was suffering. All his internal organs shut down. I decided to try and make sure it didn't happen to me.

In late 1984 I'd finished my season and had no more fights, so on 15 September I decided to go back to England. I said goodbye to Vicente – he only had a couple of fights left himself – and just before I was due to fly I turned on the TV. Vicente was on telly fighting in a bullring near Cordoba called Pozoblanco. On the bill with him were two other fighters, Paquirri and Yiyo. I remember watching it with mounting horror. At first everything was going swimmingly. They all fought their first bull and cut ears, and then the next bull came into the ring. This was Paquirri's second bull of the day and his last of the season in what was the fiftieth fight of a very successful period for him in which he had established himself as a top matador. His wife was waiting for him at home and had all the cases packed ready for them to go on holiday to Miami. Their son was waiting with her for their dad to return.

Vicente told me that Paquirri said something to him as he walked out into the ring; he shared a joke with him and was laughing when he walked out. Vicente added in hindsight that everything had just seemed a little bit too casual. Because the bull was on the small side, but with very sharp horns, Paquirri may have been a little disrespectful of it and a little too complacent, maybe because he was such an experienced bullfighter with twenty years as a full matador behind him. He was a total master and a complete professional. But on this day he got caught. The bull took him by surprise. It may have been small, but its right horn caught him in the right groin, and he ended up over the bull's head and couldn't get off. He had the horn in there all the way, and the bull ran a good 40 yards with him impaled on its horn, a freak goring really because 99 per cent of the time they catch you and put you on the deck. Everybody ran out to save him. Eventually he came off and was carried to the infirmary at the back of this little tiny bullring, where there were no medical facilities of note, and he had a massive wound. The fight was being filmed, and the guy with the camera filmed the goring and followed Paquirri into the infirmary, where another fighter, called Corbelle, desperately tried to get a tourniquet on the wound to stop the bleeding. But it was pumping out like a small fountain. As he lay there dying in an atmosphere of pandemonium, with great courage he said to the doctor, 'Doctor, please, take it easy and calm down. I am in your hands.'

There was total panic all around him. The only person who was calm was Paquirri, and he was the one who was slowly slipping away. They did manage to stop the femoral artery from bleeding and got him into an ambulance to take him the 40 kilometres to the military hospital in Cordoba, where they were waiting to operate on him. But all they did in that little infirmary in the bullring was stop the bleeding they could see. The bull's horn had gone so far in they weren't aware it had punctured the iliac artery, which is in the middle of the pelvis, and he was internally bleeding to death. His stomach was swelling up with blood like a balloon. He died halfway to hospital. If that injury had happened in Madrid they would have opened him up and dealt with it. Paquirri was buried a couple of days later, and the whole of Andalucía went into shutdown. Nobody went to work, and the funeral was broadcast live on TV with most of Spain watching it. I can only compare it to Princess Diana's funeral. That was the regard Spain held for this man. His funeral was treated with the same importance as that of a head of state. Vicente said to me, 'He might have been saved if you were there with your plasma,' but I don't think so; he needed major medical help, which just wasn't available.

Morbid as it may sound, Paquirri's death gave Vicente's career a boost for the simple reason he was in the fight where one of the most famous bullfighters of all time was killed. There was great sympathy for him having simply been in the ring with Paquirri as well as for the other fighter, Yiyo, who was only twenty-one. The year afterwards I noticed people were taking a lot more interest in Vicente, and he was getting in magazines and a lot of newspaper articles. That season went well for both of us and at the end of it I was on my way out of Madrid airport taking a flight back to England when there was a commotion with people grouped round a radio. I went over and listened to what was going on. A man turned to me and said, 'Yiyo has been killed.'

It was almost twelve months since Paquirri had died. Yiyo had a fight in Colmenar Viejo, which is just outside Madrid. Curro Romero should've been on the bill but cried off with an injury, so Yiyo took his place. He was fighting a bull that should've been used in Seville, but wasn't; then it was the reserve bull in Valencia, but wasn't used; and then there were three or four other bullrings where this animal went but wasn't used. Eventually Yiyo fought it in Colmenar. He was sensational. He was well on his way to two ears and a major triumph. He'd used every pass in his repertoire, and the bull had been outstanding. But it now came to the kill, and this is where disaster struck. Yiyo lined the bull up with the sword and placed it first time up to the hilt. He came out of the encounter and passed the bull by something like three or four yards. The bull made another charge for him. With the cloth in his left hand, Yiyo tried to move the bull away from his body and he went to the right. But with its left horn the bull caught him on the knee and tipped him over. Two *banderilleros* came out a bit too quickly, and the first one flapped at the bull with his cape, but the bull only half looked at him and was only slightly distracted. The bull was seriously wounded and didn't have the energy to follow him. Turning the other way, the bull saw the other *banderillero*, who also failed to bring him away from the stricken Yiyo. The *banderilleros* had failed to distract the bull, and Yiyo was on the floor, lying on his tummy with his hands over his head, with the bull standing over him. The bull then picked Yiyo up with his left horn penetrating his left armpit and put him back on to his feet. But when he did this the horn went so far into his body it pierced his heart. Yiyo staggered into the arms of his *banderillero*, El Pali, who swears to this day that Yiyo whispered to him, 'The bull has killed me,' before dying on the spot.

The bullfight was on live TV. Yiyo never closed his eyes when he died. They carried him out of the ring with his eyes wide open. The doctor gave an announcement only minutes later to say there was nothing they could do because the bull had split his heart in two. I couldn't believe it. Two fighters from the same cartel had been killed in the ring within twelve months of each other, and the one who had survived was my mate Vicente. It threw the bullfighting world into turmoil. The animal rights groups wrote letters to Yiyo's parents, saying he got what he deserved – this lad was twenty-one and one of the nicest people you could ever wish to meet. Then they hounded Yiyo's manager to the extent that he committed suicide two months later. It was sickening behaviour.

The world's press was focused on Vicente now, because everybody was convinced he was going to get it. They believed there was something in the cartel of 1984 that was doomed, and they all wanted to be there when Vicente died. I came back to Spain after Yiyo's death and was with Vicente for his last ten fights of the season. He was doing the most reckless things like kneeling outside the gate, waiting for the bull to come out, then not attempting to pass it. I couldn't believe it, it was almost as if he had a death wish. He was almost inviting the bull to kill him. But after all that had happened he just felt emotionally propelled to do it. It's a funny anomaly of life that the more you take risks the less danger you end up getting yourself into, and Vicente was effectively putting his head in the lion's mouth. It didn't bite. But if he had stepped back a bit and let caution rule his head, I'm sure he would've been caught. Vicente allowed himself to be tossed all over the place with little more than bumps and scratches, and he was getting ears and tails by the bucketful. It didn't matter how he fought, the crowd were just thrilled to see him fight.

But it came to the stage where Vicente had to go back to Pozoblanco to fight in a cartel that was headed by Espartaco and Emilio Muñoz. When it came to Vicente's turn the crowd hushed as he went to the gate and knelt in front of it, waiting for the bull. When the bull came out Vicente didn't move and didn't make any attempt at a pass. The bull hurtled forward towards him. By not making the pass he was inviting the bull to knock his head off, which could have effectively killed him on the spot. But the bull didn't do that; instead it jumped over him. This was nothing short of a miracle, and the crowd went mental. He was awarded two ears and a tail. After the fight the crowd left the arena still struck dumb with astonishment. The fight had so much emotion attached to it that, when he did his lap of honour, he went to where Paquirri had been killed and put flowers on the spot where he fell.

Vicente, by some miracle, had survived, and in 1994 he got a new manager and had a terrific season ahead in which he had over seventy fights booked. He started the season with two fights in Valencia, earning 15 million pesetas, and then went to Benidorm and earned another 15 million. He was on his way to becoming a very rich man. But then his knee started giving him trouble. He'd had problems with his knee throughout his career. After the Benidorm fight he booked into a hospital in Madrid for an arthroscopy. Trying to get it fixed was a huge problem. After sixteen operations he ended up crippled. His knee was fused together, and he never recovered. He's had a stiff leg ever since. In 2007 he came to England for a consultation with Mr Gutjens in Derby, the best knee specialist in the country, but the doctor looked at it and just shook his head. There was no circulation there any more. The skin had simply stuck to the bone. He said if he operated on it there was a 90 per cent chance he'd have to amputate the leg. Vicente became so dejected that he sank into periods of deep depression. His money went, and he moved back to his native village of Foyos in Valencia, where he lived, a pale shadow of his former self. His father always predicted he'd end up hanging himself. I just hope that prediction doesn't come true.

The irony is that, when he does die, he'll be fêted, and there'll be films, books and documentaries made about his life, because his life story really is a fascinating rags-to-riches-and-back-again tale. When he was growing up his family owned fields where they cultivated lettuces, and every day he had to go out with his father to pick these lettuces. Lettuce-pickers carry elastic bands round their wrists to slip round the lettuce before tossing it in a box. That was his life, and that would've been his life if it wasn't for bullfighting. When he fought he always wore elastic bands round his wrist. I once asked him why he wore them, and he said, 'They are to remind me that, if I don't fight well in the bullring today, that is the life I am going back to tomorrow, and I don't want to be pulling lettuces for the rest of my days.'

Those three years from 1984 were a weird time for bull-fighting. Strange things were happening. People were getting killed or seriously injured all over the place. I spent 1984 in Salamanca, training with cattle. In the August I was on the way to the ranch with Vicente when his father, who was driving, reversed into a truck. This was a bad omen. I'm not superstitious, but bad luck comes in threes.

When we got to the ranch I was practising with fifteen-year-old fighting cows, and one particular cow I faced had razor-sharp, almost needle-thin horns. I was making passes with it using the left hand. The cow wouldn't have it on the right horn. I knew that, and everybody who was watching me knew that, but for a split second I forgot and tried to bring it back round me on the right with a move known as a *pase de pecho*. As it charged, I realized the mistake I'd made, but I also knew it was too late to do anything, and it hit me with a bang and lifted me off my feet. The bull's horn had gone into my backside and right up my anus, so deep, in fact, that it had torn my prostate. It dumped me on the floor. The ranch handlers came running out. A searing, gnawing, throbbing pain just came, and it got gradually worse. I have never experienced pain like it.

There was no real tear in the pants, so when I was pulled out of the ring in a daze those round me thought I'd simply been tossed. Nobody could tell I'd been gored. It was only when Pedres, who owned the cattle, said let's get his gear off, because I couldn't move or walk and was in such agony, that they saw the extent of the damage. My backside was covered in blood, and it was pumping out of my bottom. They rushed me

DEATH IN THE AFTERNOON

to the local quack. I was in relentless pain. Sweat was dripping down my face, and I could barely talk because I was in
constant agony. The doctor told them to take me straight to
hospital. On the way to the hospital I was battling nausea and
the agony of a car journey which, every time we hit a bump,
was like having a thousand needles rammed up my arse. I was
also very aware that, if I was bleeding internally, they'd have to
act quickly, or I'd go the way of other matadors who'd been
gored and then failed to get the right treatment. This was serious, really serious.

At the hospital I was taken straight to the ante-room to be
prepared for the operating theatre. But before they had a
chance to do anything, Vicente's dad said, 'Let's get all this
gold off you because this lot will rob you while you're asleep.'

He said this while the doctors, nurses and surgeons were
listening, and started removing my chains and stuff. I could-
n't believe his behaviour, which was turning the procedure
into a farce. I could have been dying! But the medical staff
ignored this and as he took my jewellery they stuck a catheter
down my penis. They took out 2 litres of blood. I had been
bleeding internally, yet all Vicente's daft dad was still bothered
about was my bling. Eventually everything calmed down, and
they told me they would open me up and see what was going
on. Vicente's dad said, 'Hold on a minute. Don't let them
operate on you. I've got people in Madrid who'll operate on
you for nothing!'

I looked at him and said, 'Leave it out.'

But he wouldn't let go and said to me, 'All these sods have
done is seen your passport and they're going to get as much

money out of you as possible. You don't need opening up. It's an insurance scam.'

The surgeon, who was patiently listening to this abuse, then interrupted and said, 'We don't want any money out of anybody. This gentleman has got insurance. We don't want his money, but we do need to operate on him as a matter of urgency.'

I was in agony and desperate for them to put me to sleep so as not to be in any more pain but the surgeon left the anteroom and came back five minutes later with a document which he brought to me and said, 'Right, unfortunately, because of what this gentleman has said, we'll have to get you to sign this giving us permission to operate on you.'

I couldn't believe it. All I wanted was to be under and for my backside to be fixed, and here they were, Vicente's dad and the surgeon, having a row.

'Give it to me,' I said through gritted teeth and I scribbled my signature on it.

As they wheeled me away to be operated on, Vicente's dad was still trying to remove my rings. After I had the operation I woke to find Manolo Montoliu there with me. It was the early hours of the morning, and he was asleep on a chair. I was touched. He was prepared to stay with me all night, the only one out of everybody who had seen the goring. But he later told me it had nothing to do with wanting to be with me. Manolo was mischievous and with a twinkle in his eye he said he was simply saving having to pay a hotel bill for the night.

Montoliu was a great pal of mine from my early days in Valencia. He was a matador but didn't quite make it, despite being very talented as a good all-rounder. He just didn't have the chemistry and charisma needed to lift him above the crowd and become a star. But he did become a star *banderillero* and made his name with 'El Soro'. He went on to join Paco Ojeda's team, by which time all the top matadors wanted him, because he was regarded as Spain's number-one *banderillero*. He joined my team as senior *banderillero* for my alternative few years later and went on the following season to join José María Manzares, one of Spain's all-time leading matadors. Their last fight together was televised from the *feria* in Seville. Montoliu walked out into the ring, and the crowd fell silent, because they knew he was special.

But on that fateful day in 1992 he got it disastrously wrong. With the *banderillas* in both hands he walked across the bull's path in an arc. When the bull charged Montoliu sprinted 10 yards, and as the bull came towards him he squared off and placed the *banderillas*. But as he placed them the bull, with its right horn, caught him on the outside of his right thigh. It lifted him 3 feet off the ground and, before he could drop back down, it swung at him with its left horn and drove it through his side – through his diaphragm, through his heart and up into his neck, which forced his tongue out of his mouth. He fell to the ground virtually dead on the spot. It was horrific. The doctor indicated that there was nothing he could do, because the horn had split his heart in two.

At his funeral service Vicente was so stricken with grief that he jumped on the coffin and tried to pull it open. He found Montoliu's death hard to take. Again, the whole of Valencia stopped work for the day. *Banderilleros* often do die when they get caught because they end up being caught from the midriff upwards. Matadors, on the other hand, usually get gored below the waist. Nobody can save you if you get gored in the head or heart, and this is more likely to happen to *banderilleros*.

There's a moment in all bullfights when a matador has to test whether the bull will go for the target of the cloth and not you. The only way to find out is to let it charge. If a matador is skilful and experienced and has done everything properly he can be 90 per cent sure the bull will go for the cloth, but there has to be some element of chance that the bull won't go for the cloth and instead will take out the matador, otherwise there'd be no emotion in what they are doing. If the bull always went for the cloth then anybody could do it. There are only a few people who have this special type of courage to stand in a ring showing a cloth at a bull knowing that chance dictates that occasionally the bull will go for them and not the cloth, and that is why even the best get caught. I get lifted off my feet quite a lot, not because I'm no good, but because I don't get enough bulls to fight. When I get little runs, like I got during the 1980s, I tend not to get caught a lot, though ironically when I did get caught it was my worst injury.

Unfortunately, the day after my goring Vicente went to a ranch and got gored in his thigh. He ended up in the next hospital bed to me. In those two days the car had crashed, I'd been gored, and he'd been gored. I thought we'd be all right after that, because these things come in threes.

But I was wrong. When the season finished I went home to more danger than I ever realized I could be in. A letter bomb had been posted, and it had my name and address on it.

Chapter Eleven

LUNATIC FRINGE

I got a call from the police: 'Is that Mr Evans?'

'Yes!'

'Mr Evans, the bomb squad has intercepted a letter bomb that has been addressed to you. We need to make you aware of this, because there may be more in the post, and you need to be vigilant with regard to anything that comes through your letterbox.'

'Right,' I said, not really taking it in. 'Who has sent it?' I added.

'Although we can't be certain, we suspect it may be animal rights protestors. You're a bullfighter, aren't you?'

With those words my blood began to boil, and I ran over all the scenarios that could have happened. One of my two sons could have picked it up and it could have gone off in their hands; my wife Margaret could have opened it. How could these people be so stupid?

'Well, when you catch the bastard who did it,' I said in a rage, 'send him over to me and let me sort him out.'

They caught the guy who sent it, and then he escaped! But

once he was caught again he was sentenced to fourteen years. But I wasn't the only target. There were three bombs sent. One went off in the Post Office; fortunately no one was injured. But the other one did arrive at the house of a doctor who experimented with animals. His seven-year-old son was standing next to him and got injured when the bomb went off. That made me sick with fury. I made a vow after that – if these people ever got my family I'd follow them to the ends of the earth: I'd fight fire with fire.

It's difficult for me to be objective about animal rights groups when they do things like that. I have a difficult relationship with them that began the moment they cottoned on to the fact there was a British bullfighter. This was in 1964. Since then my dislike for them has intensified. When I began to hit the newspapers in Britain the items were invariably followed by letters to the editor from members of these animal rights groups. The letters were over-emotive and generally inaccurate. At first I mistakenly and naively thought my explanations of the bullfight would correct this. But then the letters started taking on a more sinister intention when my mam began receiving hate mail. This was ludicrous, because Mam hated bullfighting almost as much as they did! Then demonstrations were held outside my house. I couldn't get the point of this. Not that many people went past my house, because it's situated on a quiet lane, so the demonstrations were ignored. If they really thought ill of me they should have gone into the centre of Manchester or Salford and protested there. Why come and tell me?

The bottom line is these people are bullies. I've seen the

same mob that protested outside my house at protests in Spain. They're not hard to recognize because of their scruffy clothes, unwashed hair and generally unkempt appearance. And whether it's in Spain or outside my house they arm themselves with drums, whistles, horns and megaphones. When their so-called 'peaceful' demos have been kept to verbal abuse of me and my family I've always turned the other cheek. But on the one occasion they decided to get tough and brought some heavies with them to rough me up I was on the phone in a flash, bringing my mates in from all over Salford, and they got well smartened up. They've never threatened me like that since.

I tried to take them on in a more intellectual way, taking part in various discussions on TV. Probably the most famous debating show I was on was called *After Dark*. It was a late-night Channel Four show that started at midnight and ran into the early hours of the morning. This particular programme was on the issue of animal rights. Unfortunately I got lumped in with all the hunters. Since when has bullfighting been about hunting? Opposite me were animal rights groups and Animal Liberation Front activists. It didn't go well. I gave my view; I knew my profession and all the pros and cons of bullfighting. But in my opinion those I faced weren't as clued up and didn't really put across pertinent points and sensible criticism that would lead to us having an intellectual discussion. It just became something of a shouting match. When I asked if any of these people had been to a bullfight some of them shook their heads. Yet they were perfectly willing to criticize it. Well don't criticize what you haven't seen.

Certain people say my take on the anti-bullfighting brigade is extreme. With all due respect to the ones who appeared in *After Dark*, who I'm sure were sensible people, when other lunatics have had a go at your mother, wife and children and even tried to nobble your pets and send letter bombs to your house it becomes very difficult to be objective. In my eyes they are nothing more than terrorists. I'd like to say I can understand their point of view. But because of the way they've behaved towards my family and me I can't bring myself to say anything nice about them at all.

As it stands, the animal rights lobby has been pressing for an outright ban on bullfighting since 1850. It was around this time Hans Christian Andersen wrote his *In Spain*. In the book he commented that he saw a bullfight, didn't like it but assured readers not to worry, as a group of people had formed a committee and had told him they would soon get it banned. As a matter of record no anti-bullfighting group has ever been able to effect a single change to the regulations, let alone a ban. Anyone with intelligence should know an activity that takes place in a public arena under the auspices of the law-enforcement authorities cannot be totally wrong.

If we discount the ridiculous accusations of impairing the bull before it enters the bullring, by smearing Vaseline it its eyes for example, and look at what actually goes on, I don't believe there's a genuine case to criticize the way we treat the fighting bull. That is, apart from one aspect, which I'll deal with later. The bullfighting fraternity and the public at large feel awe and admiration for the fighting bull. It's common for the crowd to break into spontaneous applause when a particularly beautiful animal enters the ring. They are applauding the animal's perfect proportion, its finely developed horn shape, its speed, agility, aggression and above all its courage in the face of adversity. It doesn't take long for the follower of the bullfight to believe that the Spanish fighting bull is the finest wild animal on earth. These beautiful creatures are born and bred on dedicated bull farms spanning hundreds of thousands of acres across the Iberian Peninsula. Consider their life compared to that of an animal destined for the food market. A food bull in most cases would never see daylight, would be pumped full of chemicals to fatten it up and would live a life of stress cramped up in sheds or warehouses until the slaughterhouse calls. A fighting bull lives for over four years to full maturity in idyllic conditions. But my words tend to be ignored by animal rights groups.

I suppose I should be prepared to consider an opposing argument. The problem is I've never heard anyone who has a reasonable knowledge of bullfighting put up an argument against it. So why do so many people usually with no background in the subject raise objections? If a person has never seen an animal slaughtered or that person's only interaction with animals has been restricted to family pets, then the experience of seeing an animal put to death will be traumatic. But then what on earth would that person be doing in a bullring when he or she knows what's going to happen? Nevertheless, quite contrary to what people are sometimes asked to believe, great care is taken to present a bull on its entry into the bullring in perfect physical shape. When the bulls are brought in from the pastures they are checked by vets under the scrutiny of the police and carefully boxed onto transporters to be taken to the bullring. On arrival the police break the seals on the individual boxes, and the bulls are released into the corrals of the bullring for another inspection by the vets. The bulls normally rest for a couple of days before the day of the bullfight and on the day of the event another vets' inspection takes place and the police verify the identification documents for the bulls. After the drawing of lots to allocate the animals to the matadors fighting them they're placed in individual pens. There they wait in tranquillity until the moment each one is released into the arena for its moment of destiny. At no stage will the animal have been tampered with, and, if it had, the vets would have spotted this immediately. Unless an objection is raised to the bull being removed from its natural habitat there can be no sensible case for criticism so far.

When the bull enters the arena it has enjoyed four years of the life of Riley. It's what happens during the next ten minutes or so that differentiates the demise of the fighting bull from that of other bovines. They all end up in the meat market. But whereas the butcher-bound cow ends its miserable life being tied and killed by a slaughterman, the fighting bull is released into the control of the matador's cape, ultimately to be killed by the thrust of a sword.

In the first act, where the matador uses a two-handed cape to take the bull to the horse of the mounted picador, the aim is to teach the bull to charge. At an early stage the bull will be placed within range of the horse, which will usually result in the bull charging at its new perceived enemy, the horse. The picador then attempts to pierce the bull's tossing muscle covering its shoulders with his pointed lance. This is one of the most controversial events in the bullfight. The impact is violent, the horse is driven backwards, and the encounter is often unnerving for anyone who hasn't seen it before. But in the majority of cases the bull will charge the horse only once in an encounter lasting a mere five to fifteen seconds. At the side of the ring will invariably be the bull's breeder. He'll be taking careful notes of the bull's performance, and these details influence the strategies employed in the breeding of the fighting bull. Because if ever the fighting bull loses its fighting qualities and refuses to charge the spectacle of the bullfight will be over.

Detractors describe this first act of the picador as cruel. I answer that with the evidence of the veterinary scientists, who can prove that when the bull drives into the horse's padding and receives the picador's thrust from his lance the bull's system is filled with endorphins. The reaction is the same as in human beings in that, when endorphins are present, there's no sensation of pain from flesh wounds. How many times have soldiers gone on record to say they didn't know they were shot until they put their hand in the wound? People get stabbed in street fights and are unaware of the injury. In a similar way the bull's pain when it engages the picador is mitigated by the anaesthetizing effect of endorphins.

The second act, involving the *banderilleros*, has largely been ignored by the opponents of bullfighting, despite the fact that the aim here is largely the same as that of the picador. The *banderilleros'* job is to further tire the bull out. But the third and final act, the act of the kill, is a completely different matter. Here the detractors have had a field day. All that has gone before should have been with the intention of bringing the bull to this final phase in optimum condition. The type and number of passes made with the cape, the time the bull has spent with the horse and the strategy employed during the second act should all have had an influence on the bull's performance in this final period.

The great Juan Belmonte mischievously compared the preparation of the bull for the kill and the kill itself to making love to a beautiful woman. He said all that went on prior to the final moment was effectively the foreplay to create a scenario for the perfect kill. And he added any man worth his salt should leave his lover totally climaxed. In the modern world of bullfighting the public will base most of their interest in this final act. The matador's job is to dominate and bring the bull to the end while remaining in complete control, and with the bull under the total influence of the *muleta*. This is where careers are made or ruined. The putting together of quality work with a fighting bull by deft and skilful work with the *muleta* is complex in the extreme.

The few maestros who are capable of performing at the highest standard with a high percentage of bulls, with all the complexities that different bulls bring to the confrontation, are the matadors who earn the big pay days. Among the top echelon there are matadors who perform with the utmost grace and artistry and others who are short on style but have great technique. And the matadors who inspire the greatest interest are the ones who perform whilst exposing themselves to the greatest danger. José Tomas, the world number one in

2008, made it due to his immense strength of character and above all his frightening ability to perform whilst exposing himself to the greatest danger in this final act.

So according to the bull's condition and its inclinations to charge hard or soft, left or right, and stay near to or move away from the boards, the matador in this final act will attempt to bring the bull to a controlled position for the kill. The work with the *muleta* will usually take about eight minutes. But if he is standing by public acclaim on the brink of a major triumph, all will be lost if he fails with the sword. By fail I mean fails to kill the bull swiftly with one sword thrust. If a matador's work has been outstanding and the atmosphere he's created is euphoric, he may get away with perhaps one or two misses with the sword. But the public and the authorities will not tolerate incompetence at this stage of the fight. The rare sight of a matador incapable of dispatching the bull cleanly is horrifying. When a matador has missed an attempted kill subsequent attempts become more dangerous. The bull starts to wise up and naturally tries to defend itself. A scenario then develops which should have no place in bullfighting: of a frightened matador inflicting injuries on a stricken bull.

When Spain suffered an outbreak of mad cow disease the use of the *descabello* sword to break the bull's spinal cord at the end of a fight, or indeed when the matador has failed to kill the bull with the sword, was prohibited. The airgun with a captive bolt was used, the same as is used in a slaughterhouse. When the ban was eventually lifted the authorities missed a great chance to clean up this aspect of the bullfight. Why did they go back to allowing incompetents, who didn't and still don't have the balls for it, to bring the *fiesta* into disrepute by hacking bulls to death at the end of a bullfight? It serves no purpose anyway. The triumph is lost. No ears will be awarded, and everybody gets more pissed off the longer it goes on.

This is where these abolitionists can step in. Instead of having their puerile demonstrations that absolutely no one takes any notice of, why don't they arrange to sit down with those who administrate bullfighting? There is an association of bull breeders, an association of professional matadors with its own president, there are several syndicates representing the *banderilleros* and the picadors, and there is a national federation of bullfighting clubs. All these entities and others too numerous to mention have a direct influence and conduct the way the *fiesta* is driven. And there are many professionals like myself who'd support a change to the rules governing the kill of the fighting bull. The exposure of the fighting bull, for which we have such admiration, to the incompetence seen in some bullrings when it comes to the kill is the one aspect of the *fiesta* which I cannot defend. And it's with this in mind that the animal rights activists have got to accept the positive features of bullfighting if they ever hope to get any cooperation from the profession. Only the profession can effect any changes. The animal rights lobby have to stop saying they are going to get it banned because they are not. Hans Christian Andersen said it all those years ago, and if the activists carry on with their crass campaigns then the same rules and proceedings in place today will still be with us in another 150 years' time.

The biggest joke is these idiots seem to think that bullfighting is confined just to Spain. I have spoken to these people.

Many of them had no idea that it's an international activity – some still don't! I have to give them a history lesson. I have to tell them that in the former colonies of the British Empire British sports are played. Cricket is played in places like Australia, Africa, India and the West Indies, and rugby also flourishes in many of these places. The same influences of culture took place with the Spanish conquests in Central and South America. After Spain the country of most importance in bullfighting is Mexico. Mexico City has the biggest bullring in the world, holding 48,000 spectators. And the following of the bullfight in Venezuela, Colombia, Ecuador and Peru is on a national scale. When the animal rights plonkers tell me they want to stop the Latins from doing something that is centuries old and which has been developed from deep within the culture of these people I always ask them what they are going to replace it with. I get met by blank stares. It seems to me they haven't even thought about that. Or do they expect to replace it with something from their own culture? They should be warned if that's the case, because everybody got shut of us and our imperialism a long time ago.

They've also argued for decades that bullfighting is dying, and this has been written as fact in some publications. What these people have to do is go and get in touch with the Ministry of the Interior, who put out all the official statistics. They'll learn that more people in Spain go to bullfights than watch football matches. It's bullshit to say it's dying. The annual *feria* in Madrid, which is a month-long festival, is like the Wimbledon of bullfighting. But they get more people through the gate than for Wimbledon and Flushing Meadows put together. The ring holds 25,000 spectators, and every day for a month it is packed. And added to that is the fact that Spain is still largely composed of small villages: there are thousands of them. All these villages have their once-a-year bullfight which, when added up, means there are a hell of a lot of fights taking place in Spain. It's not something that'll go on every week in one particular village, rather it's an event wrapped around the religious festivals that all villages, towns and cities have in Spain. It's tradition, it's ingrained in the Spanish way of life and it's not simply going to go away. If religion died, these festivals might die, and only then might bullfighting take a backseat role. It'll stop when people get fed up with it, and there's no sign of that happening. If anything, bullfighting was getting even bigger and was receiving even more publicity than ever during the 1980s because a revolution was taking place, a revolution that affected me and many other bullfighters.

Chapter Twelve

MATADOR DE TOROS

The bullfighting world experienced a revolution in the 1980s when a new bullfighter, Paco Ojeda, burst onto the scene. Ojeda took Spain by storm thanks to a stunning performance in Madrid. He also changed bullfighting for ever. He was a star who not only had great style and immense courage but also introduced a new way of fighting the bull which nearly every matador, including myself, has adopted. Films from the archives of fights prior to 1980 all show a consistency of performances, with the matadors always standing in profile to the bull and their *muleta* presented at the side of them. Ojeda ignored that way of fighting. He showed his chest to the bull, advanced a flat *muleta* and stepped across the bull's perceived natural line of charge. And with his gifted sense of timing he delivered the bull to a position behind him from where he would link into a series of passes. The way *faenas* were conducted was changed for ever. Ojeda joined the ranks of the greats. He was up there with Belmonte, who was the first matador to show that the bull could be fought in a standing position, and Manolete, who was the first man to cross the bull. The style and technique that Paco Ojeda introduced to the art of *toreo* has been adopted throughout the world, and it is now the way youngsters are taught in the bullfighting academies.

I was able to perfect this technique through a lot of practice and a lot of fights. In fact throughout the whole of the 1980s the breaks were coming thick and fast, and I was becoming very well known in the Spanish bullfighting community. I knew, being as ambitious as I was, that it was only a matter of time before the urge to jump to the next level would be made.

The road to becoming a matador rather than a *novillero* effectively began in 1985 when I bit off more than I could chew and made contact with José Maria Recondo, an ex-matador who lived in Torremolinos. He had managed Miguel Marquez, the number-one matador in the 1960s and early 1970s. I arranged to meet Recondo to discuss the possibility of fighting in places like Mijas and along the Costa del Sol. We both thought there'd be benefits in putting an English matador on there in what was a series of predominately British tourist resorts. I also wanted to explore the possibility of putting on my own show as a fighter and impresario. I made contact with Pepe Luis Roman, who owned Fuengirola and Marbella bullrings, and arranged to meet him. I also arranged to meet the Galan brothers Alfonso, who would later be appointed the Spanish ambassador to Peru, and Antonio José, who was, for one year, the world number-one matador. He is famous for having killed more bulls than any other fighter without holding the *muleta* in his hand as he applied the sword thrust, an almost suicidal move that saw him tossed many times.

I was staying in the village of Foyos just outside Valencia at the Bar Paris, which was a bar with about a dozen rooms above. On the day of my trip to see them I was flying from Valencia airport and had an hour to kill. As I lay reading a magazine on my hotel bed I decided to dye my hair just to make myself look a bit more presentable. I had the dye and began painting it on, the idea being you leave it for twenty minutes and then wash it off. I then sat back on my bed reading again while I waited.

After about fifteen minutes the tannoy went off in the village to make an announcement. In those days every village had a tannoy which announced important events like weddings, funerals and fiestas; some villages still have them. I generally ignored them. Five minutes later I went to the shower and stuck my head under it; the water trickled out before coming to a stop. I realized then what the tannoy had announced: that the water had been switched off. I looked in the mirror at this hair dye, which was like paint on my head, and started to panic as I realized I only had an hour to get this muck off and then I'd have to set off to the airport, but there was no way to wash it off because there was no water! I couldn't go looking like I did with pitch on my head. This was one of the most important meetings of my life.

My mind was working overtime as I desperately searched for a solution. I looked at the toilet and then lifted the top to look in the cistern. There was still a full tank of water in there, enough for one flush at least. This really was desperation time, and I took a deep breath, plunged my head into the bowl and flushed the chain. It got some of it off, but anyone who's ever dyed their hair will know you need to run water through it for quite a while to get all the dye out. The first chain pull didn't really do much, and of course the cistern didn't fill up. But it was a hostel, and there were three floors. I knew that on each floor would be a toilet. There were about a dozen rooms open with no guests, so I went in each one and headed for the bathroom to put my head in the toilet. The big problem was some of them hadn't been flushed from previous visits and others were covered in skid marks; it was disgusting and made me retch as I did it. But I had to do it and I held my breath and went for it. I did my best to get as much dye out of my hair as possible before towelling myself down.

It didn't look that bad at the end – no worse than it had looked before I put it on anyway – so I picked my kit up and headed to the airport. My hair was dry by this time, and I could finally relax. As I was about to board the plane to Málaga a pretty girl was getting on in front of me. In those days the airport at Valencia wasn't as big as it is now, and to get to the plane you simply walked across the tarmac after checking in and hopped on. The Spaniards had a habit of taking everything with them on board, and this girl had a huge crate of oranges she was taking with her. She was struggling with them because they were quite heavy, so I asked if she needed help and took the oranges off her. Now it was my turn to struggle as I staggered with this box across the runway under the glare of the mid-afternoon sun. By the time I'd lugged the box up the steps and on to the plane I was sweating profusely, and people had started to look at me with concern and point. But I ignored them, turned to the girl and said: 'There you go, no problem.'

She looked at me and said, 'I hope you don't mind me

telling you this, but there are brown things running down your face. Your face is covered in brown streaks. Here, let me help you.'

She got out a handkerchief and wiped my face clean where my sweat had run into the dye and streaked my face. I felt like a right prat. But there's a moral to this story – when you hear a tannoy, listen to it!

I arrived at the meeting slightly flustered after all this, but it fortunately proceeded without a hitch, though I was wary of not sweating under any circumstances. I ended up arranging a number of fights in that part of Spain and agreed to buy half a dozen bulls from a second-class bull breeder in Castellon. The bulls were from Las Pedrizas. As two-year-olds they were terrific. That was the deal I did with the Galans. I provided the bulls, he and his compatriots provided the bullring and we split the till money.

The first fight we did was at Mijas, in the foothills near Fuengirola, and it was packed. The ring was rather like a rugby pitch where the spectators are seated at two ends. It was great. The crowd were boisterous, very appreciative, and a lot of them were British. It occurred to me that a lot of Brits were there because I was on the bill. We were near a British tourist hotspot, which helped. If this could be developed, I was sure I could not only have lots of fights but also make quite a lot of money. I saw an opportunity to put on my own bullfight, especially when I was then offered Fuengirola, where Henry Higgins took his alternative to become a matador.

To put on my own bullfight I knew it just needed promoting the right way but I needed backers to come in with me to hire the ring, buy the bulls, pay the teams and to help with everything else that needed to be done to put on a show. But, as I later found out, the bills never stopped coming in, and it wasn't going to be as lucrative as I had at first imagined. I got the bullring for half a million pesetas, and two pals to came in with me. One was a Manchester businessman I knew through golf. He put £5,000 in, as did Jimmy Swords, the boxing pro- moter who put on John Stone's last fight.

Jimmy is the guv'nor in Manchester. Although he never won a professional title in boxing he was a world champion as a street fighter, so much so that in the 1960s and 1970s he was the most feared street fighter in the country. A year after this fight he was implicated in the Stalker Affair, in which John Stalker, the Deputy Chief Constable of Greater Manchester Police, was removed from investigating allegations that a spe- cially trained undercover RUC team known as the 'Divisional Mobile Support Unit' had carried out a 'shoot-to-kill' policy in Northern Ireland. He was taken off the investigation after it was alleged he had fraternized with Jimmy, among others. Jimmy was named as one of Stalker's fraternity. It was said Jimmy was the head of Manchester's notorious Quality Street Gang, who allegedly offered protection to Manchester's clubs and pubs and who had bouncers on many of the doors. Stalker was also linked with local businessman Kevin Taylor, who was said to have had strong ties with the gang. But nothing ever happened; none of them was ever charged or found guilty of anything. The whole case was eventually dropped with an unhealthy suspicion of a set-up. It cost Stalker his career as a policeman, and Kevin Taylor's business collapsed and with it his health. He died a few years later. Jimmy just carried on being successful. It didn't affect him at all.

So the money was now in the pot, and we were away, but this is where I made a big mistake, I didn't get someone in to handle the promotion. I found myself dealing with officials and basically getting bogged down with the logistics of how to set up a bullfight, even down to getting the vendors to sell beer on the day, and all the minutiae and little petty things needed to put the fight on. It was worse than running a business. When I went to get the bulls, which we bought from a ranch in Salamanca, and brought them down to the coast the day before the fight I really hadn't prepared myself at all. I'd had no practice because I was too busy organizing the thing as the promoter and I was rusty as hell. Even so, I don't regret any of it, because it was a great experience. Jimmy was able to get to Spain for a couple of weeks and sold a lot of tickets. He was in and out of bars and restaurants like a whirling dervish, and we had a good crowd on the day.

Despite a lack of preparation, the whole event went beautifully, apart from when the first bull came out. It was huge for a two-year-old and had come from the ranch of Pedres in Ciudad Rodrigo. Pedres had been a great bullfighter and had become a successful breeder of cattle that were renowned as big, very good and very aggressive. This one came out, chased the *banderillero*, but smashed its head into a post known as the *burladero* barrier. The bull collapsed, semiconscious but effectively out of it. We'd paid a million pesetas for the bulls and we didn't want to put the reserve in its place because it would've added another 250,000 pesetas to the bill.

So somebody said to the President, 'Give it time to recover.'

It did eventually recover, but not enough to really fight with. After two or three passes I made a flourishing pass and watched as the bull fell over. It was almost like fighting a boxer who'd been knocked down but got up, and his feet were wobbling about all over the place. So I simply killed it, because it wasn't fit to fight. That was a good reason to me for never combining the roles of fighter and impresario. I didn't want to send it back because of the cost but as a fighter I should have demanded it go back and a new one come out.

I fought on the bill with Antonio, who was Vicente's brother. He did very well with his first bull but was very poor with the sword, so he didn't get any trophies. I fought the third bull, which was a completely different experience to the punch-drunk first one. This one was frisky and unpredictable and managed to give me a heavy toss. The crowd seemed to appreciate that, and it put emotion into the fight. It got my adrenalin pumping, because I knew that due to lack of practice I was slightly vulnerable. And the memory of my goring was still relatively fresh in my mind. But in moments like this I just dug deep into my reserves of courage and did the job. I managed a successful kill, and Antonio did a good job with his last bull, so it was a success of sorts – I do think, though, that with more preparation I could've put on a better show. Even so, we'd made some money, and after I'd got changed I sat down in the office with Jimmy. I'd got the money and divided it into three separate amounts of cash. Pushing one amount over to Jimmy, I said, 'There you go, that's yours. The other pile is our friend in Manchester's, and this pile is mine.'

Jimmy looked at me and said, 'But he isn't even here to pick his money up.'

'He's been tied up with business back home,' I said.

'Yes, but I've been working my arse off, and I've seen you in that ring risking your life, and yet that sod doesn't even bother to come.'

He put his arm around the spare pile of cash and pulled it across to his.

I said, 'Jimmy, for Christ sake, he's a mate of mine. You can't be doing this. Don't take his money.'

'Tell him to come and see me. We've done all this, me and you; we've put all this together. You can keep yours because you've done a good job, but he doesn't deserve anything.'

'Well give him his money back that he invested at least.'

'Tell him to come and see me,' Jimmy said.

And with that he put all the money in a bag and went, leaving me to make an embarrassing phone call.

It all got sorted in the end, and the money squared off, but what that experience taught me was that I didn't want to get involved in any aspect of the business of bullfighting. I simply wanted to get into the ring and fight bulls. And because that was now my main focus I began to consider stepping up to the next level and becoming a fully fledged matador. As the 1980s came to a close I'd achieved most of what I wanted to achieve as a *novillero* and I was also very aware that I was approaching fifty, and my age was becoming an issue. I was fighting with kids young enough to be my sons, or in some cases my grandsons, so I did start to get a little bit self-conscious and slightly embarrassed about the age gap that was developing. Physically

I was still as slim as them and as fit but I was fighting with teenagers. So I decided the time had come to take the alternative. I let it be known among the bullfighting fraternity that as soon as the opportunity arose I'd take it.

That opportunity came on 16 August 1991. I'd spoken to Vicente and his manager about the possibility, and they were convinced I'd be a big success, even though some bullfighters never make the transition from *novillero* to matador because they can't handle fighting much bigger bulls, which by law you have to fight if you're a matador. It was arranged to take place at a bullring in Chillon in Ciudad Real. The ceremony takes place at the beginning of the fight, when the senior matador hands over his sword to the *novillero*, which was me, and from that moment on, even if I didn't kill the bull, I'd be a full matador. My new status would be ratified by the authorities in Madrid, if they felt I was up to it, and that would be it.

It was like going back in time to my first fight. I was nervous as hell because I didn't want to mess it up and I had no experience of fighting fully mature bulls, and ITV were there to film the event for a documentary. I never got nervous before, during and after fights, apart from on my debut. But now I could feel my body jangling for the simple reason that my preparation for this momentous occasion was lacking. I'd had three months' notice that this fight was coming and I'd been promised plenty of big bulls to practise on, but the bulls never materialized. I resorted to buying my own bulls to practise on from a ranch just outside Valencia. But none of them was any good. They were all scared, and I couldn't make passes with them. So on the day I simply wasn't match fit.

The saving grace was I got offered a fight, a *novillada*, with two-year-old cattle, the day before and I took it. My bullfighting friends thought I was mad. 'What if you get injured?' they said. 'You'll miss your alternative.' But I wasn't thinking that way. I was a bullfighter. If someone offered me a fight I took it, simple as that. I didn't get injured and I did make a few passes. But even so my preparation over the whole three-month period had been poor. There were no big cattle to fight because they either didn't turn up or were unfightable.

To be on the safe side I had a doctor from England come along to the fight with 8 litres of plasma. I was fighting two bulls. When the first one came out it was massive, and I realized why many bullfighters had failed after taking the alternative. The bulls looked twice as big, and a bullfighter needed twice the bottle to take them on. I took a deep breath and faced this monster. As I made the first pass I caught the smell of the bull. It was the same smell I had detected in my first fight and every fight since. Only this time it seemed stronger.

When the bullfight starts you get the sweet, musky smell of the bull's sweat, and, combined with the movement and the action, it helps the fighter to relax and become confident in what he's doing. The very first pass is possibly one of the most important moments in the fight. If the bull comes out with frankness and the bullfighter can cope with it, then everything about the rest of the fight will go well. The first pass generates a feeling in my body I find hard to describe. Everything seems to be working at maximum capacity. The body goes into survival mode. Everything gets cranked up – smell, sight, sounds

– because the body subconsciously goes on high alert. It knows this bull could wipe it out.

The bull seemed as big as me now, and as we met it got bigger and bigger. But the sword went in, and the bull froze momentarily as though trying to comprehend the situation. Then it crashed to the floor. I had my kill and I had my triumph.

The crowd were hugely positive. There was a mad showing of handkerchiefs petitioning for an ear. It was exhilarating. When I made my lap of honour I couldn't believe it'd been as easy as it had been. But this was also mixed with relief. I was glad it was over and jubilant I was now a matador.

My second bull was even bigger. It was a monster weighing 560 kilos and was one of the best bulls I have ever fought. The bulls which are frank, which have a frankness of charge, fix on the lure – the *muleta* or cape – and not on the matador. Some bulls are not convinced the cloth is the target. They switch their focus between the man and the cloth. That's when bullfighting becomes dangerous. That's when you can get hurt. A bullfighter must convince the animal that the *muleta* is the target and not himself. My bull was fixed firmly on the cloth. But I didn't manage to kill him with the first sword thrust, and as a result only got one ear, otherwise it would've been two ears and possibly the tail.

Nevertheless, as I walked round the bullring holding the ear and receiving the cheers from the crowd, there was only one thought in my mind: I was a matador. A feeling of elation swept over me as I stood in the centre of that ring. My whole bullfighting career seemed to momentarily flash before my eyes: the triumph of my first fight in France, the agony of my return, the years spent in the wilderness and then the successful return. And all the ups and downs, all the joy and heartache, the pain and the endless hours of practice, all of this had finally paid off, and I could bask in my moment. But that was all it was: a moment. It's the same for everything in life. The joy is in getting there. Once you have reached your goal there's that brief period of elation, and then it's on to the next thing. The overwhelming knowledge that I had reached a personal summit and had achieved my sole ambition in life was very short-lived, because it was immediately followed by a backlash.

There was a huge adverse reaction to my becoming a matador that frankly left me astonished. I only later realized why this was so. In bullfighting everyone fights as a *novillero* with the ambition to fight as a matador. But most of them don't make it because they are not able to take the step up. So they take the alternative at the end of their career as a *novillero* instead and then stop. Despite never fighting fully grown bulls, they can still lay claim to be a matador, and that is what everybody in Spain thought I was doing. They were wrong. I wanted to take that step up the ladder because I wanted to fight on.

After taking my alternative, I was looking forward to reading about it in the next day's press. The backlash came, and it focused on a bull that I wasn't even pencilled in to fight. At the end of the event the reserve bull had to be disposed of. The impresario, Vicente's manager, said, 'I'll tell you what, I'll kill it, and the crowd can stay or go home if they want.' So he fought the bull, put on a nice little show, and as a symbolic gesture they cut two ears and a tail and gave it to him. But when I read the press reports they were all much of the same theme: 'The Englishman took his alternative in Chillon but was unable to kill one of the bulls, the last one, so the impresario had to come out with his suit on and kill the bull for him.' I was livid and threatened to sue everybody in sight. Then it got worse. Some papers reported I had no talent. One paper even ran with the headline 'Frank Evans – *Matador de Toros*' and the sub deck read: 'That Doesn't Mean to Say He IS a *Matador de Toros*'.

Everything I read about me was being written to do me down. Even the British press reports were negative because they were all being fed by one news story sent out by the Brown and Bond News Agency based in Madrid, which had followed up the negative criticism in the Spanish press and put their own spin on it. It was totally wrong and totally unfair, and I was fuming. But I had to take it on the chin, because they all thought I was going to walk away at any moment. Now I was desperate for more fights, this time with four-year-old bulls, because as soon as I got busy I knew it would shut them up and they'd stop attacking me. But nothing came. I expected full *corridas* in major towns and cities. All I got were offers to fight in much smaller festivals. The newspaper reports, coupled with the perception that as an Englishman I wasn't going to be as good as a Spanish matador, had done for me.

The years from 1992 to 1995 were bleak. I'd made the step up, but it was beginning to look like a backward step, because nobody was prepared to put me on. I had come all this way as a bullfighter for what? To be forgotten? To gradually fade into obscurity? No, that wasn't going to happen. I was determined I wouldn't be beaten because I knew that, if I could get that one break, I could show them. I could show the impresarios who weren't prepared to back me they'd made a big mistake. So I carried on practising and got representatives on my behalf to approach various Spanish impresarios to ask if they'd put me on. But almost every time these organizers came back with the same refrain: 'I know he is a matador, but can the Englishman kill a bull?'

It was effectively their way of saying 'no chance'. The irony of it was that killing the bull was the thing I could definitely guarantee I could do. But there was a lack of confidence in me in Spain. It was not looking good. By 1996 I'd become so disheartened I was thinking of packing it in altogether. But just as I'd given up all hope and had resigned myself to a life away from the ring there came a telephone call that would change everything and take me on a journey around the world.

Chapter Thirteen

'EL INGLÉS' IN
LATIN AMERICA

It was Juan Caparros on the phone: Caparros, my old mate, who came to see me make my debut in France and came back with me and the Austrian girls after the fight. In the 1980s he had emigrated from Spain to Venezuela when he too was struggling to get fights in Spain. He went over there and fought two fights. During that time he met and fell in love with a Venezuelan girl and never came back. When he phoned it was music to my ears: 'Frank,' he said, 'why don't you come out to Venezuela. We'd love to see you over here. I can get you a couple of fights and maybe a full *corrida*.' *Corridas* are simply fights in which fully fledged matadors fight fully grown bulls with picadors, *banderilleros* and all the pomp and ceremony that accompany this.

'I'd go to the ends of the earth to fight in a full *corrida*,' I said.

'Leave it with me. Let me see what I can do,' he added.

I had to wait a full two weeks before he telephoned me back. It was agonizing, because I knew my career effectively rested on him getting me a fight in Venezuela. When he did phone back it was to say he'd got me in at a fight on 25 August 1996, in Ciudad Bolívar, a town on the Orinoco River. I was back, but I was also slightly apprehensive. Venezuela was a mystery to me. I knew nothing about the country or what to expect when I got there. But I knew bullfighting was massive in South America, so it only made sense to turn my attention to fighting there.

I decided to take Matthew with me for support. Margaret, as she almost always did, stayed at home. Bullfighting is criticized in this respect for being chauvinistic. But I don't think it's right to take your wife or your girlfriend to the office. I've had bullfighters come on the journey to bullfights with a wife or even young kids in tow. This becomes an extra stress for everybody else in a situation that's already loaded. I find I suddenly have to be polite and considerate and give precious drops of my attention to someone who has no role to play. On the journey and on the day of the fight I want only the company of my team. We eat together and talk only about what's necessary and only about what we are all there for. There is no place for small talk. When the fight is over I still only want the company of my team. I love being with those grizzly old sods with their gruff, hoarse voices sat round a table, dissecting the afternoon's events. They don't miss a thing, and you never fail to learn something new from these impromptu chats. It helps you to bond with people you risk your life with. Margaret's presence would alter the whole set-up. They wouldn't feel comfortable talking the way they talked and the whole atmosphere would be different. But her absence was of great benefit to Matthew and Jim, because while I was away training and fighting bulls, Margaret was able to look after them and take care of their formal education.

Many people will accuse me of male chauvinism of the worst kind for this, and in some respects they'll be 100 per cent correct. But the simple fact of the matter is I don't want women anywhere near me before, during and immediately after a fight. And I find if somebody's wife is sitting there I can't relax – I can't swear and do the things I'd normally do in the company of men. So Margaret stayed at home, and Matthew came with me, a man in a man's world.

I was warned to arrive early to get acclimatized. It was so close to the Equator I was told I wouldn't be able to breathe after too much exertion. But what they didn't know was I love this kind of climate. As far as I was concerned, the hotter it was the better. I arrived two weeks before the fight and was hit by the heat as I came off the plane. It did take some people's breath away. I just smiled.

Venezuela is beautiful outside the cities. When I arrived in the capital Caracas I was met by Caparros. As we walked out of the airport we witnessed a bloke pulling another guy out of his car and pistol-whipping him. Caparros said to me, 'That's why we shouldn't hang about around here. This sort of thing goes on all the time.'

It was astonishing to see this happen and not be able to help. A few hours later I was in a chauffeur-driven car with my fight team, and we came to a set of traffic lights. A bloke walked across the road in front of our car and was making fun of us and generally taking the Mickey, so a few of our lads wound the window down and gave it him back. As they were trading insults he pulled a pistol out of his pocket and shot a passing dog. My lot shut up instantly. They didn't insult anybody after that.

But that incident summed up Caracas. It seemed a violent and nasty place. It was disappointing architecturally, and you were constantly warned that you couldn't really go anywhere alone for fear of being murdered. Everywhere I went I was warned to be careful. It was not pleasant.

But then we drove from Caracas to Ciudad Bolívar. Caparros drove the team and me there. But as we drove up the main roads we suddenly saw vehicles swerve onto our side of the road and then swerve back to their side. It was as though the drivers were drunk. It wasn't until we got a bit nearer we realized the roads were full of craters. The state of the roads was astonishing. There were 3-feet deep holes that you could only drive round, and halfway there it started raining a monsoon torrent the likes of which I've never seen before in my life. Then, twenty minutes later, it stopped as quickly as it had started. At the side of the road was hut after hut selling food and drink, but I didn't touch the food, mainly because it was unrecognizable, and I didn't have a clue what I would be eating. The countryside was vast and lush. How can Venezuela be so poor with so many resources, not to mention all that oil?

But when we got to Ciudad Bolívar it was worth the drive. The place was full of nice houses and villas, and the bullring was right on the banks of the Orinoco River, bordering a well-kept park. It looked beautiful. I got to work straight away and did a lot of training. The only problem was I didn't get any cows to practise with before the fight, so I was a bit rusty. But

I needn't have worried; the bulls I did fight at the *corrida* were what are known as *manso*, meaning they wouldn't charge. The first bull I got was quite small. When I got the *muleta* and sword out it stuck its arse right up against the boards, and I couldn't get it to come away and put up any sort of fight, so it was a question of killing it quickly and moving on to the next one.

The next one wasn't much better. I had to get the crowd on my side, because it was turning into something of a boring spectacle, so I decided to start making moves that are described as *tremendismo*. They are passes that look dangerous. With the first pass I sited the bull on my right and switched the cloth behind me at the last moment, making the bull swerve past the back of me. The bull narrowly missed me and went under the *muleta*. It looked sensational. Unfortunately it then ran off, and I spent the next ten minutes frantically chasing after it, making a pass, chasing after it again and making another pass.

Artistically it had been a failure, and I was awarded no ears. But the place was packed, and I did win the crowd over and got a lap of honour. It wasn't actually that difficult to get the crowd on my side, because they were very kind and showed great empathy towards me. Their heart was with the matador, who they wanted to do well so they could clap, cheer and celebrate his success.

On the way back to Caracas after the fight we flew over lush green forests and vegetation that seemed uninhabitable but looked beautiful. That was the best way to see the country: by air. It certainly was an experience, and I took two things back home with me: the hunger for more fights, and the knowledge that South America was another potential market to tap into for *corridas*. Though I vowed to make any return trips back there a lot shorter than two weeks.

On my return to Spain after the trip my position didn't seem to alter much with 1996 going into 1997. I was still only fighting in festivals and not getting a major *corrida*. But this changed in 1998, when Moreno came to see me about fighting in Monte Alegre, a town just outside Albacete. He'd promoted my success in Venezuela as proof that the Englishman could fight in a full *corrida* and found the response slightly less negative than before I went. The impresario of this fight was Marcelino Rodriguez. His son was on the bill with me, which was a good thing, because it almost certainly guaranteed we wouldn't be fighting dodgy cattle.

So I agreed to fight and after six years in the Spanish wilderness I was back in business, opening a major *corrida* with Javier Rodriguez, to be followed by Curro Matola, who seemed destined for stardom and was getting a huge amount of publicity. But he was a bit of a Fancy Dan in my opinion. He looked a bit too soft. I wanted to show him just how good I was. So I went out and knelt in front of the gate as the bull charged out and made a *larga cambiada*, which is where you kneel in front of the bull and swirl the cape with your hand over your shoulder to make a pass, and a number of Veronicas. The one thing I can say about making a pass on your knees is that, once you have done that, then psychologically everything else seems to become a lot easier. This is because, when the gate opens and the bull charges out, your heart literally stops beating, and you can almost chew it. It's a great confidence-booster if you can pull it off successfully. I did pull it off, and the rest of the fight went to perfection. The bull was picked, the *banderilleras* went in, and I killed it with one sword and was awarded two ears. I paraded round the ring having made my statement and settled down to watch the other two fighters.

Rodriguez came in now and put on a great little show, one-arrowed the bull and again got two ears. When Matola came out he had a bandage on his hand and wrist and he put on, in my opinion, a poor performance in which he blamed his bandaged hand for everything that was going wrong, gave the bull a hard time trying to kill it and was awarded no ears. My second bull was next. I did OK with it: one-arrowed it and got an ear. Rodriguez was again magnificent and got another two ears to take his tally to four.

Then the final bull came out for Matola to fight, and it was a monster, a real biggie. He struggled throughout, and when it came to the moment of truth he couldn't kill it. He got three warnings. This is where the rules kicked in. When you fail to kill a bull after fifteen minutes, three warning signals sound to signify you are running out of time, and if you've still failed to kill it then it's taken to the corral and dispatched by a slaughterman, and the national press get to know that you as a matador failed to kill your bull. It's the biggest disgrace a matador can suffer. But now, instead of it being taken away, I had the civil guard on my back. Their main man said to me, 'You're the senior matador here so you must be aware that it's your responsibility to kill the bull.'

I said, 'You should read the rules. The rules say, if the matador is hurt or injured within the fifteen minutes, I do indeed have to go out and kill the bull for him, but that's not the case here. This matador has failed to kill the bull in the regulation time so the bull should go to the corral for the butcher to kill it.'

'We haven't got any corrals,' he said. 'The bulls have come straight off the truck. We also haven't got any butchers to do the job, so you'll have to do it.'

I was adamant: 'I'm not doing it. It's going dark now, all the public are leaving the bullring, and it's getting cold.'

They went and had a quiet chat between them, and it had gone really dark by this time. The bull was still standing in the bullring thinking to himself that he'd cracked it and he'd had a nice little run round the ring on a Sunday afternoon and would soon be back at his ranch, but it was not to be. The civil guardsmen came back to tell me that, as it turned out, I was right in my interpretation of the law, and they would kill it, but I'd have to witness it. It was a horrible sight to see. I wished in hindsight I'd gone into the ring and done the job myself. Three civil guards came out all armed and gunned the bull down.

The matador who couldn't kill the bull did have a few more fights but failed to make it big. Instead he found stardom as an undercover reporter, investigating incidents of skulduggery in bullfighting and trying to prove that it was corrupt. To me it smacked of sour grapes. The other fighter didn't quite make it but still fought on. He just never quite took the step that you need to take to get fights in the major *ferias*. I thought I had made it. I believed that now I'd had a full *corrida* in Spain, years after taking the alternative, all the impresarios would recognize that I was serious about bull-fighting and wanted to make a name for myself as a matador, and they'd book me. How wrong I was.

The year 1999 was my worst. I got no full *corridas* and no festivals. In the back of my mind again was the gnawing feeling that it was over for me, that nobody wanted to put me on. It felt empty training on the ranches. Every couple of weeks I'd telephone my contacts: 'Did you speak to any impresarios?'

'Sorry Frank, they said no.'

I started to get that black dog feeling again that I was wasting my time staying in Spain, and there was nothing to do and nothing I could do apart from watch other people. In England all my businesses were flourishing. Everything back in Britain couldn't have been going any better. But in Spain nothing could have been worse. I was training every day on ranches and living in hope. My sons were running things back in England, leaving me all the time I needed to concentrate on bull-fighting. But nothing was forthcoming. As the new century dawned so my chances of competing as a matador on a regular basis seemed to fade. I went back to Spain in January 2000 depressed, heavy-hearted and seriously considering packing it all in. But every time I got this feeling, and just as I reached the end of my tether, the phone would ring. This time it was Morenito de Jaen. I'd worked with him in several fights, and we'd become friends. He said, 'Frank, I've just had a fight on the coast on the Costa del Sol with El Bote. The impresario is called Gaspar Jimenez. He owns the Benalmadena bullring and is going to start using it from February. He's prepared to give you a go. You only get one bull, but it's something. The deal is no money, you pay your own expenses, but he will put the team in the ring.'

Gasper Jimenez had an idea that a British bullfighter appearing in predominately British resorts might just pull in the crowds. He didn't have to say any more, I was in. I was that desperate I would have paid him to put me on, but I didn't tell him that. And on 20 February I appeared with five other matadors. My bull was excellent. It had been bred by the ex-matador 'Chamaco'. It had a huge head on it and looked magnificent; not only that, it was good to work with. I one-arrowed it and got an ear. I was delighted.

So was the impresario. When he saw me before the fight he looked me up and down and frowned. I know exactly what he was thinking. He was thinking how could this fifty-odd-year-old English bloke ever kill a fully mature bull? And he was worried. I could see it in his face. All impresarios realize the killing part is the most difficult bit, and they don't want a bull walking out of the ring alive, or a matador being carried out dead for that matter, because it would put a black mark on the event and the credibility of the impresario. But after my triumph Jimenez came up, threw his arms around me and said, 'Listen, congratulations. I didn't really expect anything like that.'

And because of that he handed me a contract for eight fights. I fought eight *corridas* that season in that little bullring, and it was fantastic. I was his house bullfighter, fighting some of the best bulls in Spain from the premier ranches. I say the best, but they had little blemishes on them, like a lump on their leg, or their tail was half cut off, meaning they didn't look right for first-class bullrings. But they were OK for ours and fought like the best.

Suddenly because I was fighting regularly I was getting exposure and the invites to fight festivals came up. The year had begun with me seriously considering quitting the game for ever, and it ended with me getting my first listing in the world rankings. The ranking system works exclusively on the number of performances a matador has had in that particular season. Ears don't count, but if you don't cut ears you don't get fights. Ears are a way to get fights, and the more fights a matador gets the higher up the rankings he'll progress. I was listed 160th, and, considering there were 10,000 bullfighters worldwide, it wasn't bad for a lad from Salford. But I had much bigger ambitions: I wanted to break into the top 100. This was a far cry from when I took my alternative and was attacked in the press. Now I'd proved them wrong. I'd fought about twenty full *corridas* since then and almost everywhere I went I cut an ear. So they had to stop criticizing me, and did, because I was doing a good job and working hard.

In 2002 the fights were coming thick and fast, and at the end of the season I checked the rankings and there I was at number sixty-five. I stared at the list in disbelief. Very few people make it as bullfighters. For me to make the rank of matador was remarkable enough. Then to become a full matador was even more of an achievement. But to break into the top 100 matadors in the world, out of a field of 10,000, was nothing short of a miracle, coming as I did from England and only taking it up in my early twenties. I kept smiling to myself as I looked at it, wondering how the hell I'd managed to get this far. But all matadors expect to make it, because we all have blind confidence in ourselves. Bullfighters are rather like boxers in this respect in that what they do is an individual thing. Because of this they have to have complete faith in their own ability to deal with anything that's put in their way. My belief comes down to my genes, personality and character. It's purely down to me. Some people are just made that way. But people in this profession have to be optimists because you can't go in a bullring having doubts. And success breeds even more optimism. This was proof I had that ability. But, as I looked at my name up there among the greats, I couldn't help thinking I could have got to this position far earlier in my career. It was only because I couldn't get enough experience with animals and had nobody to back me and look after my financial affairs that I didn't get on in those early days. I felt I was better or at least as good as 90 per cent of the fighters I have watched performing over the years. It annoyed me whenever I got in a bullring under-prepared, because with preparation I was as good as anybody. The year 2002 was proof that, with plenty of practice and plenty of fights, I could be up there with the best.

The following year was even better. This was my best-ever twelve months. I got eleven *corridas* and made number sixty-three on the list, and I also became the first English matador to fight in France – Henry Higgins had fought there, but only as a *novillero*. The fight in France was an experience in itself.

Their local lad was on the bill with me, and before the fight his senior *banderillero* came up to my team and said, 'Right, we've sorted the bulls out, and there's a big horrible five-year-old, but don't worry – we'll take that. Here's the numbers for who's fighting what, but unfortunately you won't be able to see the bulls because they're in a ranch miles away.'

My *banderillero* looked at me and said, 'Frank, we have to see the cattle.'

So we insisted on going to this ranch outside town, and the five-year-old was big, but it was also beautiful. It had well-formed horns and a good head and was just perfect. I sent my *banderillero* off to find the local lad's representative, and he told him, 'Thanks for offering to fight that bull, but we'll do you the favour and fight it, because Frank is a very experienced matador, and we don't want you to get hurt.'

'No, no,' he said, 'I will do you the favour, please, it's my favour to you.'

My *banderillero* was adamant: 'Look, we really are grateful for the offer but Frank is taking the five-year-old, and you can have the pick of the other two bulls, thanks.'

We'd backed him into a corner and got this beautiful creature, though the second bull was the ugliest of the lot. As I went into the ring to fight this magnificent bull I looked at the barrier separating me and it from the crowd: it was 2 feet high! In Spain the barriers are 4 feet high, and the bulls sometimes jump them. I couldn't believe it. If it had only occurred to the bull he could have hopped over the fence and caused havoc, but it didn't. And I had a good fight, one-arrowed the bull and got the ear. I should really have got two because it was a great bull, but there you go. A lot of Spaniards fight in France and don't get anything because the French can be quite parochial, so I suppose getting one could be construed as a major triumph. But I noticed a big difference in the French spectators as opposed to the Spanish ones. In Spain the crowd are noisy, demonstrative and generally very dramatic in their reactions. In France it almost felt as though I was fighting in front of a British crowd. They were a lot more reserved and clapped very politely whenever I made a pass they appreciated. And they kept their gobs shut while it was going on. They respected me, more so because there is a big Spanish–French rivalry that goes on. If someone fights in France who isn't Spanish they tend to try and back you a little bit more than the Spaniard. If it's their own they go nuts for them. And their local lad came out and put on a similar display to me and got two ears! Then I fought my final bull, the ugly one, which was *manso*. I just couldn't get any rhythm but managed to kill it with one sword thrust and got a lap of honour. The other lad fought his bull, killed it on the fourth sword thrust but still got two ears; if I'd done that I would've got booed out of the ring. The parochialism that sometimes predominates in bullfighting annoys me, because it occasionally takes precedence over talent. But I did get all the headlines in the French press the following day as the first English matador to fight in France.

When I returned to Spain I was really rocking and at the end of the season I was called to visit Juan Miguel Núñez, a leading bullfighting critic, Rafael Corbelle and two or three others. As I sat with them Núñez said, 'Right, you're ready for

Madrid.' And turning to the others, he said, 'Shall we put him on in Madrid?'

I was dazed and shocked. To appear in Madrid was the ultimate test for any bullfighter. It can make or break careers. A success in Madrid means untold glory to come. But it's also the toughest arena to fight in. The crowd want to see the bull fought properly – no tricks, no grandstanding, no standing in profile, no stepping out of the way of the bull when you could've stood still. They know exactly what they are supposed to be watching and how a fight should be fought. This is where bullfighters are really judged. It's the eye of the storm. Cut an ear or two in Madrid and it guarantees you at least twenty contracts on big money. To fail means a career scrubbing about for fights in the sticks.

Corbelle looked at me and said, 'Do you think you're up to Madrid?'

It was one of my ultimate ambitions to appear in this Mecca of bullfighting. But I said, 'If I'm honest, right now, no. But in the near future I might be.'

'Well, there's no point my talking to people about you unless you're 100 per cent,' Corbelle said.

For the first time in my bullfighting career I had turned down what amounted to a golden opportunity. But I didn't want to go to Madrid and make a balls of it. I walked out of that meeting wondering if I'd made a decision I'd regret for the rest of my life. But within a month I had a telephone call from Corbelle. A charity that raised money for Down Syndrome kids put on a fight every year for charity in Madrid and pack the place out. Corbelle said, 'I can get you on this bill if you want to fight.'

If you fight in Madrid you fight in Madrid, whether it is for charity or not, there's no difference. Succeed and you're a star, fail and you're yesterday's man. I'd been rueing my decision to say no to the original offer, so I wasn't going to let this chance slip away. 'Yes,' I said, 'I'll fight for you in Madrid.'

'Great,' he replied. 'The good thing is I run it and I pick the bulls, so you can have a really good class of bull to give you a chance.'

I practised like I have never practised before and tried to perfect everything in terms of technique and the way I fought. When the fight neared I went with Corbelle to the president's office in Madrid to arrange things with him. As I walked in, he was nowhere to be seen. One of his workers told me he'd been arrested the day before for stealing money from the charity. I couldn't believe it. The whole show was cancelled, and they've never put it on since. I was so close to fighting in Madrid, and it had slipped through my fingers. There was nothing for it but to refocus. I had to blank it out of my mind, otherwise I'd be thinking about what might have been for the rest of my life.

The French fight gave me the inspiration to want to fight as the first English matador in other countries, even though my one experience of fighting in a place other than Spain or France was a bit dodgy. But I wanted to break records. In 2004 I got the opportunity to fight in Mexico following a call from Paco Porras.

Porras failed in Madrid, but he did the sensible thing: he hung up his cape and went and got a job. I helped him set himself up in the tobacco business, which he was always grateful to me for. He phoned me and said, 'I've been offered a fight in Mexico. I've told them I have retired, but you're interested in going to Mexico, aren't you?'

I told him yes, and he came back to me and told me he'd got me two fights in the province of Michoacán, and I'd be based in Guadalajara, where England played their football in the 1970 World Cup. It was another country I could tick off the list. I was still in touch with José Puerto from Valencia, who'd worked for a time as *banderillero* in my team. José had retired now, but I asked him if he wanted to come to Mexico for the trip; it's not a bad idea to have people you know go to foreign countries with you. He agreed to come as my sword-handler. At Madrid airport, as soon as they discovered I was a matador, the airport authorities whizzed me to the front of the queue, and we were treated as VIPs.

I'd arranged to make a stopover in Cuba. On the plane I took a beautiful leather case with my sombrero in it that I'd need for the festival. The first cock-up came on leaving the plane in Cuba: I left minus the case. Porras, who had come as my manager, blamed José, and vice versa, because they'd both been entrusted to look after my gear. They had a huge row, and I started to get bad vibes that these two weren't going to get on. If you have a week together abroad you really need to be able to get on, or it's a nightmare.

We stayed at the Hotel Parque Central in Havana, right over Central Park. I fell in love with the place. I've never seen so many beautiful women. I couldn't believe it. If I wasn't married I would've had a field day, because I was being hit on left, right and centre. But I wasn't kidding myself: they didn't really fancy me; they just saw me as someone with a few quid who could give them a better life. Central Park was teeming with people and music and life. The cars were all 1950s relics that had been patched up, and the place was unlike anywhere I'd ever experienced. It was wonderful.

I met a business associate on our arrival, and we ended up smoking the biggest and best hand-rolled cigars in the world. They were rolled by Taulada, one of three of the best rollers in Havana. He gave me a brandy with it, and I was in heaven. I got back to the hotel at 10 p.m., and Porras, who had returned earlier for a kip, met me in the lobby. He still looked half dead. José had been on a long walk while I had my meeting and came up to me and said, 'Can I have a word with you?'

'Of course,' I replied.

'Do you really need me to come to Mexico with you?'

I thought he'd had another row with Porras and he couldn't face being with him on the trip. 'I can get another sword-handler if you don't want to come on the trip. Why don't you want to come? Has it got something to do with Porras?'

'No, no, no, no. It's nothing to do with him. I've been for a walk and met the most beautiful girl I've ever seen in my life, and she wants me to stay with her. If you let me off this trip I'm going to stay in Cuba with her.'

'José, I couldn't wish for anything nicer for you in life,' I said, and with that he was off.

He didn't go to Mexico; instead he stayed with this girl for a week and had the time of his life.

I travelled on to Mexico with Porras. On arriving in Mexico City, I suggested to Porras that we should go for a walk round.

'No, no, no,' Porras said. 'We will get robbed, mugged or raped. It's the most dangerous place on earth.'

I was getting sick of these dodgy places. So we got a connecting flight to Guadalajara, which was reputed to be safer at least. But whenever I go to these countries in South America I find that it's not Third World, it's bloody Fifth World. Architecturally they are the pits, and Guadalajara was no different. There was an absence of any nice buildings, apart from the football stadium and churches. The churches were dripping with gold and absolutely beautiful, so it seemed obvious where the little money that was floating about in that country was going.

My first fight was at a festival in Mexicali, where the bulls were four years old and were from a mixture of ranches; they were leftovers from the end of the season. Getting there was another matter. The town was on the border with the United States and was a six-hour flight, a long way to go for a festival. The plane was filled with kids in their late teens; all dressed the same way, all looking the same and all fairly subdued. I asked someone, 'Are these kids part of a football team or something?'

'Oh no,' I was told, 'They're heading to the Mexican–American border. They're going to try and get to America. Only one or maybe two of them will get through. The rest will get sent back, and they'll try and go over again. Every day this plane is packed with these sorts of young people. They know if they can just get over the fence they have made it into America.'

As I got off the plane I wished some of them luck. Then I hit Mexicali, the breeze-block capital of the world. All the buildings were made of this, and they were topped with horrible sheet roofs. Before the fight I had to get a licence. I was told to go to the licensing office and ask for El Angustias, which means 'The Anguished One'. I then discovered that all Mexicans have nicknames and are known more for their nicknames than their real names. El Angustias got this nickname when he got married; they all said he was much happier before then. He then passed my forms on to El Triste, which means 'The Sad One', and he did look a bit fed up. He had been married three times.

But the same thing happened to me in Spain when from very early on in my bullfighting career I got nicknamed 'El Inglés'. It was inevitable really, because they couldn't really pronounce Frank never mind spell it correctly on the posters advertising the fights. So to remember me they used the moniker 'El Inglés', until my comeback in 1979, when I changed my nickname to 'The Butcher', having been a butcher. But everybody ignored that and carried on calling me 'El Inglés', so it's stuck.

Having obtained my licence, I got a bit of practice before the festival at Paco Torres's ranch, which was miles away in the desert. He met us at the airport, and we all dived in his old pick-up truck and off we went, only to get a puncture as we were driving through the desert. We got out to discover there was no spare tyre, and to make matters worse we couldn't get a signal on our mobile phones. So we set off walking across the desert in the scorching heat and miles from where we wanted to be; the sun and the heat were merciless. Within minutes huge buzzards started circling round, and Paco was clearly struggling. We put him under the shade of a tree to rest. The buzzards watched, patiently; they knew we were in trouble. One of the group stayed with him while we all set off in separate directions to try and get a mobile phone signal. Without one we were doomed. Luckily one of the group managed to get through to his pal, El Chino, 'The Chinaman', because he looked Chinese, and he came to rescue us in his truck, but not before we told him to bring a couple of spare tyres. I was sorry to hear Paco has since died.

At the ranch house I was given a new sword-handler, who went by the name of El Pollo, 'The Chicken'. I said, 'Why would anyone want to be nicknamed "The Chicken"?'

El Pollo looked at me with a dour expression, shrugged and said, 'Because my dad is called "El Gallo", which translates as "The Fighting Cock".'

The bullring in Mexicali was magnificent, but the bulls themselves were misfits. They were rejects, but I was given a guarantee that all the cattle were from first-class breeders. My first bull was good, but when I put the sword in it was just a little bit slow in going down. Sometimes this happens with a bull, the sword goes in to the hilt and it doesn't seem to have a mortal effect, then suddenly, after about a minute, the bull drops and is gone. This is what happened with mine. Had it gone down quickly I would have definitely got an ear, instead I had to settle for a lap of honour.

When all the other fighters had been out and had killed their bulls, there was one bull left. Everything was announced on a tannoy in this ring, and suddenly a voice said, 'As the Englishman Frank Evans has fought his bull so well we would like to invite him to fight the last bull.'

How could I say no? So I went back into the ring, and the bull came out with a very inoffensive horn shape, which made me feel that it was going to be an easy bull to fight. But this bull was far from good; it proved to be a real struggle. It was clever. I knew I was in for a tough battle. Then the heavens opened, and while I was fighting it I kept slipping and sliding on the floor. Eventually I fought barefoot and killed it with one thrust. This impressed a group of very good-looking young women, who shouted, 'Frank, throw us your sombrero.'

They were going to catch it and throw it back. As I threw it to them some bloke snatched it as it flew through the air and ran off with it. I'd lost both my hats now, and I just stood in the middle of the ring smiling through gritted teeth. I met the girls outside the ring. They invited me out on the town with them and asked which hotel I was staying at. But as soon as I'd showered it was into a taxi and a breakneck journey to the airport at Tijuana.

My next stop was at a place called Zitaquaro. I got a plane at midnight that same night and got off it at 8 a.m. the next morning after flying through a couple of time zones. The impresario met us at the airport to take us to the *corrida*, which was another four hours' drive. I was shattered. Driving through this part of Mexico was tortuous because there were very few motorways. Arriving in Zitaquaro was like driving into Wyatt Earp's town. There were horses tied up everywhere and few cars. If the road hadn't been tarmac it would have been like going back to the Wild West. As soon as we got into the hotel I said, 'Right, I'm going to get my head down now for a few hours.'

It was 1 p.m., and I presumed the fight would start about 7 p.m., like in Spain. Torres said, 'Well don't sleep for long because the fight's at 4 p.m.'

I got thirty minutes' sleep, and then I had to prepare for the fight. My first bull was 420 kilos. It was cooperative and it had lots of passes in it; the problem was it wasn't quite threatening enough to put any real emotion into the fight. It was all a little bit too easy. But I got an ear on my debut in a full *corrida* in Mexico, so I was happy. Then I got my second bull. Torres told me it was a little bit bigger than the first one. It entered the ring, all 583 kilos of it, and for a moment I lost my breath. It was huge. But it was *manso*. When bulls are *manso* the added difficulty is they sometimes run away, looking for a way out, and in doing so they can easily run into you by mistake. But I managed to pop the sword in, and down it went. I had another triumph. I was on a high when we drove back to Guadalajara.

We had one night in a hotel, then it was off on another four-hour drive to perform in a *corrida* at Jiquilpan in the province of Michoacán. When we arrived the whole town was in fiesta mode. There were bands making processions, beauty queens were out, and the streets had been littered with flower petals. I was on the bill with two other fighters; one, El Mexiquense, was taking the alternative from the other fighter, El Fraile. The fight was in celebration of their kicking the British out of their province and reclaiming the oil fields, yet here they were with an Englishman on the bill. But the people couldn't have been nicer, and they were all looking forward to an Englishman fighting a bull, because they had this stereotypical image that the English all wore bowler hats and carried umbrellas.

In the bullring it really was party time, and this is typical of all bullfights in Mexico. The crowd are there primarily to have a good time, and they are all invariably drunk. They bring to the fight their booze and a number of cups – one to drink out of and the other to urinate into, because they can't be bothered getting up and going to the toilet. But if a bullfighter fails and has a bad time with the bull they'll think nothing of throwing these urine-filled cups at the fighter. This crowd was typical. They turned up with their litres of beer and their extra cups and were singing, dancing and generally having a raucous time. Dotted about were groups of four who'd formed themselves into trumpet bands. They're mad for trumpets. You know you're getting close to the bullring, because that's the first thing you hear. But I soon discovered they weren't hard to please. As long as you got stuck in they'd clap their hands off.

I noticed that the Mexican bullfighters who came on before me didn't really try to fight the bull properly. Instead they tried to be spectacular. One kid attempted what's known as a *porta gayola*, where you kneel 10 yards from the gate as they open it, only he didn't kneel 10 yards away, he knelt one yard from the gate! I couldn't believe my eyes: 'What the hell is going on here?' I said to Torres.

'He's going to get killed, that's what's going on,' he replied.

I watched the events unfold through gritted teeth, convinced the bull was going to gore him either through the head or through the upper body. Whatever happened it was going to be horrible. They opened the gate, and the bull came charging though and straight at this young lad. As the bull got within centimetres of him it swerved round him. It all happened in a matter of a couple of seconds. I couldn't believe it. In all my years watching and participating in bullfights I had never seen anything like it. How much nearer could he have taken it? It was barmy. The crowd went ballistic. They were on their feet cheering and clapping him. But that's not bullfighting. It's OK as a spectacle, but it's not the right way.

I was third on. The first two did OK. They livened the crowd up with their showboating but they couldn't put the sword in, and that matters. So really they set the stage for my appearance. The bulls were reputedly aggressive, and I don't mind aggressive bulls, because it makes for an exciting fight. And it was exciting. I had the place rocking, especially with the *muleta*. I called the bull for pass after pass, and the crowd were really getting into it. I looked at them and smiled. I'd taken my eyes off the bull. I'd done the one thing Pedro all those years ago had told me never to do in a bullring, and it was overconfidence that had caused me to do it. The next thing I knew I was flying through the air. I'd not given the bull enough room to go past and it had gone through me. It had given me one or two little warnings prior to this, which I had ignored because I was so euphoric and caught up in the moment. It caught me on the inside of my right leg. I got back up again, my *banderillero* had run out, but I told them I still had some work to do.

'No,' one of them said to me, 'kill it, this is a bad one, this bull. It has your number now. Get rid of it quickly.'

I made only a couple more passes and put the sword in. But then another disaster struck, as the sword went in I felt a tendon in my calf snap. It was fortunate the bull went down straight away because I was in real trouble with my leg. I could hardly stand up. Everybody thought it was from the goring, which was only a minute or two before, but I just couldn't make them understand that it was my calf. I was awarded an ear but I had to abandon my lap of honour and went straight to the infirmary, which was in the corral at the back of the bullring. In the infirmary they put me down on a petrol can. This wasn't exactly A&E. A doctor looked at me and said I was OK to go back to the hotel. When I got back to the hotel I discovered I had a haematoma in my thigh that was as big as an orange. It was caused by the whack from the bull. The horn hadn't penetrated the skin but it had caused an internal wound. It had broken a vein, and I was bleeding from the inside. So off we went to the local hospital to have it looked at. A specialist told me it would have to be operated on. Torres added, 'Whatever you do, don't let them operate on you here. You'll end up having your leg amputated if you stay here. Don't let them touch it.'

They looked like doctors would in a hospital to me, but when he said that I was frightened to death. I didn't want to get into complications, so my leg was packed in ice, and we went on a four-hour drive by ambulance to Guadalajara. Inside the ambulance I had my leg in the air, and a Mexican TV crew with me. They wanted to interview me for national TV. I was devastated to be leaving because I'd been invited to take part in the town fiesta that night. They'd invited me to a banquet with everything that went with this: great food, fantastic company and lots to drink. Instead I was in an ambulance. By the time it got to Guadalajara the doctor, a horn wound specialist, had been tipped off and was waiting to have a look at it. He said the ice had stopped the bleeding and he recommended trying to repair it without having an operation and told me he'd keep me in hospital for a couple of days to monitor it. 'No way,' I said. 'I've got a plane to catch. I'm going to Cuba tomorrow.'

'On your own head be it, then,' he said.

But I knew if I could get back to Cuba all my pals were there, and the medical facilities were second to none. And that was what I did. I got on the plane and flew with my leg in the air, to the bewilderment of other passengers. But I did wonder if I'd done the right thing because my leg by now was totally black from the top of my hip down to my foot. In Cuba the medical staff looked at it and said, 'How the hell did you manage to fly with that?'

I spent a few days recuperating in Havana before leaving for England after downing loads of blood thinners and with my leg in an anti-coagulant stocking. It took me ten days to recover, which was about right for this type of injury.

Despite the injury I was having a great time and picking up ears wherever I went. I was now living the life of an active matador, and it was great. The only downside to bullfighting I could see was in the travelling. I'd sometimes have to travel seven hours in Spain just to get some practice in. One day I'd be in Salamanca, the next Málaga and the next day Madrid. But it was a minor negative set against the huge positives I was experiencing at this time. I'd proved to everyone that, apart from the geniuses, I was as good as anybody in the bullfighting world. But I must add I'm not one to try and prove I'm better than anybody else, I just want to be as good as I can be within myself. I enjoy the aesthetic process of being a matador, of getting up in the morning and training, of not going to nightclubs and getting drunk and generally avoiding indulgence. I get more fun out of this sort of denial than from being indulgent. What makes me happy is the positive results I get from being strict.

My aim in 2004 was to break into the top fifty and maybe have a crack at Madrid. I was a minor celebrity now both in Spain and back home in England and I was getting the attention of some major stars, including David Beckham.

Chapter Fourteen

THE LAST CORRIDA

Could I really kick on in 2004 and shake things up in the world of bullfighting? That was my aim and ambition and I was starting to generate genuine interest among the media. At the beginning of that year a Spanish TV crew came over to Britain to film a one-off documentary on sporting Spaniards like Liverpool's Rafael Benitez, who'd settled in the UK, and another Spanish footballer, Javi de Pedro, who played for Blackburn. Although I wasn't Spanish they decided to dedicate a small portion of the programme to me and filmed me training in Salford. Afterwards we all went for a bite to eat at a Spanish restaurant called Harper's in Manchester. It was a great day, and we were all having a laugh and a joke, when one of the TV crew tapped me on the arm and said, 'Look at that there.'

On the wall was a photograph of David Beckham, dressed in a suit of lights. As I looked at the picture I could feel the red mist start to descend. 'I'm sorry,' I said, 'but that annoys me. Everybody can regard him as an icon if they want, but I find that photograph insulting to my profession.'

The camera crew found it hilarious as I went on and on about this picture, telling them, 'All I can say is if he wants to wear a suit of lights he should justify it by putting one on and standing in front of a bull. Until he does that he should get the suit off and stop taking the Mickey out of my game.'

Three weeks later I was sitting by the side of a swimming pool in Spain when my mobile phone started ringing. I answered it and the voice on the other end said, 'Hello, Frank, it's Paco Garcia from Madrid.'

I knew Paco – he presents the football programme for *AS Daily Magazine* – and said, 'Hi, mate, how are you doing?'

He was on his radio station going out live and said to me, 'We're live as I'm speaking to you, and I've got someone very special who'd like to talk to you.'

'Who is it?'

'I've got David Beckham. We're doing a live interview with him.'

Suddenly I had David on the phone to me. 'I hear you've been saying some things about me, Frank.'

Well I wasn't going to let him get away with that and said to him, 'I saw the photo of you in the suit of lights and found it a little bit insulting. If you want to wear a suit of lights you should go and fight a bull.'

He started laughing and said, 'Frank, calm down. That picture of me must have been superimposed because I don't ever remember putting a suit of lights on, and I'd remember something like that.'

It was all light-hearted stuff, and we ended up getting on OK, and I found him to be a charming and friendly young man, but it still wound me up. Beckham's achievements are truly astonishing for a player who I believe started with limited ability. He's pursued a career as a celebrity and become the richest footballer of all time. To me, his overachievement and his being able to maintain such a high profile outside football owes much to his dedication and unceasing commitment to a training regime that's a marvellous example to anyone embarking on a career in sport. It's only when people describe this very good player as 'great' that I, personally, have a problem. I was fortunate to see the great Alfredo di Stefano, in my opinion, the greatest of them all. I saw Diego Maradona during his stint in Spain, and how about the long reign of Pelé? Bobby Charlton and Zinedine Zidane are other names which jump into my mind when I hear the word 'great'. And I make no apology when I consider George Best to be one of the truly greats of all time.

My media encounters have been somewhat chequered. Around the same time Beckham was calling me I was invited on to the BBC's *What's My Line?* programme. I was with two other blokes and I had to stand and say, 'I'm Frank Evans. What do I do for a living?'

You had to do something that was typical of your profession, so I imitated making a pass. Jan Leeming was on the panel and straight away she said, 'I don't know what it is, but I have the idea he is a matador.'

She got it straight away and brought the house down. After the show I bumped into her in the green room and said, 'It's just come to me now. You interviewed me in the 1960s when I first started. You worked for Granada.'

Jan told me she didn't remember, and when they asked her on the show how she knew she said, 'I just guessed by the way he walked.'

But I think she remembered.

The uniqueness of my participation as an English matador has generated quite a lot of interest from the news media over the years. But I got the drift early on that some journalists were out to take the piss. One reporter came to do an article, and I told him I trained with my cape in Bule Hill Park in Salford. Then I showed him the bale of hay mounted on a shopping trolley at the back of my workshop – where I had a business manufacturing kitchens. The trolley was fixed to a wall, and I used it to practice the sword thrust. I read the article that appeared in the newspaper the following day. The gist of it was a kitchen fitter from Salford was practising to go to Spain bullfighting by chasing a shopping trolley round the local park with a cape wrapped round his neck.

But not everything has been negative, and even if I did read things about myself that I didn't like, I quickly came to accept that, as I performed in public, I wouldn't always like what was written about me. Oscar Wilde once said that there is only one thing in life worse than being talked about, and that is not being talked about.

The routine of my 'media fame' has seemed to follow a well-trodden path. I'd appear at a *corrida* which would be reported in the press, and then this would be followed up by newspapers wanting to do a feature on me. Occasionally I'd do a TV interview and sometimes be invited to appear on the more prestigious chat shows. The biggest chat show I've done was *Wogan* in the 1980s, appearing with David Frost and Tony Bennett. Wogan was great, and I thoroughly enjoyed doing the show.

The news interest in me comes in from all over the world, and of course the Spanish press always wants to know if an English matador ticks the same way as a Spanish one. I took on an appointment in Spain with Canal Sur Radio to do a Sunday-night chat programme on bullfighting and give inter-bull live commentaries. Although I enjoyed the commentating I also found it slightly frustrating because I always itched to get in the ring, and it made me long for a fight. Nothing beats the buzz of facing a fighting bull in public. If you've never been there it must be hard to imagine. I know a lot of people feel it's too hazardous to contemplate. But once you've tasted the thrill of a fighting bull gliding past in close proximity, smelt its sweet and overpowering odour and arrived at that moment of trust that comes when you know it is convinced in the *muleta*, then you are captured for ever. Bullfighting has got you then and it won't let go. You may find other worthy pastimes, as I did, but nothing can ever replace the experience of facing a fighting bull.

Nearly thirteen years after becoming a fully fledged matador I was finally beginning to get the respect in the media denied to me when I took the alternative. I'd gone from having no right to enter the bullring to a well-thought-of and in-demand matador. It even got to the stage where I began thinking: I'm actually not as good as you're making me out to be.

It had gone from one extreme to another. And just when

things looked rosy, and all talk was of an appearance in Madrid and my standings in the top 100, my past caught up with me in the most depressing way. I suddenly went from having my best-ever year in bullfighting in 2003 to my worst as an active fighter in 2004. I could never have predicted it, but it happened.

To understand just what went wrong we have to go back to the 1970s. I played rugby in the 1970s for De La Salle in Salford. I'd been watching them play one day in 1975 at their Lancaster Road ground when someone invited me to go and train with them. As so often happens in my life, I got sucked in and found myself playing for their third and fourth teams and in 1979 I'd made my way up to become first-team captain. It was great, I loved it. The nearest buzz I can compare with making a pass at bullfighting is the thrill you get from making a break at rugby and going over for a try, or timing a perfect tackle; it's good for the soul. But I ended up getting caught. I was tackled, and one lad had his arm around my ankle. My feet got stuck in the mud; as they were stuck two other players hit me and twisted me on to the deck. As I fell I heard my knee crack and knew I was in serious trouble.

If this had happened two decades later I would've had knee reconstructive surgery, but in those days you couldn't get that, and I simply strapped it up and hoped for the best. What I'd done was torn the cruciate ligament and a medial ligament, and despite getting it better I always had to wear a knee bandage after that. From that point onwards the knee was unstable. I ran two or three miles every day and did sprints, so over a period of years the training and running meant I was slowly wearing my knee cartilage away. By the time 2000 came along the knee was beginning to give me problems, but I managed to deal with it until something went wrong, badly wrong.

In early 2004 I woke up one morning in agony from the knee and found I couldn't run any distance and could barely walk on it. It felt like a never-ending toothache that gradually wore me down and left me exhausted. As the year progressed it got worse. It got to the stage where I couldn't even walk 10 yards without having to stop. The biggest problem was my inability to train properly and as a result I wasn't ready mentally or physically to fight bulls when I stepped into the ring for a *corrida* with my knee heavily strapped up. It affected my performances, and I was awful. What really jumped off the page for me was at the end of 2004, when I'd only fought five *corridas* in Spain, and I looked at the list they published to show how many ears a matador had been awarded. The ear count for my fights read a big fat zero.

It told its own story, and people in bullfighting had seen I was struggling and were telling me to get out before I got myself killed. People close to me could see it was going badly wrong. I was limping through all my fights, but bullfighting requires coordination, balance and above all confidence. All these attributes seemed to disappear bit by bit as the season progressed. When I saw my name in the bullfighting magazine with no ears next to it I began to believe I should stop.

I'd had a similar feeling when I gave up playing rugby in 1992. Then I had played thirteen games and not scored a try. In the end something tells you that you just can't do it any more. With me I've always needed a moment of shock to make me see reality. The shock in rugby came when I was playing with the fourth team away to Broughton. The second team went with us but were a player short for their game, so I was drafted in. I was delighted to be playing for the seconds until I discovered I was in with a load of muscle-bound lunatic young men who were running at me and trying to rip my head off. I had another looking-at-the-grass moment in that game, not so much through lack of enthusiasm but more because I was frightened to death. I was too old to be able to compete in these sorts of tough games, and the atmosphere was fearsome. Every time the opposition got hold of me they tried to batter me and when they ran at me with the ball I knew they were just going to go straight through me. It was time to stop playing. I'd lingered for too long in the game and I'd done my knee no favours in the process. Bullfighting in 2004 was no different. I got the drift that it was time to go. I'd come to the end of my tether with my knee and had psychologically adjusted myself to thinking of a life away from the bullring. It's rather like adjusting to old age. You don't fancy getting old but when it happens you prepare yourself psychologically for it. I simply fought my fifth *corrida* in 2004, walked out of the bullring, got changed, realized I was finished, and that was it.

But I didn't just want to go without a final farewell. I needed at least one more fight just to do something. I didn't want to walk away without at least cutting one ear. But while I was sorting out my farewell fight I began to hawk myself around Europe, desperately trying to find a knee specialist who could give me some relief from the constant pain my knee was giving me and tell me they could perform miracles and I'd be able to fight again. But it was in such a bad way I thought the chances of that happening were about 1 per cent. Every doctor I consulted couldn't give me the prognosis I was looking for. I had an arthroscopy done on it in Salford, where they went into the knee with a camera, washed it out and trimmed off some damaged cartilage. That actually seemed to make it worse! Then I went to see the bullfighting doctor in Valencia, and he said, 'I can fix you a false knee, but there's no way you'll be able to fight bulls.'

That was a bad day, made worse because I could barely walk and had to stop and sit on the wall outside his private surgery because I was in so much agony. Then for him to tell me what he told me made it one of the most depressing days of my life. It looked like the farewell fight was off, and I was going to bow out with a whimper rather than a bang. I really couldn't see any way out of it at all. Then I got a call from Peter Schofield, a physio who had treated me all my life and who worked with Freddie Griffiths at Salford Royal Hospital. He said, 'Frank, I've got the man for you. He works in Derby. Go and see him. He has just operated on someone in the Royal Family and he only does knees. If anyone can help you, he can. He'll sort you out. His name is Mr Guido Gutjens.'

I made the journey south to Derby to see this guy, who listened to me while I explained my problem and told him I wanted at least one more fight. He X-rayed the knee and did all the things to check out a knee that orthopaedic surgeons do, then he gave his prognosis and said, 'I can fix your knee and I won't rule out you're ever fighting bulls again. All I can say is I won't be recommending that you do. I have clients who play tennis, and I've recommended they don't play tennis, but they do. So after the operation I will have a look at your knee and we'll simply take it one step at a time. But your knee does need replacing. There's no other remedy for it.'

I said, 'Is there any way the operation could be postponed while I fight one more bullfight? Is there anything you can do short term to allow me to get this last fight in?'

'In that case I'll give you a cortisone injection. I can't keep giving you these injections, but as a temporary measure it'll take away the pain.'

I arranged four fights for 2005 in July and August, the last one being my final fight, which would climax with my pigtail being cut off in the ring to signify that I had retired from bull-fighting. Two weeks before the first of these fights I went to Derby, Mr Gutjens put a needle into my knee to inject the cortisone, and I walked out of the hospital without limping. I couldn't believe it. I immediately rang the specialist when I got home and said, 'Why can't you just keep doing this?'

'It softens the bones and the tissues around the knee. You can only do it so many times,' he told me.

But I felt like a new man. I was completely revitalized and went off to Benalmadena for the first of my four fights in July and cut three ears. It was brilliant. I was running around the ring as though I'd just started again. The knee felt brilliant, and now psychology started playing its part again because I began to believe that after cutting ears and tails galore this couldn't be the end of it. The devil in my mind began to tell me that if I could fix the knee and it felt like it did with the cortisone I'd be back. In the two fights in July I cut six ears. It was a massive triumph.

Then came my final two fights, which the press got very busy with; TV, radio and the newspapers gave me a brilliant send-off, and the bullfighting fraternity organized a great big farewell dinner for me as well with tributes galore. But during my final fight, although there was a party atmosphere and all my friends and acquaintances from the bullfighting world were there, I couldn't help but feel a sense of anticlimax. I just wasn't myself during that fight and I didn't put on a particularly good show. Two ears were awarded to me, but they were more out of sympathy than for anything I'd done in the bullfight. It just didn't feel right. At the farewell dinner I felt uncomfortable and awkward. When everybody had gone home I walked through the town and found a late-night café still open. I sat alone in this café, nursing a coffee and thinking: what am I walking away from? Why am I walking away from this?

I hated quitting, even though my family and friends close to me seemed relieved. I just wasn't a quitter by nature and never have been. It was interesting that no one seemed to sense my heart was not in leaving. I felt certain that, with the right doctors who could cure my ailments and get me back into a physical condition where I could fight bulls again, I'd be back. No one knew me better than myself, and I knew that, if I got the green light to fight bulls once more, I would. It was my life and nothing else was of more importance to me.

I got a call shortly after my retirement from my impresario friends to say I could join their team organizing bullfights. I agreed to do this just so I didn't lose touch with the bullfight-ing world. But it was a slightly Machiavellian gesture, because I knew that to keep in touch with them would always leave the door open for a comeback. When I returned to England at the end of August with the curtain seemingly down on my bull-fighting career I went to see my Derby doc and said, 'Right, I've retired; now let's go ahead with the operation.'

But I needed to wait six months for all the cortisone to leave my system. By the time the six months was up they'd pion-eered a new knee to replace the titanium one, which normally lasted ten years. In lab tests the new one appeared to last thirty-five years, and I was going to be one of the first to have this new type fitted. I had a spinal injection to numb the pain and I did-n't feel a thing. The operation took just over an hour. At the end of it my man pulled his gloves off and said to his team, 'Congratulations, that is the best knee I think we've ever put in.'

I was due to stay in hospital for five days to make sure there was no infection, but they said they'd keep me in longer if I couldn't bend the knee 90 degrees and walk unaided up about four stairs. They also said they'd let me out sooner if I could manage this. I'd got myself very fit before going to hospital, and when the anaesthetic had worn off after the op I started to move my leg and get it going again. I wanted out of that hospital. The following morning when the physio came to do his round I said, 'What are these tests that you want me to do to justify my going home?'

They told me again and I said, 'Right, I'll do them for you.'

The physio said, 'Don't be silly, you've just had your operation.'

'No, I'll do it for you now.'

So I bent my leg 90 degrees and stood up. The physio called over his colleagues and said, 'Look at this over here.'

They couldn't believe it. 'Where's the stairs,' I said. 'I'll climb the stairs.'

The physio was astonished but he said, 'Hang on, we can't just let you go home like that.'

'But I've done everything you said. I can bend my knee 90 degrees, I can walk up and down stairs unaided and I want to go home.'

A hospital isn't the place to linger if you can help it with things like superbugs and MRSA. They got Mr Gutjens to see me now and as he walked in I was walking about and I said to him: 'You said it's the best knee you've ever put in, so there you go, I have just proved you right.'

I was out of hospital within the hour and I got going again as soon as I got home. I began by doing light exercises and took the view that, if my knee didn't hurt, then I should move it. The results of my moving my knee and getting it back to normal were astonishing. I knew from that moment that I was going to have another crack at bullfighting. In one sense I was elated, absolutely on top of the world, but in another I did feel I'd cheated a lot of people with my retirement.

Within three weeks of the op I was legging it round Worsley Golf Club and I felt reborn. I'd been putting on fights in Spain as an impresario so I was still involved in that respect but I now started putting out the feelers for a potential comeback. An ex-matador called Miguel Marquez had come out of retirement to do charity fights, so I used him as inspiration for my return.

By December 2006 I was ready to fight and I was doing shuttle sprints now on my knee. It was functioning at 100 per cent and it felt better than at any time since the 1970s. I started training at El Ventorillo in Toledo with Marquez, who fought four cows and was all over them. Miguel looked sharp, keen and was as good as he'd ever been. He was practising for a charity festival in Fuengirola in aid of Alzheimer's. I left to go back to Salford ten days before the fight. A week later Miguel dropped dead at the ranch of a massive heart attack. It hit me hard, because he was of a similar age to me. Suddenly, for the first time in my life, I began to feel mortal. Something told me that could've been me. And with my family's history of heart problems and my blood pressure scare I decided to go for a full check-up, just to make sure everything was OK.

I was recommended to go and see a cardiologist called Dr Alan Fitchet and booked in to see him at Hope Hospital. I told him all about the bullfighting and the blood pressure tablets and added, 'A good friend of mine has just dropped dead from a heart attack, and I want to make sure I'm fit and healthy because I do quite vigorous training and I need to know that I'm OK for my own peace of mind.'

I told him about the gym and the weights and the sprints; nothing was left out. He did all the checks of my blood pressure and my heart rate and put me on a treadmill with an oxygen mask and on an ECG machine, registering my performance in and out of stress. All the tests showed no abnormalities, and I came through it with flying results, but he said: 'With your family history I'm not quite happy that we've bottomed everything out so what I'd like to do is give you an angiogram. This means we go through the femoral artery with a dye and a camera and have a look at how your coronary arteries are performing.'

I could sense he couldn't quite put his finger on something, so he said to me, 'Let's give it the full check. If it was anybody else I'd tell them to go home and get on with their life. But you're telling me you want to go and fight bulls again, so let's do the angiogram.'

On the day of my results I sat with these little old ladies in the waiting room of the hospital and chatted to one of them who said, 'I've had a bit of a heart attack, that's why I'm here.'

All these people had something go wrong with them which made them get in touch with their doctor. But in my case there was nothing wrong with me, and I did begin to wonder what the hell I was doing sitting with all these old people. I felt like an athlete stuck with a bunch of geriatrics. We all got moved to cubicles for the results with a curtain round each one and I listened to the doctor in the next-door cubicle say to this old woman: 'I'm really sorry, but you have serious problems and we'll have to operate.'

This lady was very polite and said, 'Well, whatever you think is best, doctor. If you need to operate that's fine, just as long as you can make me better.'

I couldn't believe he was going to say the same thing to me. When he came into my cubicle I was expecting him to say, 'Right, you're fit as a fiddle, Frank, off you go.'

Instead he looked at me with a frown and said, 'Frank, I've got some bad news. You have serious blockages in your arteries. One of them is 94 per cent blocked and the other 99 per cent blocked. The other arteries are carrying the load.'

I couldn't believe what he was saying, but I've never really been one to panic. Every problem has a solution, and I said: 'Right, accepted, the question is, what is the answer?'

'You'll need a heart bypass operation.'

'OK, NHS, when?'

'Probably five to six months.'

'If I pay for it, when?'

'Now, this week.'

'Right, let's pay for it.'

It cost me money, but I preferred paying to having the money in the bank and me being six feet under. There was no way I was going to wait with a thing like that. I felt like a dead man walking. I also had a heart murmur, which is caused when a valve fails to close properly and blood escapes a little bit. I was placed in the hands of the eminent Mr Keenan, who decided to repair the valve at the same time as having the heart bypass. I gave him the thumbs up because I really didn't expect there to be any major drawbacks. I was just glad I was getting it done without having had a heart attack to warn me first. There was nothing wrong with my heart, it was in good shape; it was just the valves and arteries that were knackered.

What I didn't know until after the operation was the heart bypass didn't involve stopping the heart, but fixing the heart murmur did, and my reaction to this part of the operation was pretty traumatic to say the least. I was dead beat when I came round after the op. I have never known a sensation like it. I was absolutely shattered. I couldn't even comb my own hair without feeling totally gone, and to get out of bed just to go to the toilet was an absolutely massive job. When my family came to see me shortly after the op I was still on a ventilator, but bit by bit they eased me off it. Then the tubes that were in my neck and down my throat and here, there and everywhere, were withdrawn, and I was put back in a room out of intensive care.

Having had such a huge success with the knee I really did think I would be Jack the lad and be up and out of bed within days of the operation. But they told me it'd take at least ten days, and it did. I came out nine days after the op and went walking around Worsley Golf Club the day after. The members were horrified when I turned up because I looked like a ghost. But I felt that the best way to get going effectively was to get going. The first thing I did when I got home was walk out of my house and up a small hill about 100 yards in length. I managed 20 yards and had to turn round and come back. The next day I got a little bit further up this hill and bit by bit I managed to make it to the top. Three weeks later I suddenly started to feel a little bit livelier again. But I couldn't run or do sprints so I went to see the doctor to say things were progressing a bit too slowly for my liking. He blasted me and said, 'What the hell are you doing here? It's only been three weeks since your operation. What do you expect?' He added, 'Your heart was stopped for nearly an hour. That caused an incredible trauma to your body which it'll take months to recover from. It's almost like having a terrible car crash, and your body is still trying to recover from it. It needs a long, long time. They cut your breastbone open with a saw, stopped your heart and started it again. You'll need plenty of rest.'

Three months after the op I started light training, which was just jogging, and I got my cape out, but I could hardly hold it up. All this was done out of the way of any prying eyes and on my own because it really did feel like I was starting over again. Every time I finished I had this feeling of being absolutely shattered. But I noticed the day after I was never as shattered as the day before and I began to benefit from the exercise. It was a full twelve months after the operation before I felt fit again. I had recovered. The comeback was now on. My breastbone could take a knock and was actually stronger than it was before the op. The cardiologist said, 'You do what you need to do. As soon as it feels right that's your body telling you it's OK to do it, so off you go.'

Throughout 2008 I'd been busy putting bullfights on, buying the bulls, putting the bullrings up or hiring them – all organizational stuff that goes with putting on a fight. I soon realized this was the last thing I wanted to do. I'd been told by my impresario partners that I'd make a few quid and still be involved in bullfighting, but this was different. This was just like selling kitchens or buying and selling houses or any of the things I'd done in life that may have made me money but that I didn't really enjoy doing. I'd have people involved in bullfighting that didn't turn up for work for one reason or another and it became far too stressful to ever be enjoyable. I'd not turned my back on bullfighting, but I hated being an impresario. I wanted to fight bulls again. It would mean I'd probably lose money rather than make it, but I'd rather lose money and be happy than make money and be doing my head in. So in 2008 I started telling people I was making a comeback and that I'd be reappearing again. The response to this was surprising. My partner, Juan Carlos Carreno, and his partner, Alberto Lucas, had bought me a full fighting suit worth £4,000 when I retired, and Carreno said, 'I'm presenting this to you on the condition that you fight once in it and then hang it up for ever when you have had the fight.'

It was such a lovely touch. But when I told him I was coming back his reaction was totally different. He screamed at me, 'You're mad! Why don't you get a life? Where do you think you are going with this? You'll do what all the others have done: you will come back and mess up a great reputation that you've built up over the years. You cannot do any more than you've already done, and a bull will get hold of you and seriously harm you.'

This was the sort of response I was getting from everybody in bullfighting. They were all saying don't stand in front of a bull because it'll hurt you and probably kill you. I'd had loads of respect when I retired, now they were worried I was going to mess everything up and saying to me, 'Why are you doing this at your age?'

'Other fighters have gone on past sixty,' I told them. 'Cordobés did it, and Romero as well, and neither of them was as fit as me.'

It's not common for a bullfighter to go on into his sixties but it's certainly not unusual. Most fighters when they get to forty go and do something else in life. The secret is: do they like doing whatever they've given up bullfighting for? This is what people didn't understand about me. The one thing I loved to do and still do is to stand in a bullring and fight a bull. Everything else connected to life simply pales into insignificance. Nothing can beat that little bit of fear and adrenalin that fighting a bull instils. And if I didn't want to do it, if it no longer became enjoyable, I would've got out long ago. It ended with Carreno saying to me, 'All I can say to you is I will not collaborate in any way whatsoever with this come-back, because you're mad.'

And he added, 'I want my suit back,' but he chuckled as he said this, so I knew he was only joking.

But I made a deal with him. I said, 'OK, you may think I'm mad, but I think you're mad for smoking, so I'll make a deal with you: you stop smoking, and I'll stop fighting bulls.'

We shook hands on it, but I know he can't stop smoking, so I'm safe. I managed to get myself a fight in a village called Arcos de la Frontera in August 2008. I was ecstatic. It was a full *corrida*. It was a new chapter in my life. Out of respect I telephoned Carreno and told him, 'I've got a fight booked but I'd like you to find the bulls for it to make sure the cattle are right.'

He went mad at me again and said, 'You're aggravating me. What if I get a bull and it does you in? You are asking me to find you a bull that will do you in.'

'I'm only asking you out of respect,' I said.

That fight didn't come off, much to Carreno's relief and my dismay. But instead I teamed up with Porras to fight at a festival in Villanueva de la Concepcion just outside Málaga on 15 August. The fight was only against two-year-olds, but my bull weighed 420 kilos. It was massive for a two-year-old and it was ideal for my comeback. Channel Four came to do a little feature on it, and all the Spanish and English press arrived en masse. I soon realized they weren't coming to see the great matador reappear, they were going to see a granddad with a false knee and a heart operation try and take on a bull and probably get killed or seriously hurt. Very few people had seen me prepare for it, so they didn't realize just how focused and ready I was. Some of them probably thought I was going to enter the ring with a walking stick.

But the fight went beautifully because the bull was ideal for a comeback in that, despite having a slight problem with cutting inside, it was slightly *manso*, so I had lots of time to get my breath. In that respect I enjoyed the fight, and it went well. Within the first few minutes of the fight all my apprehensions had disappeared – I was slightly nervous because I knew people had turned up to see if I might fail. There was a little bit more responsibility on my shoulders to make sure I didn't come unstuck. But I'd been on a ranch fighting lots of cows, so I knew I was ready, and ready I was, killing the bull with one sword thrust and claiming two ears. As I took my lap of honour I knew I couldn't have stage-managed it better. But in my eyes it wasn't a comeback.

The big comeback would come when I reappeared at a major *corrida* in a professional fight. I had one booked at the end of the 2008 season, then came the credit crunch, and all of a sudden there was no money to put on fights, and everybody was cancelling. When you fight in a village there's not enough money sometimes to cover the full cost of a *corrida*, even if the venue is packed to capacity, so the shortfall is subsidized by the local mayor's office. As soon as the credit crunch hit things changed, and I was approaching mayors who'd offered me a *corrida*, and they were saying, 'Frank, we'll pay for the band and you can have the ring for free, but we haven't got any more money to give you.'

It basically amounted to a £15,000 shortfall, and I wasn't going to give that sort of money away just for the sake of re-appearing. So I didn't reappear. In the last five years up to 2007 bullfighting in Spain had attracted more spectators than La Liga, the Spanish football league. But figures for the first half of 2008 painted a different picture. They showed something like 400 fewer bullfights than for the corresponding six months of 2007. Things had got bad. In 2008 there were sixteen bullrings in the north of Spain that didn't see a fight.

But I knew that, if Spain was in difficulties and I couldn't get a fight there, I could always turn my attention to South America. What I've learned over the years is to be patient, because things happen in this profession when you least expect it. I was on a roll from 2000 onwards when really I should've been going home for ever, and now I'm back again after a couple of setbacks – older, wiser and in lots of ways even better for it. And because of the interest generated in me there's more motivation among impresarios to put me on. The future for me holds a non-ending fading-off into the distance, fighting bulls. I fully intend to fight on until the day comes when I just can't do it any more. If I didn't enjoy it I'd stop, but I simply can't get the poison out of my system.

Margaret has never said a word about it. She just smiles. When she retired she had her life renewed with the advent of our five grandchildren. I bought a boy's bullfighting kit for my grandson Tom's eighth birthday. It was a cape and a toy sword. I left it in the house ready to wrap up. It disappeared. Somebody got rid of it. I don't know if it was Margaret, Jim or his wife who threw it away, but they didn't want him to have it. I spoke to Margaret about it and asked her what had happened to it. She just shrugged and said, 'Dunno.'

'You have to be exposed to everything in life,' I said to her. 'And if one of them wants to be a bullfighter, then so be it.'

She smiled at me and walked off.

This is why I doubt there could ever be another British bullfighter. I don't think it's necessarily any more difficult now than it was then. In many respects it's a bit easier in that there are more schools set up by the government in all the major cities where would-be matadors pay per week to be trained before being put in with six-month-old cows. A lot more than when I first started. But the chances of someone from Britain first of all being able to speak the language fluently and then going over there long term to be trained are slim. Then they have to be able to do it. And bullfighting is tough. As I've written, hardly anyone makes it. It is nigh-on impossible for a Brit to do this.

There must be some youngster somewhere with a British passport and all the ingredients to function in this most complicatedly beautiful profession of them all. It is a small needle in a giant haystack. For now, I am the last British bullfighter.

ACKNOWLEDGEMENTS

I world like to thank my wife Margaret for her unwavering support throughout our life together, for her perseverance in putting up with me and all this. It has been one way and without her calm and steadying presence neither I nor the family would have had such a charmed existence. I thank my brother Bob for showing me how to overcome adversity. My two sons Matthew and James have always been there for me and our continued interaction with their new families is a constant joy.

From the world of the bulls I have had the benefit of meeting many lifelong friends. I may never have persevered without the initial support of Patricio Garrigos 'Graneret'. José Puerto has stayed loyal with me from my very beginning. Juan Caparros, since he followed me into my debut in 1966, has continued to promote my cause. My gratitude to Paco Ramirez who kept the shops alive during my spell with George. I am indebted to Vincente Ruiz 'El Soro' and his family. Vincente included me in all his endeavors until his catastrophic injury and it was his father 'Pedro' who passed on to me the invaluable secret of the sword thrust. Ramon Cabo, the most knowledgeable aficionado I know supported me with kindness and advice and pulled out money for me when I was in need. I have to say thanks to Pedro Magaña. Life was chaotic with Pedro, but he put me into almost all my activity as a *novillero* and I think even liked me.

My thanks to the taurine writer Juan Miguel Nuñez who

writes nice things about me and for introducing me to Morenito de Jaen who has become my 'peon de confianza' and to whom I am grateful for the hours of training and coaching to be whatever I am in a bullring. I thank Rafael Corbelle for his professional advice and support and Francisco José Porras, my friend and erstwhile manager.

I offer special thanks to Gaspar Jiménez, the impresario who had faith in me and put me in front of more bulls than I ever dreamed possible.

Alberto Lucas and Juan Carlos Carreño look after me in Salamanca and their ongoing input is invaluable.

Ray Wood, the late founder president of the Peña Fiesta Brava of Manchester, gave me sound advice and introduced me to the right people. Today's president, Tim Hardman, is a great help in my public relations with the taurine elite. My mentor, George Erik, founder president of the Club Taurino of London, was a wonderful friend and promoter of my course, and I grateful to his taurine offspring's the CTL president Dr Ivan Moseley and Brian Harding for their cooperation and support. The Allen family have treated me as another son and provided me with some hairy moments in the form of their son Steve as my chauffeur. Bob Rule is the only English sword handler in the history of bullfighting and I thank him for his loyalty and attempts at keeping the swords sharp.

And my heartfelt thanks go to Joaquin Bueno who kindly allowed us to use his photographs.